APEX ACADEMIC RESOURCES

SIE Exam Success

Securities Industry Essentials Exam Prep

Fully FINRA-Aligned Study Prep Guide with Full-Length Mock Exams, Detailed Explanations and e-Learning Platform Access

First Edition

Table of Contents

Chapter 1 Introduction to the SIE Exam

1.1 Purpose of the SIE Exam

1.1.1 What the SIE Covers

The Securities Industry Essentials (SIE) Exam tests a broad range of foundational topics, ensuring that newcomers to the financial industry possess a working knowledge of essential concepts before taking on more specialized roles. At its core, the SIE covers the major building blocks of securities regulation, market operations, product knowledge, and ethical obligations. This scope allows individuals from various backgrounds—whether they have direct experience in finance or not—to enter the industry on relatively even footing in terms of baseline competence and understanding.

Because the aim of the SIE is to measure a candidate's readiness to engage responsibly in a regulated environment, the exam assesses knowledge in four key areas: the functioning of capital markets, the characteristics and risks of different financial products, the essential rules surrounding trading and customer accounts, and the regulatory framework that governs the industry. These four pillars form a cohesive picture of how securities businesses operate day to day, how investments themselves work, and what safeguards exist to protect both investors and the markets. By laying such a comprehensive foundation, the SIE helps ensure that all future registrants share a common language and set of reference points when discussing industry practices.

A noteworthy aspect of the SIE's coverage is the emphasis it places on basic compliance standards and investor protection. Candidates are introduced to the roles of regulatory bodies, such as the Securities and Exchange Commission (SEC) and self-regulatory organizations (SROs), as well as the principles behind major securities laws. It also highlights high-level prohibitions—like insider trading and market manipulation—so that new entrants are immediately aware of their professional responsibilities. Although more advanced exams will delve deeper into specific rules and procedures, this exam ensures everyone enters those advanced studies fully aware of why these rules exist and how they maintain fair and orderly markets.

In addition to regulatory awareness, the SIE assesses knowledge of how various financial instruments function, including equities, bonds, options, and investment company products. By testing candidates on both common and less familiar categories—such as municipal fund securities or direct participation programs—the exam encourages breadth of understanding. It does not, however, demand specialized mastery of any single product type. Instead, it ensures that a candidate can identify and explain how general product features align with investor needs and what corresponding risks might apply. The end result is a well-rounded foundation that prepares aspiring professionals to tackle deeper, more niche competencies in subsequent qualification exams or on-the-job training.

Key Coverage Areas	High-Level Focus
Capital Markets	Structure and participants in the primary and secondary markets, roles of regulators, and market types
Products and Their Risks	Characteristics of equity, debt, and more complex investment vehicles, along with the fundamentals of risk
Trading, Customer Accounts, and Prohibited Activities	Essential trading practices, rules for handling customer accounts, and regulatory prohibitions such as insider trading
Overview of the Regulatory Framework	Core federal securities laws, roles of agencies like the SEC, and foundational compliance requirements

Each coverage area is integral to the exam's mission of evaluating whether candidates are suitably prepared to uphold standards of ethical conduct and informed service. By combining all four into a single, entry-level assessment, the SIE fosters a consistent level of industry knowledge—a benefit not just for test-takers and prospective employers, but also for the investing public that places its trust in securities professionals.

1.1.2 Who Must Take It (Open to the Public)

1.1.2 Who Must Take It (Open to the Public)

Unlike many prior entry-level securities exams that required firm sponsorship, the SIE Exam is open to a much broader group of test-takers. Any individual who wishes to demonstrate a foundational knowledge of securities—even if they are not currently employed by, or seeking employment with, a broker-dealer—may opt to register and sit for the exam. This open-access approach lowers the barrier to entry, allowing college students, career switchers, and aspiring financial professionals to prove their competence before actively pursuing roles in the securities industry. Essentially, the exam serves as a standardized benchmark, confirming that a candidate possesses the necessary building blocks to move forward in a compliance-oriented environment.

In practice, most individuals who plan to become registered representatives or associated persons at broker-dealers eventually must take the SIE, typically as a prerequisite before moving on to more specialized qualification exams. Still, the possibility of taking the SIE entirely independently—and well ahead of formal employment—has expanded opportunities for early career exploration. Students majoring in finance or business frequently leverage this exam to stand out in internships or entry-level job applications. Others might consider the SIE for personal growth or as a steppingstone to more advanced designations. Regardless of the candidate's motivation, the key point remains that the exam's open structure allows any interested party to demonstrate industry readiness in a formal, recognized manner.

For many individuals, the flexibility of taking the SIE first, without sponsorship, can reduce the time and risk involved in a potential career change. Rather than waiting to be hired and then scrambling to learn industry rules under tight deadlines, prospective professionals can develop their understanding of essential concepts on their own schedule. This approach benefits not only newcomers, but also the firms that may one day hire them. Employers value prospective hires who already grasp crucial regulatory mandates and industry fundamentals, as it means less initial training and a faster ramp-up to full productivity.

Though passing the SIE alone does not grant one the authority to act as a registered representative, it remains a non-negotiable entry point for anyone seeking to become licensed down the road. By setting this foundational standard, regulators and industry participants alike help ensure that new entrants thoroughly understand the ethical obligations and structural underpinnings of the securities markets from day one.

1.1.3 Passing Score and Validity Period

Candidates must earn a minimum score of 70% to pass the Securities Industry Essentials (SIE) Exam. This percentage indicates the baseline level of knowledge that regulators and industry stakeholders have deemed necessary for entry into a highly regulated profession. While the exam itself does not grant full registration for specific roles, achieving at least the 70% threshold is viewed as a clear demonstration of foundational competency in core securities laws, product types, and investor protection concepts. Once a candidate's results are released, their score generally reflects a pass/fail outcome rather than a detailed breakdown of performance in each content area, although future sections in this book will discuss how candidates might glean insights into any weaker areas of understanding and address them before advancing to more specialized examinations.

Beyond simply passing, it is critical to recognize the four-year validity period attached to an SIE Exam pass. During this window, individuals can pursue further qualification exams—such as those required to become a General Securities Representative—without having to retake the SIE. This arrangement not only motivates aspiring professionals to build upon their foundational knowledge within a reasonable timeframe, but it also provides flexibility for those who may be uncertain about their immediate career path in the securities field. Should a candidate's four-year period expire without taking any subsequent steps toward registration or additional exams, they would need to complete the SIE once again to maintain an active baseline of industry knowledge. This requirement helps ensure that anyone practicing in the securities environment is conversant with the most up-to-date rules and practices in an ever-evolving marketplace.

Finally, while passing the exam remains a key milestone, holding an active SIE credential by itself does not authorize an individual to transact business as a registered representative. Instead, it should be viewed as a robust jumping-off point—an essential credential for those who wish to demonstrate readiness to meet the demands of any role that requires a deep respect for both regulations and ethical standards. The four-year validity period thus strikes a balance between giving candidates ample time to decide how to apply their foundational learning and ensuring that people entering the field are working with knowledge that remains both current and relevant.

1.2 Exam Structure and Format

1.2.1 Number of Questions and Time Allotment

A critical aspect of preparing for any standardized exam is understanding its length and how much time you are given to complete it. The SIE Exam consists of a total of 85 questions, all of which must be answered within a single testing session. These questions are designed to test your grasp of the foundational knowledge necessary for entering the securities industry. Whether you come from a financial background or are completely new to the field, being aware of the exact number of questions helps you pace yourself during practice sessions and on test day. Test-takers who recognize how many questions they will face tend to manage their time more effectively, thus reducing the risk of running out of time near the end of the exam.

In terms of the official time allotment, candidates are granted 1 hour and 45 minutes (105 minutes in total) to complete the exam in one sitting. No additional breaks or stopping of the clock is provided, so you should approach this window with a clear strategy for time management. Some individuals find it helpful to divide the exam into smaller segments—perhaps completing a fixed number of questions every 15 to 20 minutes to stay on track. Others prefer to work at a steady pace, ensuring they read each question carefully without dwelling too long on any single item. While personal approaches to timing will vary, the common goal is to ensure all 85 questions are addressed thoroughly within the 105-minute duration.

Because this exam uses a computer-based format, you can move through questions at your own pace, and you have the option to review flagged items if time permits. Nonetheless, each candidate should be mindful of the clock to avoid letting a few challenging questions consume too many valuable minutes. If you finish early, you typically have the opportunity to revisit questions you may have skipped or marked for review, which can be particularly beneficial if you encountered any uncertainties along the way. Balancing speed with accuracy is a learned skill, and gaining familiarity with how much time you spend per question during practice will be instrumental in optimizing your performance when it counts.

1.2.2 Scoring Method (75 Scored + 10 Unscored Pretest)

The SIE Exam features a total of 85 questions, but only 75 of those are actually scored. The remaining 10 questions, often referred to as "pretest" items, are experimental in nature and do not affect your final result. Exam administrators use these pretest questions to gather statistical data on item clarity, difficulty, and overall performance before deciding whether to introduce them as scored questions in future tests. Because pretest items are embedded randomly throughout the exam, you cannot distinguish them from the scored ones. Consequently, it's best to give each and every question your full effort, since you won't know which ones will count toward your final score.

In calculating your score, only your responses to the 75 scored questions are factored into the final percentage. Each correct answer contributes equally—there is no partial credit for multi-part questions or any weighted points. In other words, the total number of correct answers out of those 75 scored items is what determines your mastery of the tested material. This consistent approach allows for fair comparisons among candidates, as everyone's performance is measured on the same set of validated questions. Although you might be curious about how you did on the unscored items, exam results generally will not indicate which questions were pretest, and you will not receive a separate tally of how many of those you answered correctly.

One important byproduct of including unscored questions is that test developers can keep the exam content up to date, reflecting new regulations or shifts in industry practices without constantly overhauling the entire test. Because the pool of pretest items is tested in live exam conditions, they receive a "real-world" evaluation for clarity and fairness, ensuring that future scored questions maintain a balanced level of challenge. While you won't know which items are part of this evaluation process, being aware of the reasoning behind these pretest questions can alleviate concerns if you encounter something that seems atypical or unfamiliar. By approaching every question with equal diligence, you effectively cover both the officially scored content and any experimental items that may eventually shape the exam for future candidates.

1.2.3 Question Distribution by Topic Area

Each question on the SIE Exam falls into one of four major content areas, reflecting the breadth of knowledge new entrants to the securities industry are expected to master. While the exact weighting of these areas may shift slightly over time as regulators update the exam, the fundamental structure remains consistent. These four domains ensure that candidates gain exposure to the broadest possible range of foundational concepts—from an understanding of capital markets and the different products they offer, to the specific rules that govern trading, customer relationships, and the broader regulatory framework. This distribution of content helps maintain an equitable balance between theoretical knowledge and the practical considerations professionals will encounter in day-to-day operations.

In practice, the largest portion of the exam typically focuses on the characteristics and risks of various financial products, followed by rules related to trading, customer accounts, and prohibited activities. These two areas together constitute a significant majority of the questions, underscoring how critical it is for securities professionals to understand both what they are offering to clients and how those transactions must be conducted. A smaller but still meaningful portion of the exam tests knowledge of capital markets—encompassing market participants, regulatory roles, and basic economic factors—while the final section examines the regulatory framework in more detail, ensuring that all new entrants are conversant with key industry rules and requirements.

Content Area	Approximate Weight
Knowledge of Capital Markets	16%
Understanding Products and Their Risks	44%
Understanding Trading, Customer Accounts, and Prohibited Activities	31%
Overview of the Regulatory Framework	9%

The table above offers a snapshot of how exam questions are divided among these critical domains. By taking note of this breakdown, candidates can tailor their study plans to align with the emphasis placed on each section. Some areas may feel more intuitive based on a candidate's background or interests, while others will require dedicated effort to master unfamiliar concepts or rules. Overall, this balanced approach to content distribution serves to confirm that all individuals who pass the exam possess not only a strong grasp of financial instruments and operations, but also the regulatory context within which these transactions must take place.

1.2.4 Question Style and Difficulty

Many of the questions in the SIE Exam are presented in a straightforward multiple-choice format, yet they can vary in complexity and the type of knowledge they demand. Some questions will ask for direct recall of definitions or concepts, requiring you to recognize industry terminology or outline the basic features of a security. Others may be more situational, prompting you to apply a concept to a real-world scenario or to interpret information about a hypothetical client and decide on a suitable course of action. These scenario-based questions can be especially nuanced, as they test not only your ability to memorize facts but also your comprehension of how various regulations, products, and practices intersect in practical contexts.

Difficulty is generally consistent with the exam's purpose of establishing a solid foundation for beginners in the securities industry, but it is not uniform across all items. You may encounter straightforward factual questions that feel relatively simple, interspersed with items that require careful reading and analysis. Often, the more challenging items hinge on subtle distinctions between similar products or rules, making it crucial to read every detail of the question and answer choices. The intent behind this variety in difficulty is to ensure that those who pass the exam have a balanced grasp of both the factual underpinnings of the industry and the judgment needed to navigate basic client or compliance situations.

In many cases, the test designers use plausible distractors—answer choices that resemble the correct one in some way—in order to gauge whether you truly understand the concept being tested. For instance, a question might present multiple regulatory guidelines that sound similar, requiring you to pay close attention to the precise wording or context that differentiates them. Adopting a methodical reading strategy, which involves carefully parsing each question and breaking down the relevant regulatory or product details, often makes the difference between a hasty incorrect response and an accurate selection. By recognizing the range of question styles and the calibration of difficulty throughout the test, you can better prepare yourself to adapt and respond effectively, regardless of whether a given question calls for simple recall or more in-depth critical thinking.

1.3 Registration and Logistics

1.3.1 Eligibility Requirements (Age, no Sponsor Required)

To sit for the SIE Exam, you must be at least 18 years of age. This age threshold is one of the few concrete prerequisites set forth by the regulators, ensuring that individuals entering the securities industry in any capacity are legally recognized as adults. Because the exam is a serious undertaking that opens the door to numerous professional opportunities, this minimum age requirement also underscores the industry's focus on entrusting financial knowledge and potential customer interactions to those who have reached a certain level of maturity. Importantly, having this age-based eligibility criterion places the SIE on par with many other professional qualification pathways, which similarly stipulate that applicants must be of legal adult status.

Unlike older series exams that often required association with a registered broker-dealer before scheduling, the SIE does not mandate firm sponsorship. This means you do not need to be employed by or affiliated with any specific financial firm to register and take the test. From a practical standpoint, this open format allows college students, career switchers, and individuals exploring the securities sector to gain official credentials on their own terms, without the added pressure of immediate employment demands. While pursuing the exam independently is certainly an option, doing so can be especially beneficial for prospective job seekers: demonstrating initiative by taking the SIE ahead of formal hire can set a candidate apart in a competitive job market.

1.3.2 How to Schedule the Exam

Before scheduling the SIE Exam, you will need to complete the necessary registration paperwork, which typically involves submitting personal information through the appropriate FINRA form. If you already have a sponsoring firm, they will handle the registration through FINRA's systems on your behalf. However, because the SIE does not require sponsorship, many individuals file Form U10 independently. Once the required registration details are processed, you will receive a unique enrollment or tracking number that authorizes you to proceed with exam scheduling. This step is essential because it confirms your eligibility and ensures the testing center or online proctoring service can verify your information correctly on exam day.

After receiving your enrollment confirmation, scheduling is generally done online or over the phone with a testing vendor authorized by FINRA. You will have the option to select a convenient test date, time, and location, provided there are seats available. Some candidates opt for a traditional physical testing center, while others may be able to take the exam via remote online proctoring if that feature is supported in their region. During the scheduling process, it is wise to consider your current study progress and any obligations that might interfere with your ability to sit for the exam on a particular day. Allocating enough time for review and practice exams can make a critical difference in your performance, so choose a slot that not only fits your schedule but also allows for final exam preparation without undue stress.

Because testing center availability may vary by region, it is advisable to book as early as you feel prepared to commit to a date. This approach helps secure a preferred spot and gives you a firm target to work toward, motivating you to finalize your study schedule. You can often reschedule if an unforeseen circumstance arises, but you should be mindful of the guidelines governing changes or cancellations to avoid incurring additional charges. Likewise, candidates planning to test remotely should familiarize themselves with any special requirements, such as having a reliable internet connection and a private workspace free from distractions. With a clear understanding of the registration pathway and scheduling process, you can confidently map out your study timeline and approach the exam date with readiness and minimal logistical hurdles.

1.3.3 Exam Fees and Retake Policies

Exam fees for the SIE are set by FINRA and must be paid at the time of registration. Candidates who are employed by a firm often see these fees covered by their employer, but individuals registering independently must bear the costs themselves. While the exact amount may occasionally change, you can expect the fee to be in line with typical entry-level certification exams. For the most up-to-date information, it is best to consult official FINRA resources or the testing vendor's website. Because these fees are nonrefundable, you should be certain of your exam date and your readiness before finalizing payment, to avoid incurring unnecessary expenses if circumstances require rescheduling.

Retake policies for the SIE are also governed by FINRA guidelines. If you do not pass on your first attempt, you must wait a minimum of 30 days before taking the exam again. This same 30-day waiting period applies between your second and third attempts. Should you not achieve a passing score on the third try, however, the waiting period extends to 180 days. Each subsequent failure will reset that six-month interval. Keep in mind that every time you retake the exam, you will be required to pay the same registration fee again. This structured retake schedule underscores the importance of thorough preparation, as rushing into repeated attempts can quickly become both time-consuming and costly.

It is worthwhile to approach the SIE with the goal of passing on your first attempt, not just from a cost perspective but also to maintain momentum in your career development. A thoughtful study plan—one that includes multiple practice exams and adequate review of material—can vastly improve your odds of success. While the retake windows offer a clear path forward if you do fall short, it is helpful to view them as a fallback rather than part of your primary plan. By understanding the financial and time implications of the exam process in advance, you can approach the test itself with greater confidence and a well-structured strategy.

1.4 Test-Taking Strategies and Study Tips

1.4.1 How to Use This Book (Reading Material + Practice Exams + Online Platform)

This book is designed to guide you through every facet of the SIE Exam in a logical, progressive manner. You'll first encounter in-depth reading material that aligns closely with the official exam outline, ensuring you have full coverage of the knowledge areas tested. Because the SIE spans a variety of topics—from fundamental regulatory principles to more detailed discussions of specific product types—it's best to work steadily through each chapter, verifying your understanding of one section before moving on to the next. In doing so, you'll gain a step-by-step grasp of the subject matter, building a foundation that will serve you well as you begin more hands-on practice. While you may be tempted to skip ahead to practice questions right away, reading thoroughly before testing yourself can help you better identify which areas need additional review later.

Alongside the reading material, we've included a series of full-length practice exams that simulate the format and difficulty of the actual SIE. By periodically measuring your progress with these practice tests, you'll develop insight into your strengths and weaknesses and learn to manage the multiple-choice format with increasing confidence. Detailed answer keys are provided to clarify why a particular choice is correct or incorrect. Reviewing the rationales behind each question is just as important as getting the question right in the first place; it ensures that you understand the underlying concepts thoroughly and can apply them even when a question is framed differently. This cyclical process of studying, testing, and reviewing allows you to refine your focus, zeroing in on any gaps in comprehension.

To supplement the reading material and practice exams, the accompanying online platform offers additional interactive features. You'll find digital flashcards to reinforce your memory of key terms and concepts, as well as an exam simulator that closely mirrors the conditions you'll face on test day. For those who learn best through repetitive quizzing or prefer a more gamified approach, these resources can help keep your studies fresh and dynamic. Ultimately, the blend of structured reading, self-assessment through practice exams, and interactive online tools will give you a multi-angle approach to mastering the SIE's diverse topics, setting you up for both immediate exam success and a strong long-term grasp of essential industry principles.

Resource	Purpose	Benefit
Reading Material	In-depth coverage of SIE topics aligned with the exam outline	Builds conceptual understanding before quizzing
Practice Exams	Full-length simulations mirroring question count and complexity	Identifies knowledge gaps and polishes exam strategy
Online Platform	Flashcards, exam simulator, and downloadable full-length mock exams	Reinforces learning through varied study techniques

By combining these three elements, you create a continuous feedback loop that helps you deepen your expertise with every study session. Investing time in each component—reading first, testing yourself second, and then leveraging online tools—can systematically boost your knowledge and confidence as you move closer to exam day.

1.4.2 Time Management During the Exam

Making the most of your allocated exam time starts with having a structured plan. Rather than answering each question in a reactive or haphazard manner, consider deciding in advance how you will pace yourself through the entire test. For some, this means moving question by question at a consistent speed; for others, it involves an initial pass to tackle the most straightforward questions quickly, followed by a return to any items that require additional thought. Regardless of which strategy you choose, the key is to maintain forward momentum so that you avoid running out of time before you have attempted every question. Because missed or unanswered questions cannot earn any points, it is always better to provide your best guess than to leave a response blank.

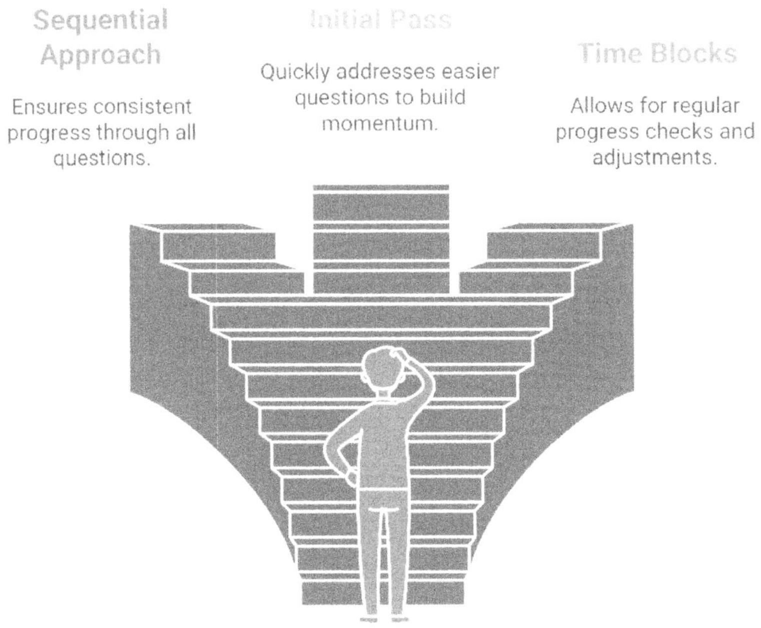

A practical first step in pacing is to familiarize yourself with how long it typically takes you to read, interpret, and answer a question. By timing your practice sessions, you can gauge whether you need to adjust your reading speed or change how you handle more involved items. Some candidates find it useful to break the exam into smaller time blocks, pausing at regular intervals to check whether they are on track. Others prefer a more flexible approach, focusing on maintaining an even, unhurried cadence throughout. Either way, keeping a watchful eye on the clock can reduce the risk of a last-minute scramble, which often leads to careless mistakes.

Pacing Strategy	Description
Steady Pace	Allocate a consistent amount of time per question. Monitor your progress regularly to avoid drifting too fast or too slow.
Two-Pass Method	Quickly answer the easiest questions on your first pass, then use remaining time to revisit and solve more challenging or time-consuming items.
Time-Chunk Approach	Divide the exam into equal segments (e.g., every 15 or 20 minutes), ensuring you reach a certain question number by each time checkpoint.

If you finish before the official test period ends, a final review of any uncertain answers can prove invaluable. During that review, give special attention to questions you initially found tricky. Briefly revisiting the rationale behind your original choice can sometimes reveal a misunderstanding or oversight. On the other hand, lingering too long on every question you might second-guess can be counterproductive, so it's wise to strike a balance—confirm answers you're fairly confident about, and concentrate your energy where your instincts tell you something may be amiss. By developing a clear, personalized strategy for time management and practicing it in simulated exams, you'll be far more likely to keep a steady pace and submit well-considered answers for every question.

1.4.3 Approaches to Multiple-Choice Questions

One of the most effective strategies for tackling multiple-choice questions is to read each question stem thoroughly before looking at the answer options. Pausing to understand what precisely is being asked can prevent the confusion that arises from hastily skimming answer choices. Pay special attention to keywords like "except," "not," or "best," as these can drastically alter the correct response. Once you have a clear grasp of the question, consider paraphrasing it in your own words. This simple habit helps you internalize the scenario and confirm that you truly understand what the examiner wants to test. After solidifying the question in your mind, scan the answer options deliberately—eliminating any that are clearly off base, and using your knowledge of financial terminology and regulations to narrow down plausible candidates.

If you encounter two or more choices that appear correct, compare them by referring back to the question stem's exact wording. In the SIE Exam, it's not uncommon for distractors to be factually correct statements yet still not answer the specific question posed. In such instances, focusing on the subtleties of the question—whether it asks for a "primary" regulatory goal or an "appropriate" product recommendation—can make the difference between an educated guess and an outright error. When you feel uncertain, it's often beneficial to pick the option that aligns most consistently with overarching industry rules or the fundamental principles you've studied. Further, maintaining calm and trusting your process of elimination will help you avoid overthinking. By systematically breaking down each prompt and answer choice, you can reduce the likelihood of misreading a question or falling into common exam pitfalls.

Keyword/Indicator	What It Signals
"Except" / "Not"	You're seeking the choice that does **not** fit the scenario or regulation described.
"Most Appropriate" / "Best"	The question may have multiple plausible options, but only one is the optimal or overarching solution.
"Primarily"	Focus on the main or leading factor, rather than supplementary reasons or minor details.

By honing these approaches in your practice sessions—carefully dissecting question stems, ruling out incorrect responses with confidence, and watching for subtle phrasing—you'll develop a sharper eye for how the exam is structured. This methodical approach to multiple-choice items complements solid content knowledge, ensuring that you're well-positioned to navigate even the most nuanced SIE questions on exam day.

1.4.4 Managing Exam Anxiety

Feeling nervous or apprehensive before taking the SIE Exam is completely normal. A certain level of stress can even be beneficial, heightening your focus and sharpening your mental acuity on test day. However, excessive anxiety can undermine your performance by clouding your judgment or causing you to rush through questions without fully analyzing them. One key to managing anxiety is solid preparation: if you know you have thoroughly studied the material, taken practice exams under timed conditions, and refined your test-taking techniques, much of the uncertainty that fuels worry will disappear. Confident familiarity with the exam format and your own pacing strategies can anchor you in what might otherwise feel like an unpredictable environment.

Another powerful approach involves integrating short mental and physical relaxation techniques into your study routine, as well as during the exam itself when permissible. Deep breathing exercises, for example, can help counteract the physical symptoms of stress, such as a racing heartbeat or clammy palms. Some individuals find it useful to take a brief "mental break" after every 10 or 15 questions, closing their eyes for a few seconds to refocus. Even something as simple as a quick stretch can interrupt escalating tension, enabling you to return to the next question with a calmer, clearer mindset. The key is to experiment with small, easily implemented techniques during your study sessions, so that by the time you're in the testing environment, these methods feel like second nature.

Coping Strategy	Description
Deep Breathing	Inhale slowly for a count of five, hold briefly, then exhale for a count of five to calm nerves.
Brief Mental Breaks	Pause for a few seconds between groups of questions to reset and clear your mind.
Positive Visualization	Picture yourself achieving your desired score, reinforcing self-confidence and focus.

Cultivating a positive mindset also plays a significant role in alleviating exam-related stress. While it's vital to be realistic about areas that still need improvement, try to acknowledge the progress you've already made. Remind yourself of the practice scores you've achieved, the familiarity you've built with the content, and the strategies you've honed for challenging questions. Framing the exam as an opportunity to demonstrate your knowledge—rather than as a high-stakes hurdle—can dramatically shift your emotional response. By pairing thorough preparation with straightforward stress-management techniques, you'll be better positioned to approach the exam calmly and effectively, transforming what could be an intimidating experience into a manageable and even empowering one.

Chapter 2 Knowledge of Capital Markets

2.1 Regulatory Entities, Agencies and Market Participants

2.1.1 The Securities and Exchange Commission (SEC)

The Securities and Exchange Commission (SEC) serves as the primary federal regulatory authority overseeing the securities markets in the United States. Established by the Securities Exchange Act of 1934, it holds broad powers to ensure that issuers, broker-dealers, and other market participants adhere to federal securities laws. Through various regulations and enforcement actions, the SEC seeks to maintain market integrity, protect investors from fraudulent practices, and foster an environment where capital formation occurs within a fair and orderly framework.

In practical terms, this means that the SEC reviews and approves registration statements for new offerings, monitors ongoing disclosure requirements, and investigates alleged violations of the securities laws. While its role extends to numerous aspects of the financial ecosystem—ranging from corporate disclosures to oversight of national exchanges—the SEC typically collaborates with self-regulatory organizations (SROs) to handle day-to-day market supervision. The SEC, however, retains ultimate authority when it comes to interpreting and enforcing the federal statutes that underpin investor protection and transparent market operations.

2.1.1.1 Purpose and Mission of Securities Regulation

Securities regulation exists primarily to protect investors, safeguard market integrity, and facilitate efficient capital formation. These goals reflect a fundamental principle: individuals and institutions participating in the financial markets should be able to do so in an environment that is transparent and fair. By requiring issuers to disclose accurate and timely information, regulatory frameworks help market participants make informed decisions about where to put their money. This transparency in turn reduces the risk of fraud and other deceptive practices, thereby bolstering public trust in the financial system. The end result is a more stable marketplace in which capital can flow more freely, ultimately fueling economic growth and innovation.

Historically, many of the key U.S. securities laws were enacted during the aftermath of major financial crises, when public confidence in the markets had been seriously undermined. Lawmakers recognized that investors would be hesitant to commit funds if they believed the markets were rife with manipulation, insider dealing, or inadequate disclosure. Modern securities regulation, therefore, is built on the twin pillars of mandating clear, consistent disclosure and enforcing rules that prohibit dishonest conduct. While specific regulations or enforcement approaches can vary over time, the underlying mission remains constant: to ensure that those who seek to raise capital in the public markets do so under rules that promote fairness, accuracy, and accountability.

Key Objectives of Securities Regulation	Description
Investor Protection	Ensuring that individuals have access to accurate information and safeguards against fraudulent practices.
Market Integrity	Maintaining fair and orderly markets by prohibiting manipulation and fostering transparency.
Capital Formation	Encouraging businesses to raise funds efficiently while balancing the need for thorough disclosure.

By enforcing these objectives, regulators strive to cultivate a level playing field on which investors can trade with confidence. In turn, companies are more likely to find willing buyers for their securities when the marketplace is viewed as credible and well-policed. This balance between regulatory oversight and robust market activity is what ultimately underpins the ongoing viability and success of the capital markets.

2.1.1.2 Definition, Jurisdiction, and Authority of the SEC

As an independent federal agency, the Securities and Exchange Commission (SEC) is charged with administering and enforcing the primary statutes governing the issuance and trading of securities in the United States. Established under the Securities Exchange Act of 1934, the SEC operates separately from executive departments, giving it latitude to develop and implement regulatory policies based on evolving market conditions. In broad terms, its function spans rulemaking, oversight, and enforcement: the SEC writes regulations that interpret existing federal securities laws, supervises industry participants to promote compliance, and takes action against those who violate these standards. By maintaining a clear boundary from other government bodies, the SEC can focus its efforts solely on issues that directly affect U.S. securities markets.

The SEC's jurisdiction covers a vast range of market participants and activities. Publicly traded companies must file periodic reports disclosing financial and operational information; broker-dealers, investment advisers, and other intermediaries are required to register and adhere to regulations that safeguard the investing public. The commission also examines exchanges and certain over-the-counter trading platforms to ensure they comply with the federal securities laws. When suspected violations arise—be they insider trading, accounting fraud, or other unlawful conduct—the SEC has the authority to investigate, subpoena relevant information, and bring civil enforcement actions in federal court or through administrative proceedings. Although it often collaborates with self-regulatory organizations and other government bodies, the SEC retains top-level authority to interpret securities laws, approve or disapprove of proposed rules by industry groups, and ultimately guide the evolution of regulations that keep the markets fair, orderly, and efficient.

2.1.2 Self-Regulatory Organizations (SROs)

Self-Regulatory Organizations (SROs) play a pivotal role in the securities industry by handling day-to-day oversight duties and enforcing standards among their member firms. Rather than relying solely on government agencies like the SEC for all supervisory functions, the industry itself steps in through these bodies to monitor and regulate member activities. SROs are thus empowered to create and enforce rules specifically tailored to the nuances of their markets, a structure that combines industry expertise with a mandate to uphold integrity and investor protection. By leveraging their intimate familiarity with how firms operate, SROs can respond more swiftly to emerging market trends or issues, which helps keep oversight agile and up-to-date.

Although SROs function with a degree of independence, they remain subject to the ultimate authority of federal regulators. This collaborative framework allows the SEC to focus on overarching regulatory matters, while SROs manage ongoing membership oversight and rule compliance on a granular level. It also provides a system of checks and balances: SROs develop and enforce rules, but their rulemaking and disciplinary actions often require approval or review at the federal level. This dual-layer approach aims to ensure that each participant in the securities ecosystem—from large broker-dealers to specialized trading venues—adheres to uniform standards of conduct, maintaining public confidence in the markets.

2.1.2.1 Purpose and Mission of SROs

At their core, Self-Regulatory Organizations (SROs) strive to uphold the integrity of the financial markets by enforcing rules and ethical standards among their member firms. Unlike governmental agencies that receive funding through public budgets, SROs are often financed by dues or fees paid by the member firms they regulate, giving these organizations a distinct blend of industry insight and regulatory oversight. This insider perspective allows them to craft guidelines that are closely aligned with current market realities, helping to prevent misconduct and instill best practices without imposing unnecessary hurdles on legitimate business activity. In this way, the SRO model offers a form of decentralized governance, drawing upon the collective expertise of industry participants while still answering to overarching statutory requirements.

Beyond setting and enforcing rules, SROs devote resources to fostering market confidence. They typically conduct routine examinations of member practices, investigate complaints of potential rule violations, and, when necessary, administer disciplinary measures. By proactively identifying potential sources of fraud or conflict of interest, SROs can address threats to market stability before they escalate. The presence of an industry-led regulator also lends credibility to the standards by which firms operate; professionals regulated by an SRO often find that compliance obligations are both more precise and more flexible than if they had been mandated exclusively by a federal authority. This close alignment with day-to-day industry operations helps SROs maintain a practical, real-time approach to oversight, reinforcing public trust in the financial services sector.

In addition to rulemaking and enforcement, many SROs further their mission by educating both market participants and, in some cases, investors. Training programs, guidance letters, and rule interpretations issued by these organizations can clarify best practices, highlight emerging risks, and promote uniform implementation of new regulatory mandates. This educational role is crucial, as it bridges gaps in understanding and ensures that even smaller firms—those without extensive compliance resources—can stay abreast of evolving standards. By offering guidance in tandem with the power to enforce rules, SROs create an environment where compliance is viewed not merely as a legal requirement but also as a shared commitment to a healthier, more transparent marketplace.

Finally, it is important to note that SROs function within a framework defined by federal securities laws and remain accountable to the Securities and Exchange Commission (SEC) or other relevant agencies. This accountability ensures that SROs do not become insular or overly permissive toward the industries they oversee. Periodic reviews and rule-filing obligations maintain a balance that supports meaningful self-governance while preventing conflicts of interest from undermining investor protections. By combining specialized expertise with a structured approval and oversight mechanism, SROs meet their essential purpose: safeguarding the markets they serve and fostering an environment in which both firms and investors can operate with confidence.

2.1.2.2 Jurisdiction and Authority of Key SROs

FINRA (Financial Industry Regulatory Authority)

FINRA serves as the primary self-regulatory organization overseeing broker-dealers and their registered representatives in the United States. It is responsible for writing and enforcing rules governing the ethical and operational conduct of its member firms, which include both large, internationally recognized broker-dealers and smaller independent shops. These rules cover critical areas such as advertising standards, suitability requirements, and recordkeeping protocols. While FINRA derives its authority partly from the Securities Exchange Act of 1934, it also operates under close oversight by the Securities and Exchange Commission (SEC). This means that any new rule or amendment FINRA proposes must be submitted to the SEC for review and approval, ensuring that self-regulation remains aligned with broader federal mandates.

From an enforcement standpoint, FINRA has the power to investigate suspected violations, conduct disciplinary hearings, and impose sanctions—ranging from monetary fines to suspensions or even permanent bars from the industry. FINRA also administers mandatory arbitration and mediation forums for resolving disputes between customers and their broker-dealers, as well as disputes among members themselves. By centralizing these regulatory, enforcement, and dispute resolution functions, FINRA not only promotes uniform standards but also relieves federal agencies from the burden of day-to-day oversight, allowing them to concentrate on systemic risks and higher-level policy concerns.

MSRB (Municipal Securities Rulemaking Board)

The MSRB is tasked with regulating the municipal securities market, encompassing entities that issue, underwrite, sell, or advise on municipal bonds and other public sector debt instruments. It formulates rules designed to protect investors and municipal entities alike, aiming to ensure transparent and fair dealings in a market that finances crucial public projects across the country. Unlike some other SROs, however, the MSRB does not enforce its own rules directly. Instead, it relies on the SEC and certain banking regulators—such as the Federal Reserve Board and the Office of the Comptroller of the Currency—to oversee compliance among different categories of market participants.

Although its jurisdiction is limited to activities in the municipal securities domain, the MSRB plays an essential role in standardizing disclosure and professional conduct for underwriters, dealers, and municipal advisors. It also develops guidelines for electronic trading platforms, trade reporting, and pricing transparency. The combination of these rules and reporting requirements helps investors evaluate the creditworthiness and risks associated with a municipal issue, thereby supporting the broader goal of ensuring that municipalities can efficiently raise funds for public works while fostering confidence among those who invest in these projects.

CBOE (Chicago Board Options Exchange)
As the largest U.S. options exchange, the CBOE holds the authority to write and enforce rules for the listing and trading of options contracts on its marketplace. Its jurisdiction extends to member firms and individual traders who execute options transactions on its platform. Although the CBOE is well-known for pioneering standardized, exchange-traded equity options, its regulatory scope has evolved to include oversight of index options, volatility products, and other derivatives. Any proposed rule changes by the CBOE—such as new contract specifications or margin requirements—must be filed with the SEC, which retains final approval to ensure these rules do not conflict with federal securities laws.

Through its regulatory arm, the CBOE monitors trading activity for signs of market manipulation or other infractions, cooperating closely with the SEC and FINRA to detect and address unusual patterns. This collaborative framework allows the CBOE to respond quickly to real-time market developments, such as halting trading in certain contracts if anomalies or extraordinary volatility arise. By combining deep expertise in derivatives markets with a recognized rulemaking function, the CBOE remains a pivotal SRO in maintaining the integrity, transparency, and orderly operation of the U.S. options industry.

2.1.3 Other Regulators and Agencies

Beyond the Securities and Exchange Commission (SEC) and Self-Regulatory Organizations (SROs), several other federal and state entities influence the regulatory landscape of the securities markets. Each of these entities carries out a distinct mandate, whether that involves overseeing the fiscal and monetary environment, safeguarding investor assets, or promoting uniform licensing standards. They generally intersect with the securities markets in ways that either shape investment behavior—such as through tax policy—or provide additional layers of security for participants. By working alongside the SEC and SROs, these agencies strive to create a cohesive framework that upholds market stability, protects investors, and ensures consistent practices among financial intermediaries.

While not all of these regulators directly craft rules governing broker-dealers or issue specific securities-related guidance, each plays a pivotal role in maintaining the broader structure within which the industry operates. For example, some focus on preventing systemic risks in the banking system, while others ensure individual investors' accounts remain protected up to certain limits. In upcoming sections, we'll explore how each of these agencies or departments contributes to the overall health of the capital markets, from shaping monetary policy to backing deposit insurance. By understanding their various roles, candidates can appreciate the interplay of different governmental and quasi-governmental bodies that together maintain public trust and economic stability.

2.1.3.1 Department of the Treasury / IRS

The Department of the Treasury is a critical arm of the U.S. government, tasked with managing the country's finances and formulating fiscal policy. It oversees the production and issuance of U.S. currency, while also managing federal debt through instruments like Treasury bills, notes, and bonds. These debt offerings are a staple of the capital markets, providing a benchmark for interest rates and a relatively low-risk investment option for individuals and institutions. Because Treasury securities influence everything from lending rates to global foreign exchange flows, the department's actions can have wide-ranging effects on liquidity and risk perception in the broader marketplace. Furthermore, Treasury's oversight of economic sanctions and anti-money laundering initiatives can affect how financial firms structure their compliance programs to meet both domestic and international regulatory obligations.

Under the larger Treasury umbrella, the Internal Revenue Service (IRS) plays a leading role in administering and enforcing the nation's tax laws, including those directly tied to investment income and securities transactions. The IRS develops policies on how gains and losses from stock sales, dividends, and interest payments are taxed, thereby influencing investor behavior. For example, favorable tax treatments on capital gains can encourage longer holding periods, while higher dividend tax rates may steer investors toward growth stocks or other investment vehicles. In practical terms, financial professionals and their clients must navigate reporting requirements (e.g., Form 1099 for interest and dividends) and adhere to IRS guidelines for cost basis tracking to ensure accurate tax calculation. These rules are crucial to maintaining the integrity of the markets, as they reduce incentives to evade tax obligations and help stabilize investment flows by creating predictable frameworks for how returns will be treated.

By working in tandem, the Department of the Treasury and the IRS shape essential economic conditions that directly affect the securities industry. Treasury debt issuance provides liquidity and benchmark rates, while the IRS's tax policies determine how investors approach risk, reward, and the timing of transactions. In doing so, these institutions not only guide day-to-day financial activities but also set the tone for broader market confidence, supporting the capital formation process that underpins economic growth.

2.1.3.2 State Regulators (NASAA)

State regulators serve as a crucial layer of investor protection alongside federal authorities, focusing on the specific needs and concerns of residents within their respective jurisdictions. At the forefront of coordinating these state-level efforts is the North American Securities Administrators Association (NASAA). Though "North American" in name—encompassing members from the United States, Canada, and Mexico—its impact is most directly felt in the U.S., where state securities agencies enforce "blue sky" laws. These laws require that securities offered or sold within a state be registered, unless a specific exemption applies, and they impose licensing requirements for broker-dealers and investment advisers at the state level. By taking a more localized approach to enforcement, state regulators can address investor complaints and oversee smaller intrastate offerings that may not necessarily draw the attention of larger federal entities.

NASAA itself operates as a forum for information exchange among state regulators, fostering uniformity where possible. It develops model rules and exam protocols, such as those governing the Series 63, 65, or 66 licenses. These model rules not only streamline the registration process across multiple states but also standardize the basic proficiency requirements for individuals selling securities or offering investment advice to the public. While the Securities and Exchange Commission (SEC) maintains broad federal jurisdiction, the states often have the final say in how securities are marketed to local investors, and they ensure that firms and representatives meet ethical and disclosure standards aligned with their specific statutory frameworks. This close attention to local market conditions—combined with NASAA's focus on aligning regulations across borders—helps safeguard smaller or niche investor segments that might otherwise slip through the cracks of federal oversight.

In practice, the collaborative dynamic between NASAA and state regulatory agencies allows for quick responsiveness to region-specific problems, such as emerging scams or specialized offerings that primarily affect local communities. Because these agencies are embedded within each state's legal and cultural context, they can tailor enforcement to address unique issues—for instance, widespread real estate development offerings in a particular area or localized business ventures reliant on community-based investments. Meanwhile, NASAA's development of uniform procedures and educational resources ensures that these regulations, while state-specific, adhere to baseline professional standards. Ultimately, this blend of local knowledge and broader regulatory coordination amplifies investor confidence at every tier of the market.

2.1.3.3 The Federal Reserve

The Federal Reserve (often referred to as "the Fed") serves as the central bank of the United States, wielding considerable influence over the nation's monetary policy and overall financial stability. Through its Board of Governors and twelve regional reserve banks, it works to promote maximum employment, stable prices, and moderate long-term interest rates—goals collectively mandated by what's known as the Fed's "dual mandate." Although the Federal

Reserve operates within the framework of congressional oversight, it maintains a high degree of independence in its day-to-day decisions. This autonomy enables the institution to set policies aimed at stabilizing the financial system without direct political pressure, ensuring that interest rates and credit availability reflect economic conditions rather than short-term political considerations.

A central aspect of the Fed's authority lies in its ability to manage the money supply and influence interest rates. It does this primarily through open-market operations—buying or selling U.S. Treasury securities to affect the amount of money circulating in the banking system. By adjusting the federal funds rate (the rate at which depository institutions lend balances at the Federal Reserve to each other overnight), the Fed can either encourage economic growth or rein in inflationary pressures. Furthermore, it sets the discount rate, which is the interest rate at which banks can borrow directly from the Federal Reserve's discount window. These tools not only shape borrowing costs for consumers and businesses but also ripple through capital markets, affecting everything from stock prices to bond yields.

Key Monetary Policy Tools	Description	Market Impact
Open-Market Operations	Buying or selling U.S. Treasuries to regulate the monetary base	Influences short-term interest rates and liquidity in the market
Federal Funds Rate Target	Setting a target rate for overnight lending between depository institutions	Guides broader borrowing costs for consumers and businesses

Discount Rate	Rate at which banks borrow from the Federal Reserve's discount window	Affects short-term credit availability and signals monetary policy
Reserve Requirements	Mandated fraction of deposits that banks must hold in reserve (used infrequently as a policy tool)	Impacts how much banks can lend and thus the money supply

Beyond setting interest rates, the Fed also supervises and regulates many of the nation's banks, ensuring they remain safe and sound in their lending and investment practices. This supervisory role serves as a critical backstop against excessive risk-taking that could destabilize the broader financial system. In times of financial crisis, the Federal Reserve often steps in as a lender of last resort, providing emergency funding to institutions facing liquidity constraints. Such interventions are intended to calm market sentiment and prevent local disruptions from spreading throughout the entire economy.

From the perspective of the securities industry, shifts in Fed policy can dramatically alter market conditions. A decision to raise or lower target rates not only influences borrowing costs but also shapes investor sentiment regarding stocks, bonds, and alternative assets. For instance, in a low-interest-rate environment, equities and longer-dated bonds may become more attractive to investors seeking higher yields, while an environment of rising rates can moderate speculative behavior. In this way, the Federal Reserve's actions reverberate through capital markets, guiding capital flows and risk preferences in ways that professionals in the securities field must continuously monitor.

2.1.3.4 Securities Investor Protection Corporation (SIPC)

The Securities Investor Protection Corporation (SIPC) was established under the Securities Investor Protection Act of 1970 to protect investors if a broker-dealer fails financially. Although it works alongside regulatory agencies, SIPC is not a governmental entity; rather, it is a nonprofit membership organization funded by broker-dealers that are required by law to join. Its principal function is to oversee the liquidation of insolvent brokerage firms and ensure that customers' missing securities and funds are restored up to certain limits. In essence, SIPC coverage seeks to maintain public trust in the securities markets, assuring investors that, in the event of a broker-dealer collapse, they will not lose their holdings simply because of the firm's insolvency. However, SIPC does not protect against declines in the market value of securities; it only replaces the stocks, bonds, and cash that are held in an account if they are lost or misplaced due to a firm's failure.

When a member broker-dealer goes under, SIPC steps in to coordinate the claims process with a court-appointed trustee, who examines customer accounts to determine what each investor is owed. SIPC's standard coverage is up to $500,000 per separate customer, which includes up to $250,000 in protection for cash balances. The term "separate customer" extends to individual accounts, joint accounts, and certain other account categories, allowing an investor to benefit from multiple layers of coverage if they hold different types of accounts. If a client's account cannot be fully satisfied by the remaining assets of the failed brokerage, SIPC funds make up the shortfall within the specified limits. Once customers receive their proportionate shares of cash or securities, they are generally treated as unsecured creditors for any amount that goes beyond SIPC's coverage threshold.

Coverage Aspect	Amount
Total Coverage	Up to $500,000 per separate customer
Cash Coverage Sub-Limit	Up to $250,000
Protection Focus	Missing securities or cash due to broker-dealer failure (not market losses)

SIPC's existence underpins the broader stability of the U.S. securities industry by mitigating the fallout from brokerage failures. It works closely with self-regulatory organizations and the SEC in monitoring member broker-dealers, maintaining updated lists of members, and educating investors about the extent and limits of their coverage. Though rare, high-profile brokerage liquidations underscore the importance of SIPC's role, as it ensures a swift, organized resolution for clients who might otherwise face prolonged legal battles to recover their holdings. By providing a safety net in these circumstances, SIPC bolsters investor confidence, enabling capital to flow more freely in the financial markets.

2.1.3.5 Federal Deposit Insurance Corporation (FDIC)

The Federal Deposit Insurance Corporation (FDIC) is an independent U.S. government agency created in 1933 during the aftermath of widespread bank failures. Its primary mandate is to maintain stability and public confidence in the nation's banking system by insuring deposits, examining and supervising financial institutions, and managing receiverships when banks fail. Unlike the Securities Investor Protection Corporation (SIPC), which protects investor assets in brokerage accounts, the FDIC focuses on deposit insurance for bank accounts such as checking, savings, and certificates of deposit (CDs). This distinction is critical for investors and consumers alike: while SIPC coverage applies to securities positions within a brokerage, FDIC coverage addresses the risk of a bank's insolvency, ensuring depositors' funds remain safe up to specified limits.

By law, the FDIC insures deposits up to $250,000 per depositor, per FDIC-insured bank, for each account ownership category (such as individual, joint, or certain retirement accounts). When a bank fails, the FDIC steps in as a receiver, working to liquidate the institution's assets or arrange a merger with a healthier bank so that customers retain prompt access to their insured funds. In many cases, depositors remain largely unaffected by a bank's closure, aside from a brief transition period as the FDIC facilitates a transfer of accounts. Though coverage limits may occasionally be revisited by Congress, deposit insurance remains a cornerstone in fostering public trust in the U.S. banking system—a trust that is essential to encourage consistent saving habits and healthy levels of credit activity.

Because the FDIC also supervises and examines member institutions, it helps guard against excessive risk-taking that could undermine both individual banks and the broader financial ecosystem. These supervisory roles often involve reviewing lending practices, capital adequacy, and risk management frameworks. By promoting sound banking operations, the FDIC reduces the likelihood of institutional failures, thereby limiting the potential cost to its deposit insurance fund. Taken together, deposit coverage and supervisory functions establish the FDIC as a key pillar in maintaining the integrity and stability of the nation's financial landscape, ensuring that the flow of funds through insured banks remains a reliable backbone of the U.S. economy.

Key Functions of the FDIC	Description
Deposit Insurance	Insures eligible deposits up to $250,000 per depositor, per insured bank
Bank Supervision	Reviews and examines banks to ensure sound financial practices and legal compliance
Receivership Management	Takes over failed banks, sells assets, and protects insured depositors

Such a framework complements the other regulatory bodies discussed in this chapter: while agencies like the SEC focus on securities and investor protection, and the Federal Reserve oversees monetary policy and systemic financial stability, the FDIC stands watch specifically over depositors' funds, mitigating bank runs and reinforcing a robust foundation on which capital markets can flourish.

2.1.4 Market Participants and Their Roles

At a fundamental level, capital markets bring together a variety of players whose combined actions help shape the flow of funds and the pricing of securities. These participants range from individual retail investors to large institutional entities, each with their own motivations and constraints. Broker-dealers stand in the middle of this interplay, matching buyers and sellers or executing trades for their own accounts, while investment advisers and municipal advisors guide clients through portfolio decisions and public financing strategies. From the issuer's perspective, underwriters help raise capital by pricing and distributing new security offerings, whereas custodians and trustees oversee the protection and administration of those assets once sold. In addition, certain entities—like transfer agents and depositories—take on operational roles to keep the market's back-end functions running smoothly.

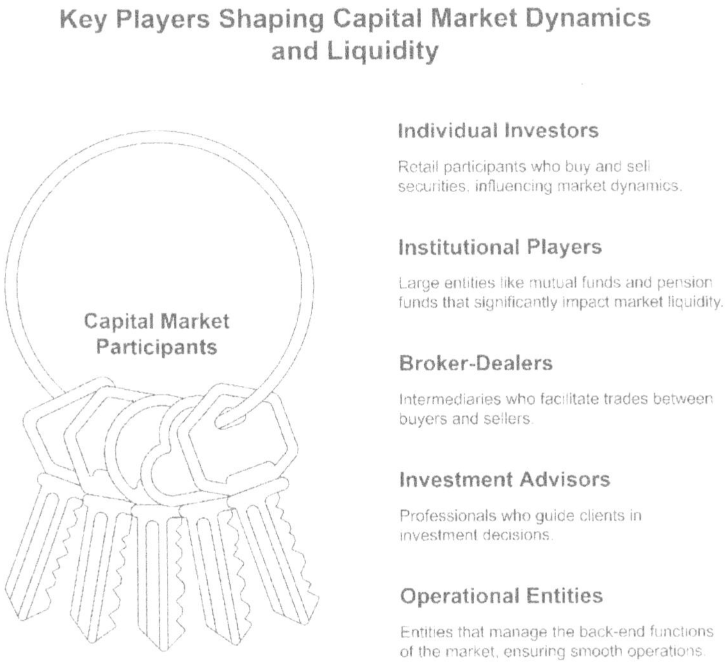

Understanding the unique responsibilities and interactions of each participant is critical to grasping how the financial ecosystem maintains both liquidity and integrity. Those who trade in a principal capacity, such as traders and market makers, supply ongoing price quotes and inventory for trading venues, thereby ensuring that securities remain readily exchangeable. On the other hand, agencies charged with holding or transferring securities focus more on recordkeeping and safeguarding client interests. By collaborating in these specialized capacities, market participants enable transactions of all types and sizes to occur in a timely, orderly manner. The upcoming sections will delve further into the nuances of each participant's role, clarifying how their functions collectively uphold efficiency and trust within the capital markets.

2.1.4.1 Investors (Accredited, Institutional, Retail)

Investors form the backbone of the capital markets, providing the funds that fuel economic growth and enabling companies and governments to raise money for various initiatives. While these market participants all share the goal of seeking returns, they differ in terms of financial sophistication, risk tolerance, and regulatory requirements. Understanding the distinctions between accredited, institutional, and retail investors is essential for grasping how each group influences securities offerings, pricing, and liquidity. From high-net-worth individuals who meet certain wealth or income thresholds, to large entities managing billions of dollars in assets, to everyday people saving for retirement, each category of investor plays a distinct role in shaping market behavior and driving capital formation.

Accredited investors typically include those who satisfy specific net worth or income criteria set forth by regulatory authorities, as well as certain entities like banks and trusts with substantial assets. Because they are presumed to have the resources and expertise to conduct their own due diligence, accredited investors often enjoy access to private placements and other unregistered offerings that are not open to the general public. Institutional investors, such as pension funds, mutual funds, insurance companies, and endowments, wield considerable influence due to the sheer size of their investable assets. These institutions can sway market sentiment, especially if they shift large allocations from one asset class to another. Retail investors, on the other hand, are everyday individuals who invest for personal goals—ranging from short-term speculation to long-term retirement planning. While each retail investor may deploy relatively small amounts of capital, taken collectively, they form a massive segment of the market and can drive significant demand for publicly traded securities.

Category	Typical Criteria or Definition	Market Impact
Accredited	Net worth over $1 million (excluding primary residence) or income over $200,000 ($300,000 jointly) for prior two years; also includes certain institutional entities	Access to private placements and unregistered offerings, can assume greater risks
Institutional	Large organizations (pension funds, mutual funds, insurance companies, etc.) that invest substantial sums	Influence market liquidity and price formation due to sizable trades
Retail	Individual investors who do not meet accredited thresholds; invest personal funds for various objectives	Aggregate market force; often pursue mutual funds, ETFs, or direct stock ownership

From a regulatory perspective, rules governing disclosure, advertising, and suitability often differ based on which category of investor is being served. Private placements, for instance, may require far less disclosure than a public offering, yet they are restricted to accredited or institutional investors. Retail investors benefit from mandatory disclosures and protections designed to help them navigate markets with fewer resources or less professional guidance. Understanding these investor segments, and the strategies and protections tailored to each, sheds light on why certain securities are made broadly available, while others remain the province of a limited audience. Each group, by virtue of its size, sophistication, or regulatory standing, drives a different slice of demand in the markets, collectively fueling the vibrant, multifaceted ecosystem that defines modern finance.

2.1.4.2 Broker-Dealers (Introducing, Clearing, Prime Brokers)

Broker-dealers operate at the center of securities trading, facilitating the exchange of assets while often providing ancillary services such as research, margin lending, and portfolio analysis. On the most basic level, a broker-dealer will act as a broker when it brings together buyers and sellers, earning a commission for executing trades, and as a dealer when it trades securities from its own inventory, profiting from markups or markdowns. Within this broad category, however, distinct types of broker-dealers cater to different client bases and perform specialized roles to ensure the efficiency and safety of transactions. Two essential subtypes—introducing brokers and clearing brokers—work in tandem to handle trades and manage the myriad back-office tasks that accompany them, whereas prime brokers often serve as the one-stop financial service platform for large, sophisticated clients.

Introducing Broker-Dealers typically interface directly with customers, offering advice, trade execution, and various other client services. However, they do not maintain custody of customer funds or securities, passing that responsibility on to a clearing broker. This arrangement allows the introducing firm to focus on front-end operations, like building client relationships and tailoring product offerings, rather than wrestling with operational intricacies. The division of labor also adds an extra layer of risk management: because the clearing broker holds client assets, it is better positioned to handle complex settlement functions and maintain robust compliance systems around recordkeeping and safekeeping. Through such a partnership, introducing brokers can compete with larger firms while minimizing capital requirements and operational overhead.

Clearing Broker-Dealers take on the back-office responsibilities essential to completing trades. Once a security is bought or sold, the clearing broker confirms trade details, settles funds, delivers the securities, and keeps records of all transactions. Clearing brokers must meet heightened regulatory thresholds—including higher net capital requirements—given their vital part in preventing settlement failures and ensuring the stability of the securities markets. They also provide technology platforms that introducing brokers use to place orders and manage client positions. By consolidating clearing and settlement functions among a limited number of firms, the industry can maintain a more standardized, secure environment for recordkeeping and transfers of ownership.

Prime Brokers stand out as specialized broker-dealers offering a suite of sophisticated services typically geared toward hedge funds, large institutional investors, and other active trading entities. In addition to the usual clearing and settlement, prime brokers offer services like securities lending, margin financing, risk analytics, and operational support. These capabilities enable professional investors to manage complex strategies—from short selling to derivatives trading—under one central hub. Often, a hedge fund will execute trades through multiple broker-dealers but use a single prime broker to aggregate and track positions, handle portfolio financing, and streamline reporting. This arrangement improves operational efficiency, since all trades eventually reconcile through a single prime broker, reducing errors and ensuring that performance data and risk metrics are consistent and consolidated.

While introducing and clearing brokers together ensure that everyday transactions run smoothly for a wide array of clients, prime brokers take on more intricate tasks for entities that demand institutional-level tools and financing options. All three types of broker-dealers play vital roles within the securities industry's larger infrastructure, helping maintain a stable, efficient trading environment while tailoring their services to client size and complexity. Through this specialization, broker-dealers collectively form the backbone of trade execution and asset custody, enabling investors and institutions alike to pursue diverse investment strategies with confidence in the mechanics of the market.

2.1.4.3 Investment Advisers

Investment advisers play a distinct yet integral role in the financial markets by offering personalized guidance on securities and portfolio strategies. Unlike broker-dealers, who may earn transaction-based compensation, most investment advisers charge advisory fees—such as a percentage of assets under management (AUM) or a flat fee—for the ongoing management and monitoring of client portfolios. Their services can range from formulating comprehensive financial plans to executing day-to-day investment decisions on behalf of individual or institutional clients. In many cases, the adviser exercises discretionary authority, allowing them to buy or sell securities in a client's account without prior approval for each transaction, provided they stay within the bounds set by the client agreement. This close alignment of economic interests, wherein an adviser's compensation often rises or falls with the client's portfolio value, is designed to foster a sense of partnership in pursuit of the client's financial objectives.

One of the key legal frameworks governing this profession is the Investment Advisers Act of 1940, which, among other requirements, imposes a fiduciary duty on advisers. This fiduciary responsibility compels them to place the interests of their clients above their own, making full disclosure of any conflicts of interest and ensuring recommendations are suitable in light of each client's objectives, risk tolerance, and overall financial situation. Depending on the amount of assets under management, an adviser may have to register at the federal level with the Securities and Exchange Commission (SEC) or with one or more state securities authorities. Larger advisers—those with over $100 million in AUM—are typically overseen by the SEC, while smaller advisers often fall under state jurisdiction. Regardless of the registration channel, all advisers must maintain detailed records of their advisory activities and adhere to advertising and performance reporting standards that promote transparency.

Because investment advisers frequently handle a range of complex tasks—such as ongoing portfolio rebalancing, retirement planning, and estate considerations—they rely heavily on clear, ongoing communication with clients. Advisers may also specialize in particular niches, like socially responsible investing or managing the portfolios of nonprofit organizations, tailoring their approach to the unique goals and constraints of the client base. This emphasis on personalized service helps differentiate advisers from other market participants and reinforces their fiduciary mission: to guide clients toward long-term financial well-being through informed, conflict-free counsel. By operating under this model of undivided loyalty, investment advisers serve as a key pillar of investor protection and confidence in the broader securities ecosystem.

2.1.4.4 Municipal Advisors

Municipal advisors occupy a specialized niche in the securities markets, focusing exclusively on the needs and interests of public entities such as state governments, cities, counties, and other municipal issuers. Their core function is to provide guidance on financial matters tied to municipal offerings, including the issuance of bonds for infrastructure projects, revenue anticipation notes, and other public debt instruments. Unlike investment advisers, whose client base often includes private individuals or institutions, municipal advisors concentrate on ensuring that government entities secure financing under terms that align with both budgetary constraints and long-term community goals. Their fiduciary duty requires them to act in the best interests of the municipality, helping to structure deals that promote cost-effective borrowing while mitigating potential risks—whether that involves choosing a fixed- or variable-rate issue, determining an optimal maturity schedule, or evaluating credit enhancement options.

From a regulatory standpoint, municipal advisors fall under the purview of the Municipal Securities Rulemaking Board (MSRB), which establishes rules of conduct specifically tailored to municipal finance professionals. The MSRB's regulations require municipal advisors to register with the SEC, adhere to professional qualification standards (including licensing exams), and comply with recordkeeping and supervisory obligations that protect municipalities from conflicts of interest or deceptive practices. Because municipal issuers often have unique budgeting cycles, tax revenues, and political considerations, municipal advisors must balance technical financial expertise with a deep understanding of public policy and stakeholder coordination. For instance, they may advise on statutory limitations for debt issuance, assist with credit rating presentations, or work with underwriters to design a bond structure that resonates with potential investors.

These responsibilities place municipal advisors at the intersection of finance and governance, where decisions about capital formation can have long-lasting impacts on public services and community development. An effective municipal advisor not only crunches the numbers but also communicates complex financing strategies in a transparent way, facilitating consensus among elected officials, community members, and potential bondholders. By guiding the decision-making process with specialized insight into municipal bond markets, municipal advisors help their clients achieve the delicate balance of securing the needed funds for public projects while maintaining fiscal prudence and accountability.

2.1.4.5 Issuers and Underwriters

Issuers are organizations—ranging from corporations to municipalities—that seek to raise capital by offering securities to the public or through private channels. When a company decides to go public via an initial public offering (IPO) or expand its shareholder base with follow-on offerings, it issues equity in the form of stocks. Similarly, a municipality or government entity might issue bonds to fund infrastructure projects or other public works. The proceeds from these offerings typically support growth initiatives, debt refinancing, or operational needs. In the equities space, these moves often provide investors an opportunity to become part-owners of a company, sharing in both its risks and potential rewards. In the case of bonds, issuers borrow money from investors and promise to repay the principal plus interest, thus offering a structured income stream to the bondholders.

Underwriters play a central role in these transactions, acting as intermediaries who bridge the gap between the issuer and the investing public. Typically investment banks or specialized broker-dealers, underwriters conduct due diligence on the issuer's financial health, the broader market environment, and the target audience for the securities. Their goal is to price the offering in a way that generates sufficient demand while still providing attractive terms for the issuer. Once pricing is set, the underwriter often commits to purchasing the securities from the issuer and then reselling them to the public. In a "firm commitment" arrangement, the underwriter assumes the full risk of not selling all the shares or bonds at the agreed-upon price—meaning they may be left holding unsold securities if demand fails to meet expectations. In a "best efforts" arrangement, on the other hand, the underwriter agrees only to market the issue and sell as many shares as possible at a specified price but does not guarantee the entire amount will be sold. This division of risk and responsibility is critical because it influences how quickly the issuer can access capital, as well as the overall market reception.

Beyond the actual sale, underwriters often provide additional services essential to a successful offering. These can include coordinating legal and regulatory filings, conducting investor roadshows, and furnishing research coverage that informs the market about the security's features and potential. Underwriters also typically manage the syndicate process, wherein multiple firms cooperate to distribute large offerings that a single institution might not handle alone. By shouldering responsibility for distribution and pricing strategy, the underwriting syndicate ensures that the issuer gains access to a wide range of potential investors—from large institutions to individual participants—within a relatively short time frame.

The interplay between issuers and underwriters shapes the primary market, where new securities are sold for the first time. This relationship not only determines how much capital the issuer can raise but also influences the security's post-offering performance in the secondary market. A well-structured underwriting process can generate positive momentum and liquidity, bolstering investor confidence. Conversely, mispricing or poor syndicate coordination might lead to undersubscribed offerings, which can dampen demand for future issues from the same entity. Thus, issuers and underwriters work in tandem to balance price, risk, and market conditions, setting the stage for the security's lifespan in the broader financial ecosystem.

2.1.4.6 Traders and Market Makers

Traders are individuals or entities that buy and sell securities with the objective of profiting from short-term market fluctuations, long-term trends, or a combination of both. In the most general sense, traders may operate on behalf of broker-dealers, institutional investors, or themselves (as proprietary traders). Their methods can include systematic approaches—like algorithmic trading—or more discretionary strategies based on market research and technical or fundamental analysis. Although traders may represent different motivations and time horizons, they share a common goal of executing orders efficiently and at prices that reflect—or improve upon—prevailing market conditions. Some traders specialize in specific asset classes, such as equities, fixed income, or derivatives, honing specialized skills or insights that enable them to navigate the unique microstructures and risk profiles of each market.

Market makers, on the other hand, perform a more structured function in the marketplace, continuously standing ready to buy or sell securities at publicly quoted bid and ask prices. By doing so, they help maintain liquidity, ensuring that investors can transact quickly without experiencing significant price disruptions. Unlike many traders, market makers almost always hold inventory and are compensated by the spread between the bid and ask prices. The narrower the spread, the more competitively they are pricing a given security, which in turn helps enhance market efficiency. Market makers often register with exchanges or electronic communication networks (ECNs) under contractual obligations to remain active participants, even when short-term conditions introduce volatility or reduced liquidity. Because they're routinely at risk of adverse price movements in the inventory they carry, effective market makers rely on hedging strategies, risk models, and rapid trade execution. In exchange for assuming these risks, they collect the bid-ask spread and may also receive incentives from trading venues aiming to foster tight quotations and robust transaction flow.

Behind the scenes, technology and regulatory standards heavily influence how both traders and market makers operate. The widespread adoption of electronic trading platforms has substantially reduced transaction times and given rise to high-frequency trading (HFT) firms, whose algorithms place multiple orders within fractions of a second. While such tools can improve liquidity and price discovery, they also heighten competition among market makers and demand rigorous compliance frameworks to prevent manipulative practices like spoofing or quote stuffing. On the regulatory side, entities such as FINRA and the SEC impose rules on best execution, position reporting, and fair dealing to ensure that traders and market makers conduct themselves transparently and in alignment with broader market integrity goals. Consequently, the interplay between these sophisticated trading technologies and comprehensive regulatory oversight serves to refine the role of traders and market makers, contributing to a capital market environment that—under healthy conditions—remains liquid, efficient, and reflective of underlying asset values.

2.1.4.7 Custodians and Trustees

Custodians serve a vital function in the capital markets by safeguarding clients' securities and other financial assets. While broker-dealers often handle transaction execution, custodians focus on the secure storage and accurate recordkeeping of those securities once purchased. In practice, custodians maintain detailed records of asset ownership, reconciling positions with transfer agents and depositories to ensure that each holding is properly accounted for. This meticulous documentation not only protects investors from administrative mishaps but also helps reduce operational risk. Because custodians typically operate under strict regulatory requirements and often employ sophisticated technology systems, they can provide clients—ranging from retail investors to large institutions—with confidence that assets are safe from theft, fraud, or clerical errors. In many cases, custodians may also handle ancillary tasks, such as collecting dividends or interest payments, managing corporate action events (e.g., stock splits, mergers), and providing portfolio statements or tax reporting.

Trustees, on the other hand, oversee assets held in trust for the benefit of third parties, such as beneficiaries of a family trust or bondholders in a debt issuance. Acting under a fiduciary duty, trustees must at all times prioritize the interests of these beneficiaries above their own. For example, in the realm of corporate or municipal bonds, an indenture trustee might verify the issuer's compliance with debt covenants, hold collateral (if the bond is secured), and facilitate the timely distribution of principal and interest payments. Trustees in personal or family trusts may be responsible for prudent investment of trust assets, tax planning, and making disbursements in accordance with the terms laid out by the trust's creator. Regardless of whether the trust context is public or private, the trustee's role is one of high legal and ethical accountability, entailing careful oversight of asset allocation, recordkeeping, and risk management.

Both custodians and trustees maintain close alignment with regulatory frameworks that govern financial integrity, transparency, and consumer protection. This includes complying with antifraud provisions, adhering to best execution standards if they facilitate any type of transaction, and meeting requirements for annual financial audits or periodic reviews by regulatory authorities. In many jurisdictions, custodians are subject to capital requirements aimed at bolstering their resilience, while trustees—particularly those overseeing large pools of assets—must demonstrate robust internal controls to protect beneficiaries' interests. By fulfilling these responsibilities conscientiously, custodians and trustees help preserve market confidence, ensuring that investors can enter into transactions with the assurance that their assets and entitlements remain protected in both ordinary and extraordinary circumstances.

2.1.4.8 Transfer Agents

Transfer agents occupy a critical role within the securities markets by managing and recording changes in ownership for corporate stocks, bonds, and other registered securities. When an investor buys or sells shares in a company, the transfer agent updates the official record of who holds those shares—commonly referred to as the shareholder register—and ensures that stock certificates (in physical or electronic form) are properly issued, canceled, or transferred. This process may sound straightforward, but it involves numerous considerations, such as verifying signatures, ensuring compliance with state laws or corporate policies, and coordinating with depositories or broker-dealers to process trades effectively. Transfer agents also track the number of authorized shares and watch for any errors or duplications that could compromise the accuracy of the issuer's records.

Beyond handling routine ownership changes, transfer agents frequently administer distributions such as dividends, interest payments, or corporate action proceeds (e.g., cash from mergers, spin-offs, or rights offerings). In this capacity, they gather and maintain the necessary banking information for shareholders, calculate distribution amounts based on the shareholder's position as of a specified record date, and arrange payments either by check or electronically. Handling dividends and corporate actions is no small task, given that companies might have thousands or even millions of shareholders. Accuracy and timeliness are paramount, since any lapses could jeopardize shareholder confidence or expose the company to legal and regulatory risks. As an added layer of complexity, international shareholders may require special tax withholding procedures, currency conversions, or disclosures in accordance with local regulations.

In addition to updating ownership records and distributing payments, transfer agents often serve as a communication channel between issuers and their shareholders. They might process shareholder inquiries, organize shareholder meetings, or facilitate proxy voting, which is especially important for publicly traded corporations seeking to gauge investor sentiment on corporate governance matters. This interaction demands a combination of technological infrastructure and data management expertise, ensuring that communications—from proxy statements to annual reports—reach the correct individuals and reflect accurate ownership information. Moreover, transfer agents must operate under a variety of regulatory frameworks, including federal securities laws enforced by the Securities and Exchange Commission (SEC) and any applicable state laws. They can also be subject to oversight by self-regulatory organizations if the securities they service trade on registered exchanges.

By diligently maintaining the accuracy, privacy, and efficiency of recordkeeping and transaction processes, transfer agents help uphold overall market confidence. Their behind-the-scenes management of shareholder records reduces confusion, prevents double-counting or misallocation of shares, and expedites corporate actions. Whether working with large multinational firms or smaller private issuers, the transfer agent's function remains a cornerstone of operational integrity in the securities domain, ensuring that all stakeholders—from public investors to corporate boards—can navigate the capital markets with clarity and trust.

2.1.4.9 Depositories and Clearing Corporations (DTCC, OCC)

Depositories and clearing corporations serve as the foundational infrastructure for settling trades and safeguarding securities in modern capital markets. Their primary mission is to ensure that once buyers and sellers agree on a transaction, the movement of money and the transfer of ownership occur smoothly and reliably. In the U.S., the Depository Trust & Clearing Corporation (DTCC) stands as a central pillar for most equity, corporate bond, and other debt instrument settlements, whereas the Options Clearing Corporation (OCC) performs a parallel function in the options market. Through robust technological systems and risk mitigation protocols, these entities reduce the possibility of settlement failures and protect market participants from counterparty defaults or clerical discrepancies.

The Depository Trust & Clearing Corporation (DTCC)

DTCC traces its roots to the early 1970s, when "paper crunches" threatened to overwhelm broker-dealers with an ever-growing volume of physical certificates. By converting those certificates into electronic book-entry form, DTCC dramatically streamlined the post-trade process, effectively eliminating the risk of lost or forged paperwork. In a typical equity or bond trade, DTCC simultaneously transfers securities from the seller's broker to the buyer's broker and moves cash in the opposite direction—an arrangement known as delivery versus payment (DVP). This electronic system reduces transaction costs, expedites settlements (commonly within two business days, though further reductions in settlement times are in progress), and provides a transparent audit trail for regulators and firms. Moreover, DTCC's subsidiaries, such as the National Securities Clearing Corporation (NSCC), act as intermediaries that guarantee trades, absorbing counterparty risk so that participants can rely on a centralized process rather than having to manage dozens or hundreds of bilateral settlement relationships.

The Options Clearing Corporation (OCC)

In the derivatives domain, particularly options on equities and indexes, the OCC takes on a similar clearing function. After an option contract is executed on an exchange, the OCC becomes the buyer to every seller and the seller to every buyer, effectively "novating" the trade and assuming counterparty risk. This not only reassures traders that they can realize their gains without relying on the creditworthiness of individual counterparties, but also empowers the market to function with tighter bid-ask spreads and more frequent transactions. The OCC employs sophisticated margin requirements—calculating initial and variation margin—to protect against the risk of large losses from volatile markets. In doing so, it ensures that sellers of options maintain sufficient capital or collateral to cover potential obligations, thereby mitigating the possibility of a widespread default event. Additionally, the OCC facilitates the option exercise and assignment processes, ensuring that contracts are settled according to established rules and on time.

Although DTCC and OCC specialize in distinct segments of the market, they both promote standardization, efficiency, and stability. Each clearing corporation maintains comprehensive operational controls, including a layered approach to cybersecurity, backup data centers, and contingency plans for extreme events. They also coordinate closely with regulators, self-regulatory organizations, and financial institutions worldwide to evolve clearing and settlement practices in step with technological advancements and market developments. In this way, depositories and clearing corporations remain a linchpin of the financial ecosystem, ensuring that trades executed in markets large and small conclude with confidence, precision, and minimal systemic risk.

2.2 Market Structure

2.2.1 Types of Markets

Broadly speaking, the securities markets can be divided into distinct categories based on how and where transactions take place. In the **primary market**, new securities are offered to the public for the first time, typically through initial public offerings (IPOs) or bond issuances. By contrast, the **secondary market** handles the buying and selling of existing securities once their initial distribution has occurred, providing ongoing liquidity and an avenue for investors to adjust their portfolios.

In addition to these well-known venues, there are specialized segments referred to as the **third** and **fourth** markets. The third market involves over-the-counter transactions of exchange-listed securities, often among larger institutional investors seeking more direct trade execution. The fourth market, meanwhile, refers to direct institution-to-institution trades, frequently facilitated by electronic communication networks that match large block orders without using an exchange's public quote. Although each of these markets caters to different participants and needs, together they ensure a diverse ecosystem where investors can purchase new offerings, trade seasoned securities, and handle private, large-scale transactions.

2.2.1.1 Primary Market

The primary market is the arena in which new securities are sold to the public for the very first time, enabling issuers—whether corporations, municipalities, or governments—to raise fresh capital. In this setting, underwriters often play a pivotal role in pricing the securities, gauging investor demand, and managing the risk of distributing these new shares or bonds. The most prominent example of a primary market transaction is the initial public offering (IPO), where a privately held company offers its stock to the investing public and "goes public." However, primary market sales also include follow-on offerings, such as secondary or shelf registrations, where established public companies issue additional shares or bonds. In either case, the key distinguishing factor of the primary market is that the proceeds from the sale go directly to the issuing entity, financing corporate expansion, debt repayment, or other organizational objectives.

Issuers commonly rely on multiple methods for bringing securities to market, each reflective of their specific goals and risk tolerance. For instance, in a firm commitment underwriting, the underwriter guarantees to purchase the entire offering from the issuer at an agreed-upon price—shouldering the risk if demand falls short. Alternatively, in a best efforts arrangement, the underwriter commits only to marketing and selling as many securities as possible at a target price, without guaranteeing the entire issue will be sold. Exempt offerings, such as private placements under Regulation D, also take place in the primary market but are sold to a more limited pool of qualified or accredited investors, bypassing many registration requirements in exchange for restricted distribution. Regardless of the distribution approach, primary market activities set the stage for how a security will ultimately be perceived in the broader financial ecosystem. By determining the initial price, supply, and structure of the offering, the primary market offers a glimpse into both the issuer's capital needs and the market's appetite for new investment opportunities.

2.2.1.2 Secondary Market (Electronic, OTC, Physical)

Once securities have been issued in the primary market, they begin trading in the secondary market, where existing shares or bonds change hands among investors. The key hallmark of secondary market activity is that the issuer does not receive proceeds from these trades; rather, one investor sells to another at a mutually agreed price. This ongoing exchange not only creates liquidity—allowing investors to quickly convert holdings into cash—but also provides real-time feedback on how the market values a company's prospects or the creditworthiness of a debt issuer. Over time, secondary market trading patterns can influence corporate decision-making, as issuers monitor share price performance to gauge market sentiment or plan additional capital raises.

Secondary markets can take several forms. **Physical exchanges**—exemplified by historic trading floors like the New York Stock Exchange (NYSE)—once relied on floor brokers to match buy and sell orders through open outcry. Today, these venues have largely transitioned to **electronic platforms** that match orders algorithmically, though they may still maintain a partial physical presence for ceremonial or high-profile events. Other stock exchanges, such as the Nasdaq, have been electronic since inception, relying on a network of dealers and market makers to quote prices and fill orders. Beyond exchange-listed trading, **over-the-counter (OTC)** markets handle securities not listed on formal exchanges. Here, broker-dealers negotiate transactions directly via telephone or electronic networks, often for less-liquid stocks or bonds. Although OTC trades are less transparent than exchange-based transactions, regulatory frameworks still require brokers to report and disseminate pricing information within specified time frames, ensuring that investors have access to essential data. By accommodating different security types, liquidity needs, and investor preferences, these various secondary market structures together help maintain a dynamic, continuously priced environment that underpins the broader functionality of the financial system.

Secondary Market Segment	Defining Traits	Examples
Physical (Floor-Based)	Historical open outcry; now mostly electronic/hybrid	NYSE (partial floor presence)
Electronic Exchange	Fully digital matching of bids/asks via electronic books	Nasdaq
Over-the-Counter (OTC)	Decentralized dealer networks; often for less-liquid securities	OTC Bulletin Board, Pink Sheets

Through these channels—physical, electronic, and OTC—investors can buy or sell previously issued securities at times and prices that reflect evolving market conditions. Their activity drives the price discovery process, ensuring that share or bond valuations respond to news, earnings announcements, interest rate changes, and broader economic indicators. Ultimately, the depth and liquidity of the secondary market promote confidence in the capital-raising process, since prospective issuers and investors alike can anticipate stable, continuous trading avenues for newly created securities over the long run.

2.2.1.3 Third Market

The third market refers to the over-the-counter (OTC) trading of listed securities—i.e., stocks and bonds that are listed on formal exchanges such as the NYSE or Nasdaq. In this segment, broker-dealers and large institutional investors can execute trades away from the exchange's central order book, often negotiating prices directly or through electronic communication networks. One of the main attractions of the third market is the potential for narrower spreads or lower transaction costs, particularly when large block trades are involved. Institutions that frequently engage in high-volume trades may opt to go through third-market broker-dealers to minimize the market impact that can occur when attempting a sizable order on a traditional exchange. By operating outside the central exchange framework, these trades can remain somewhat more discreet, limiting the risk that other market participants will detect (and potentially exploit) large orders.

Although conducted away from the primary exchange, these transactions are still subject to regulatory requirements designed to ensure transparency and protect investors. Broker-dealers that participate in third-market trades must report their trades in a timely manner so that pricing information becomes publicly available, preserving a level playing field for market participants. Moreover, these firms are guided by best execution obligations, which require them to seek prices for clients that are at least as favorable as—or better than—those available on the listing exchange. In effect, the third market complements exchange trading by offering an alternative venue that can facilitate large or specialized transactions. Its existence reflects the principle that securities markets function best when they allow participants multiple pathways to achieve liquidity, so long as each pathway remains anchored in fair and transparent practices.

2.2.1.4 Fourth Market

In the fourth market, large institutional investors trade directly with each other, circumventing traditional exchanges and broker-dealers. This direct approach can be particularly beneficial for block trades, where orders involve exceptionally large volumes of shares or bonds. Institutions such as pension funds, mutual funds, hedge funds, and insurance companies often turn to the fourth market to execute these trades discreetly, aiming to minimize the market impact that can occur when extensive orders are placed in a public forum. Transactions in the fourth market typically occur through proprietary electronic communication networks (ECNs), dark pools, or private crossing networks, each designed to preserve anonymity while providing a mechanism for matching orders internally. Because price quotes are not displayed to the broader public, participants can adjust positions without alerting competitors or triggering adverse price movements.

In many respects, the fourth market pushes the concept of over-the-counter (OTC) trading to an institutional extreme, in that the trades do not go through the usual exchange mechanisms. Nonetheless, most of these trades must still follow best execution guidelines and abide by post-trade reporting rules that regulators set for off-exchange transactions. While the absence of a central marketplace might raise concerns about transparency, sophisticated market participants rely on advanced reporting and settlement protocols to ensure that transactions clear seamlessly. The overall effect is that institutions can negotiate terms and execute sizable transactions with minimal disruption to market prices—an arrangement that can foster deeper liquidity for professional investors while highlighting the increasingly multifaceted nature of modern securities markets.

2.3 Economic Factors

2.3.1 The Federal Reserve Board's Impact

As the primary decision-making body within the U.S. central bank, the Federal Reserve Board significantly influences economic conditions through its ability to shape the nation's money supply and guide short-term interest rates. By adjusting the cost of borrowing and regulating how freely credit flows, the Board's policies can either encourage economic expansion or temper inflationary pressures. These decisions are critical not just for banks and lenders, but also for everyday consumers and businesses seeking loans or looking to invest. Over time, shifts in interest rates can affect market sentiment, impacting everything from stock prices to the bond market's appetite for risk.

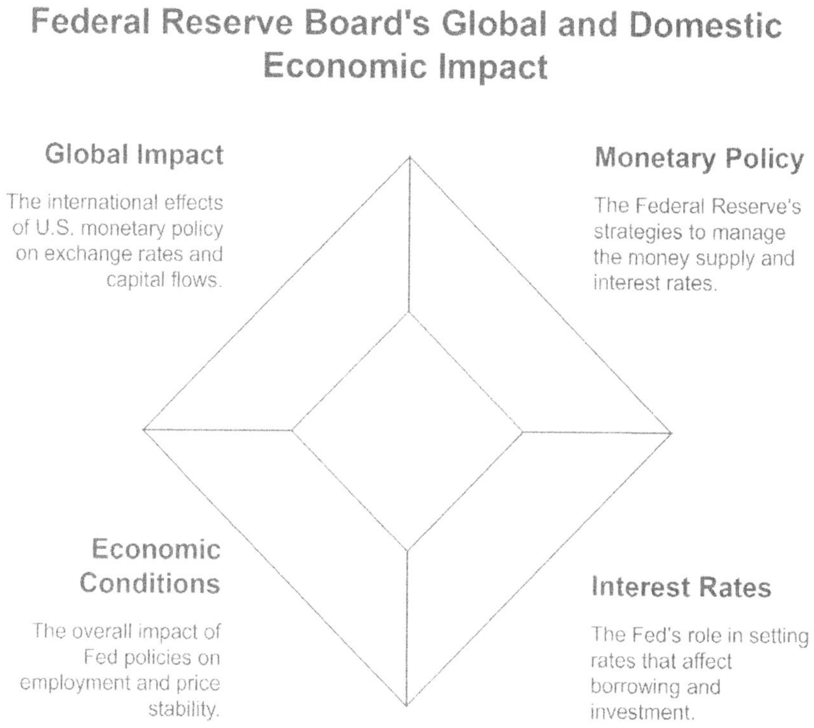

Although the Federal Reserve operates with relative independence, it remains accountable to Congress, which established its dual mandate of promoting maximum employment and stable prices. In practice, this means the Federal Reserve Board often acts pre-emptively, raising or lowering its target rates before economic imbalances grow too large. The board's influence also extends internationally, since U.S. monetary policy can affect exchange rates and global capital flows. Even a minor interest-rate adjustment may reverberate through international financial markets, demonstrating just how intertwined the Federal Reserve's policies are with broader economic stability.

2.3.1.1 Monetary vs. Fiscal Policy

Monetary policy and fiscal policy are two distinct levers through which economic objectives can be shaped, each managed by different arms of government. **Monetary policy** falls primarily under the purview of a nation's central bank—in the United States, the Federal Reserve Board. It focuses on controlling the money supply, managing interest rates, and influencing credit conditions. By adjusting these parameters, central banks aim to achieve goals such as stable prices, low unemployment, and moderate long-term interest rates. Common tools include open market operations (buying and selling government securities), setting reserve requirements for banks, and altering the discount rate or the federal funds rate. These changes, while typically incremental, can ripple through the financial system, affecting everything from consumer lending costs to investment activity. Because monetary policy decisions can be enacted relatively quickly and fine-tuned in response to incoming economic data, they often serve as the first line of defense against inflation or recessionary pressures.

Fiscal policy, on the other hand, is enacted by legislative bodies—such as Congress—and executed by the executive branch of government. It concerns the collection of taxes, the allocation of public spending, and the issuance of government debt. Through measures like adjusting tax brackets, creating stimulus packages, or funding infrastructure projects, fiscal policy can redistribute resources, encourage growth in targeted sectors, and mitigate negative economic shocks. Unlike monetary policy, which can be changed by central bank committees without extensive legislative debate, fiscal policy often requires political consensus and can thus involve lengthy deliberation. Consequently, fiscal policy changes may occur less frequently but can have large, direct effects on employment, consumer demand, and public services. By balancing these two forms of intervention—monetary measures for shorter-term liquidity management and fiscal measures for broader, structural shifts—policymakers can cultivate a more resilient economy that responds to emerging challenges while laying the groundwork for long-term stability.

Aspect	Monetary Policy	Fiscal Policy
Key Decision-Maker	Central Bank (e.g., Federal Reserve Board)	Legislative and Executive Branches (e.g., Congress, President)
Primary Tools	Interest rate adjustments, open market operations, reserve requirements	Taxation, government spending, government borrowing
Speed of Implementation	Generally quicker due to fewer decision-makers	Often slower due to political processes
Focus	Managing liquidity, controlling inflation, stabilizing currency values	Influencing aggregate demand, employment, and income distribution

Monetary and fiscal policies thus operate in tandem, each complementing the other's strengths and limitations. While the Federal Reserve can rapidly adapt interest rate targets to guide short-term economic cycles, broader fiscal initiatives set by Congress can address structural or social priorities, such as education, infrastructure, or social safety nets. In an ideal scenario, central bankers and elected officials coordinate to maintain balanced growth, steering the economy away from extreme boom-bust cycles and ensuring a healthy environment for investors, businesses, and consumers

2.3.1.2 Open Market Operations and Impact on the Economy

Open market operations (OMOs) stand at the heart of the Federal Reserve's monetary policy toolkit, enabling the central bank to inject or withdraw liquidity from the financial system in real time. Through its trading desk at the Federal Reserve Bank of New York, the Fed buys and sells U.S. Treasury securities and other approved instruments with primary dealers. When the Fed **purchases** securities, it credits the dealers' reserve accounts, effectively adding new money to the banking system. This addition of reserves tends to lower short-term interest rates because banks have more funds available to lend. Conversely, when the Fed **sells** securities, it debits the dealers' reserve accounts, removing funds from circulation and exerting upward pressure on rates. By carefully calibrating the volume and timing of these transactions, the Federal Reserve can steer the federal funds rate—a benchmark for interbank lending—toward its desired target, influencing borrowing costs and financial conditions across the economy.

The immediate effect of an open market operation manifests in how banks interact with each other and with their customers. In an environment where the Fed is actively purchasing securities (an expansionary stance), banks find it cheaper to obtain reserves, prompting them to lower the interest rates they charge on loans to businesses and consumers. This usually stimulates economic growth, as cheaper credit can encourage higher levels of consumption, investment, and production. On the flip side, selling securities (a contractionary stance) can pull liquidity out of the system, raising rates and discouraging rapid expansion or speculative bubbles. Beyond interest rates, these operations also ripple out to other markets: bond yields adjust in response to new supply-demand dynamics, equity valuations can shift due to changing borrowing costs, and foreign exchange rates may fluctuate if capital flows respond to new rate differentials. Taken together, open market operations are a powerful lever the Fed uses to fulfill its dual mandate of fostering maximum employment and maintaining stable prices.

Fed Action	Reserve Impact	Likely Effect on Rates	Typical Economic Objective
Buys Securities	Increases bank reserves (liquidity)	Downward pressure on interest rates	Stimulate growth, counter deflation
Sells Securities	Decreases bank reserves (liquidity)	Upward pressure on interest rates	Slow inflation, cool overheated economy

Because OMOs can be conducted swiftly and reversed if needed, they provide a high degree of control over the day-to-day availability of money. Policymakers track economic indicators—such as unemployment, inflation, and GDP growth—to decide whether to add reserves, remove them, or leave the system in equilibrium. Banks, financial markets, and corporations closely monitor the Fed's signals in open market operations, as any shift in direction may herald broader changes in lending conditions, capital investment decisions, and consumer confidence. By fine-tuning the scale and pace of securities transactions, the Federal Reserve seeks to guide the economy toward steady growth without letting inflation spiral out of control.

2.3.1.3 Interest Rate, Discount Rate, Federal Funds Rate

Interest rates serve as one of the Federal Reserve's primary tools for guiding economic activity, influencing borrowing costs for consumers, businesses, and financial institutions alike. When the Fed adjusts its monetary stance, it typically aims to affect the overall interest-rate environment—*particularly* short-term rates—so as to either stimulate or temper economic growth. A lower interest-rate climate encourages households to spend and businesses to expand, whereas higher rates typically curb excessive speculation or inflationary pressures. While numerous interest rates exist in the economy (including those on mortgages, auto loans, and corporate bonds), the Federal Reserve focuses most directly on the federal funds rate and, to a lesser extent, the discount rate as levers for managing liquidity and credit availability.

The **federal funds rate** is the rate at which depository institutions lend reserves to each other overnight. Although this rate emerges from an interbank lending market, the Fed exerts considerable influence over it by conducting open market operations and setting a target range that it communicates to the public. This target rate becomes a benchmark for myriad other short-term rates, including interest on commercial paper and some adjustable-rate loans. Slight shifts in the federal funds target can translate quickly into changes in how banks price credit for businesses and consumers, ultimately rippling into broader asset prices and investment decisions. Meanwhile, the **discount rate** is the rate the Federal Reserve charges banks that borrow directly from its discount window—a backup source of funding meant to ease short-term reserve shortfalls. Because borrowing from the discount window generally implies a more urgent liquidity need, the discount rate is often set slightly higher than the federal funds rate. Doing so encourages banks to rely primarily on interbank lending, resorting to the discount window only in exceptional circumstances. These two rates, taken together, outline the boundaries of overnight borrowing costs for depository institutions, thus shaping the scaffolding upon which other interest rates in the economy are built.

Rate	Definition	Set By	Primary Influence
Federal Funds Rate	Interbank overnight lending rate	Market (guided by Fed target)	Benchmark for other short-term rates (e.g., prime rate)
Discount Rate	Rate at which banks borrow directly from the Federal Reserve's discount window	Federal Reserve Board	Backup funding source; typically above federal funds rate

Changes in these rates affect everything from personal savings yields to the cost of corporate borrowing. For instance, if the Fed raises its target for the federal funds rate, banks may soon elevate their prime lending rates—used to price small business loans and credit cards—making credit more expensive. Conversely, if the Fed lowers its target, an influx of cheaper credit can encourage economic expansion. While these mechanisms are not instantaneous and can be swayed by external global factors, they remain central to how the Federal Reserve moderates economic cycles and pursues its dual mandate of stable prices and maximum employment. Through this intricate interplay of liquidity management, overnight rates, and market responses, the Fed wields significant, if indirect, power over the velocity and direction of the nation's economic activity.

2.3.2 Business Economic Factors

A variety of economic factors influence businesses and the broader market environment in which they operate. These range from the foundational purpose of financial statements—providing stakeholders with transparency about a company's assets, liabilities, revenues, and costs—to the cyclical nature of the overall economy, where businesses and investors experience phases of contraction, trough, expansion, and peak. Tracking specific data points such as earnings, debts, or inventory levels offers insights into a firm's operational health. On a larger scale, analyzing business cycles clarifies whether broader economic conditions are likely to support growth or indicate a downturn, shaping both corporate strategies and investor sentiment.

Economic indicators further refine the picture of how businesses might perform in various conditions. Leading indicators, like building permits or consumer expectations, can foreshadow shifts in the market, while lagging indicators, such as employment rates, confirm trends after they have materialized. Coincident indicators track real-time conditions, and inflation measurements help evaluate the purchasing power of money and potential pressure on interest rates. From the viewpoint of asset allocation, understanding whether bonds or equities are more favorable in a particular stage of the business cycle becomes crucial—growth stocks may excel during expansion, whereas defensive stocks or certain bonds might better withstand a contraction. Across these dynamics, differing schools of thought—Keynesian, Monetarist, and others—offer frameworks for interpreting how government policy and economic forces shape corporate profitability and market performance.

2.3.2.1 Purpose of Financial Statements (Balance Sheet, Income Statement)

Financial statements are critical tools that offer a transparent snapshot of a company's fiscal health. By providing standardized information, they enable investors, creditors, regulators, and even competitors to gauge an entity's stability and profitability. Among the various statements a company publishes, two of the most fundamental are the **balance sheet** and the **income statement**. The balance sheet details a firm's assets, liabilities, and shareholder equity at a specific point in time. It effectively answers the question, "What resources does this entity possess, and how are they financed?" The income statement, on the other hand, captures the firm's performance over a given period—often quarterly or annually—by showing revenues earned and expenses incurred, culminating in the net profit or loss. Taken together, these two documents convey both a firm's current financial position and its recent operational success or struggles.

The **balance sheet** is commonly divided into three main sections: **assets**, **liabilities**, and **shareholder equity**. Assets typically include everything from cash on hand, inventory, and receivables to long-term resources like property and equipment. Liabilities may range from short-term obligations—such as accounts payable and accrued expenses—to long-term debt. Shareholder equity comprises items like common stock, retained earnings, and additional paid-in capital, reflecting the residual interest in the company's assets after liabilities have been accounted for. Observers often use the balance sheet to assess liquidity (the firm's ability to meet short-term commitments) and leverage (the degree to which a firm relies on borrowed funds). Meanwhile, the **income statement** focuses on the flow of revenue and expenses. Revenues represent money earned from products sold or services rendered, while expenses reflect costs like salaries, utilities, and materials. Subtracting total expenses from total revenues yields net income (or net loss), which is a key indicator of operational effectiveness and profitability. This figure is frequently compared against industry peers or prior periods to gauge whether the firm's profitability is improving or declining. Because both statements adhere to standardized accounting principles—like GAAP (Generally Accepted Accounting Principles) in the U.S. or IFRS (International Financial Reporting Standards) internationally—they facilitate apples-to-apples comparisons across different companies and time frames.

Statement	Key Elements	Primary Question Answered
Balance Sheet	Assets, Liabilities, Shareholder Equity	"What does the company own and how are those assets financed?"
Income Statement	Revenues, Expenses, Net Income (or Loss)	"How did the company perform financially over a specific period?"

For market participants, the information found in these statements offers vital clues about a company's capacity to generate future cash flows, pay dividends, or service its debt. Investors commonly analyze trends in revenue growth, profit margins, and balance sheet ratios—such as the current ratio or debt-to-equity—to determine whether a security is undervalued or overvalued relative to its perceived risk. In this manner, financial statements become the bedrock of fundamental analysis, informing decisions about portfolio allocation, risk management, and long-term investment strategies. By laying bare a company's financial operations, these documents fulfill a regulatory mandate for transparency while also fostering a level playing field among all stakeholders seeking to evaluate or compare different investment opportunities.

2.3.2.2 Business Cycle Phases (Contraction, Trough, Expansion, Peak)

The business cycle represents a pattern of expansions and contractions in overall economic activity, typically measured by key indicators such as GDP, employment, and industrial production. Although each cycle is unique and does not unfold at precise intervals, these fluctuations tend to follow a recognizable sequence of four primary phases: **contraction, trough, expansion, and peak**. Understanding where the economy sits within this cycle helps businesses and investors anticipate shifts in consumer demand, credit availability, and labor conditions, which in turn shape corporate earnings and market valuations. Policymakers, such as the Federal Reserve, also pay close attention to cyclical movements, adjusting monetary policy to combat excessive inflation during expansions or alleviate economic distress during contractions.

1. **Contraction**
   During a contraction, economic growth slows or turns negative, and businesses often experience declining revenues and profits. This phase can manifest as a recession if it extends over two or more consecutive quarters of shrinking GDP. High unemployment rates, weaker consumer confidence, and reduced investment typically characterize this stage. Companies may focus on cost-cutting measures, including layoffs, in response to sagging demand. As a result, equity markets often exhibit bearish tendencies, and bond prices may rise if investors seek safer assets. Contractions can vary in severity—from mild slowdowns to deep recessions—depending on factors like the health of the financial system, consumer debt levels, and the global economic environment.

2. **Trough**

   The trough denotes the turning point at which the economy stops contracting and begins stabilizing. Demand, production, and employment usually stop declining, though they may remain relatively weak for some time. Policymakers often deploy expansionary measures during or just before this stage—lowering interest rates, enacting fiscal stimulus—to lay the groundwork for recovery. Businesses and consumers who reduced expenditures during the contraction might begin to see conditions easing, leading to incremental improvement in spending. In financial markets, the trough phase can present investment opportunities, as assets may be undervalued and positioned to benefit from a forthcoming rebound.

3. **Expansion**

   Following the trough, the economy progresses into a period of expansion. Unemployment falls, consumer spending and industrial output increase, and corporate earnings typically improve. Confidence returns, prompting businesses to invest in growth initiatives such as new product lines, facility upgrades, or acquisitions. Equity markets frequently rally during expansions, reflecting optimism about future profits. At the same time, central banks monitor inflation pressures that might arise in a robust economy, potentially raising interest rates if growth appears likely to overheat. This interplay of rising demand and cautious monetary policy can be a defining feature of the mid- to late-expansion stage.

4. **Peak**

   The cycle reaches a peak when overall economic activity hits its high point. Employment levels may be near full capacity, and consumer demand is strong, often pushing corporate earnings and stock valuations upward. Yet, this phase carries risks:

excessive growth can stoke inflation, resource shortages, and overinvestment in certain sectors. Companies might overestimate market opportunities, leading to possible imbalances—such as inflated real estate prices or stock bubbles. As credit tightens or consumer sentiment softens, the economy becomes vulnerable to another downturn, eventually sliding toward contraction and restarting the cycle. Timing and recognizing these inflection points remain a constant challenge for investors, as shifts from peak to contraction often materialize faster than expected.

Navigating the Business Cycle

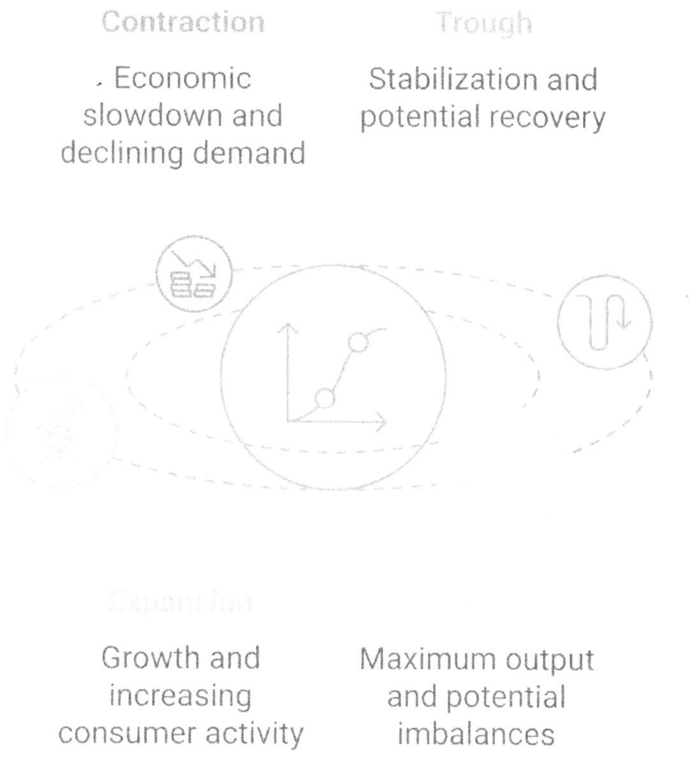

Phase	Key Traits	Market Implications
Contraction	Reduced output, rising unemployment, falling demand	Bearish equities, potentially higher bond prices (flight to quality)
Trough	Stabilizing output, minimal or no growth	Possible investment opportunities (undervalued assets)
Expansion	Rising demand, higher output, falling unemployment	Bullish equities, potential inflationary concerns
Peak	Maximum output, potential overheating or imbalances	Elevated equities, risk of correction if growth proves unsustainable

Monitoring the business cycle phases is crucial for both corporate and investment strategies. A well-timed expansion of production can position a firm for success, while delaying capital expenditures may be prudent if indicators suggest a looming contraction. Similarly, investors may rotate between asset classes—such as moving from growth stocks to defensive stocks or bonds—depending on prevailing and anticipated economic conditions. By staying attuned to these macroeconomic signals, participants can better navigate volatility and harness the cyclical nature of the markets.

2.3.2.3 Economic Indicators (Leading, Lagging, Coincident, Inflation)

Economic indicators are statistical measures that help market participants, policymakers, and businesses understand current conditions and anticipate future trends in the economy. By grouping these indicators into categories—leading, lagging, coincident, and inflation-related—analysts can better interpret where the economy might be heading and how various sectors could respond. Taken together, these metrics inform decisions ranging from corporate expansion plans to central bank interest-rate policies, directly affecting asset prices in capital markets.

Leading Indicators

Leading indicators often shift direction before the broader economy does, making them useful for forecasting turns in the business cycle. Examples include **manufacturing orders**, **building permits**, and certain **consumer confidence** surveys. These data points may rise or fall months before a widespread change in economic activity becomes evident, since they capture business and consumer plans that haven't yet translated into actual spending or hiring. Investors watch these indicators to reposition portfolios, sometimes rotating into defensive assets if signs point to an impending slowdown, or moving into growth-oriented sectors if the data suggest a strong expansion. Because leading indicators can also generate false signals—spiking or dipping briefly without a sustained trend—relying on more than one measure helps create a fuller, more reliable picture.

Lagging Indicators

In contrast, lagging indicators confirm shifts in the economy after they've already occurred. Common examples include **unemployment rates**, **corporate earnings**, and **consumer debt levels**. These metrics can take time to adjust because employers might delay layoffs or hiring, and accounting practices often report earnings only after a quarter has ended. While lagging indicators don't offer predictive insights, they are extremely valuable for assessing the depth or durability of an existing trend. Policymakers and businesses often use them to evaluate the success of measures taken during a contraction or expansion. For instance, a declining unemployment rate may validate that an economic recovery is truly underway, reinforcing the trajectory suggested by leading indicators.

Coincident Indicators

Coincident indicators track real-time movements in the economy. Measures like **nonfarm payroll employment**, **industrial production**, and certain aspects of **personal income** can reveal the current state of growth or contraction without the time lag seen in other data sets. Because these indicators closely mirror aggregate output and consumption, they serve as a baseline for gauging whether the economy is expanding or contracting at any given moment. If coincident measures begin to weaken while leading indicators are also trending downward, it strengthens the case for an impending slowdown. Conversely, robust coincident data combined with buoyant leading indicators suggests a sustained or even accelerating growth phase.

Inflation

Although inflation isn't always categorized in the same manner as leading or lagging indicators, it significantly impacts both business cycles and market sentiment. Inflation measures how the average level of prices changes over time, eroding consumers' and businesses' purchasing power if it climbs too quickly. Policy tools like open market operations or interest rate adjustments often aim to keep inflation within a target range—too low a figure can signal weak demand, whereas too high a figure risks destabilizing the economy. Market participants watch inflation indicators such as the **Consumer Price Index (CPI)** and the **Producer Price Index (PPI)** to gauge whether the Federal Reserve might alter its monetary stance. A sudden spike in CPI might prompt the central bank to raise interest rates, thereby influencing bond yields and equity valuations. Conversely, persistently low inflation could lead to a more accommodative policy stance, stimulating borrowing and potentially boosting asset prices.

Indicator Category	Examples	Primary Use
Leading	Manufacturing orders, building permits, consumer confidence	Early warning of turns in business cycle
Lagging	Unemployment rate, corporate earnings, consumer debt levels	Confirmation of established trends
Coincident	Nonfarm payrolls, industrial production, personal income	Real-time gauge of economic performance
Inflation	CPI, PPI, core inflation measures	Assesses price stability, guides policy decisions

By synthesizing data from these categories, analysts can build a nuanced view of macroeconomic conditions. For instance, if leading indicators point upward while inflation remains subdued, equity markets might rally in anticipation of corporate profit growth. Should lagging indicators then confirm a robust expansion, further capital flows may reinforce those gains. On the other hand, a divergence—say, strong leading indicators offset by rising inflation—could create uncertainty, driving more cautious strategies among investors and businesses. In this manner, economic indicators serve as an ongoing diagnostic, revealing the economy's underlying momentum and foreshadowing the policy actions or shifts in investment allocation likely to follow.

2.3.2.4 Effects on Bond and Equity Markets (Cyclical, Defensive, Growth)

Bond and equity markets respond differently to shifting economic conditions, largely because investors view these asset classes through the lens of risk, return, and time horizon. **Bonds** typically represent a claim on a steady stream of interest payments plus the eventual return of principal, making their returns more predictable. Consequently, bond prices tend to rise when investors seek safety—often in periods of slowing economic growth or heightened volatility. In contrast, equity valuations are heavily influenced by corporate earnings prospects, which are linked to overall economic momentum. If economic indicators suggest robust expansion, equities often rally, especially in sectors that benefit from rising consumer demand and business investment. Conversely, when forecasts turn negative, equity markets can experience broad sell-offs as earnings expectations deteriorate.

Within the equity market, **cyclical, defensive, and growth stocks** each exhibit distinct behaviors in response to macroeconomic shifts. **Cyclical stocks**, found in industries such as consumer discretionary, automotives, and travel, typically thrive when the economy is strong because consumer and corporate spending is higher. These companies may see revenues spike during expansions, but they are also more vulnerable when growth tapers off, causing earnings to drop precipitously. **Defensive stocks**, in contrast, belong to sectors like utilities, healthcare, or consumer staples—areas of the economy that maintain relatively stable demand regardless of business cycle fluctuations. Because people still need basic goods and services, defensive stocks often display less earnings volatility and can outperform when recessions loom or the market turns risk-averse.

Meanwhile, **growth stocks** represent firms—often in technology, biotech, or innovative industries—that are expected to expand at above-average rates. They typically reinvest earnings to fund future development instead of paying substantial dividends, so investors focus on future cash flows and market share potential. During expansionary environments with low interest rates, growth stocks can command premium valuations, but their prices can be sensitive to shifts in monetary policy or any slowdown in expected growth.

For bond markets, interest rate movements—tied closely to both central bank actions and investor sentiment—play a central role in determining pricing and yield. If policymakers raise rates to curb inflation or cool an overheated economy, the yield on newly issued bonds rises, causing existing bonds with lower coupons to drop in price. This dynamic can also pressure equities, especially growth-oriented names whose valuations hinge on discounting long-term cash flows at relatively low rates. Conversely, when rates are cut or remain low, bond prices typically increase (yields fall), and the equity market may find renewed vigor in sectors dependent on cheap credit and strong consumer demand.

In this broader context, cyclical, defensive, and growth equity segments interweave with bond market conditions to create a diverse mosaic of investment strategies. During an economic upturn, cyclical stocks and certain growth-oriented sectors often deliver impressive returns, supported by increasing consumer and business spending. At the same time, bond investors may see limited price appreciation if interest rates drift upward, although higher coupons on new issues could become attractive. Alternatively, in a downturn, defensive equities and high-quality bonds often play a stabilizing role in portfolios as flight-to-safety investments attract capital flows. Investors who skillfully blend these asset types—understanding how cyclical, defensive, and growth stocks each behave under shifting economic conditions—stand a better chance of weathering volatile markets and achieving long-term objectives.

2.3.2.5 Principal Economic Theories (Keynesian, Monetarist)

Economists have long debated the best ways to stimulate growth, manage inflation, and stabilize economic cycles. Two influential schools of thought in this arena are **Keynesian** and **Monetarist** economics. While both seek to understand and guide macroeconomic performance, they diverge sharply in their prescriptions for policy intervention, the role of government, and the drivers of economic well-being. These theoretical differences shape everything from central bank decisions to fiscal policy debates, highlighting how deeply held assumptions about consumption, investment, and money supply can produce contrasting strategies for growth and stability.

Keynesian economics, often associated with the ideas of British economist John Maynard Keynes, posits that aggregate demand—encompassing consumption, investment, government spending, and net exports—is the primary engine of economic activity. When aggregate demand falters, as in a recession, Keynesians argue that government intervention can counteract the downturn by increasing public spending or cutting taxes, thus stimulating demand and reducing unemployment. The rationale is that private sector spending alone may not rebound swiftly enough after a sharp contraction, and that the public sector must fill the void to jump-start the economy. Moreover, Keynesians maintain that wages and prices can be "sticky," meaning they do not adjust quickly enough to restore full employment on their own. Consequently, proactive fiscal policies, such as infrastructure projects or targeted tax incentives, can help reinvigorate growth and maintain employment levels. Although monetary policy also plays a role in the Keynesian view, it often serves as a supportive tool: if interest rates are already near zero, fiscal stimulus may prove more effective than further monetary easing.

Monetarist economics, most famously championed by Milton Friedman, centers on the money supply as the key determinant of economic stability and price levels. Monetarists believe that inflation arises primarily from an overexpansion of the money supply, while inadequate money growth can stifle economic output. This view underscores the importance of steady, predictable monetary policy over fine-tuned fiscal interventions. Rather than adjusting public spending based on the business cycle, monetarists recommend that central banks adhere to a consistent rule—such as allowing the money supply to grow at a fixed rate correlating with long-term potential GDP growth. In this framework, government attempts to "time" the economy or run large deficits risk destabilizing markets and fueling inflation, because fiscal measures can be slow to implement and often extend beyond the scope of immediate need. By focusing on money supply management and letting market forces determine consumption, investment, and wages, monetarists expect the economy to self-correct more efficiently over time.

Although Keynesian and Monetarist theories appear to present contradictory approaches, policymakers often adapt elements of both, crafting a blended strategy that employs fiscal stimulus in times of severe recession while relying on prudent monetary controls to keep inflation in check. The balance between these viewpoints can shift with changing economic conditions, political climates, or the emergence of new economic data. In practice, central banks and governments weigh multiple factors—such as unemployment rates, inflation trends, and global market dynamics—when deciding whether to stimulate, restrain, or merely stabilize the economy, reflecting a real-world pragmatism that draws on both schools of thought.

Aspect	Keynesian View	Monetarist View
Key Driver of Economy	Aggregate demand (government spending can close demand gaps)	Money supply (stable, rule-based growth is crucial)
Policy Emphasis	Fiscal policy (stimulus during recessions), supportive monetary policy	Monetary policy (controlling inflation via money supply)
Role of Government	Active intervention to stabilize employment and output	Limited role; markets self-correct if money supply is well-managed
Inflation Cause	Excess aggregate demand; can be managed by reducing spending or raising taxes	Excessive money supply growth leading to too much liquidity chasing goods

This comparison highlights that while Keynesian theorists lean toward government-led solutions to jump-start or moderate economic cycles, monetarists believe in minimal intervention, placing trust in predictable monetary policy rules. Both viewpoints continue to shape modern economic discourse, influencing how politicians, central bankers, and other stakeholders tackle issues like recession, inflation, and fiscal deficits.

2.3.3 International Economic Factors

International economic factors can significantly influence domestic markets, even for purely U.S.-based investors. One of the most critical gauges is the **balance of payments**, which tracks all economic transactions between a nation and the rest of the world. This record includes the flow of goods, services, investment income, and financial transfers, offering a bird's-eye view of how money and resources move in and out of the country. Persistent imbalances—such as a large trade deficit—may affect currency strength, interest rates, and foreign investor sentiment.

Another key consideration lies in comparing **GDP (Gross Domestic Product)** with **GNP (Gross National Product)**, each highlighting different angles of national economic output. GDP measures the total value of goods and services produced domestically, regardless of ownership, while GNP includes output generated by a country's residents and businesses both at home and abroad. Alongside these measures, **exchange rates** and currency fluctuations play a pivotal role in determining the competitiveness of exports, the cost of imports, and the overall purchasing power of both consumers and businesses on the international stage.

2.3.3.1 U.S. Balance of Payments

The U.S. Balance of Payments (BOP) is a comprehensive record of all economic transactions between the United States and the rest of the world over a specified period, typically a quarter or a year. It not only tracks trade in goods and services but also captures cross-border flows of investment income, financial assets, and transfers such as foreign aid or remittances. Because these data show how dollars enter or leave the country, the BOP offers critical insights into the United States' international economic position and influences policymakers' decisions on trade, tariffs, and currency arrangements. In essence, the BOP reveals whether the nation is a net lender or borrower on the global stage, highlighting areas where the U.S. might depend on foreign investment to fund domestic consumption or government expenditures. When trade deficits become a large component of the BOP, for example, they are often offset by capital inflows—money invested by foreigners in U.S. stocks, bonds, real estate, or direct business ventures—underscoring the interlinked nature of trade and capital markets.

Structurally, the BOP is divided into two broad accounts: the current account and the capital and financial account. The current account covers the export and import of goods and services, along with net income from abroad—such as interest, dividends, and wages—plus unilateral transfers like remittances. A persistent deficit in the current account suggests that the country is importing more than it exports, or paying out more investment income than it receives. In turn, the capital and financial account records cross-border flows of capital, including foreign direct investment (FDI), portfolio investment in equities and bonds, and changes in official reserves held by central banks. A surplus in this account indicates that foreign entities are investing more in the United States than Americans are investing abroad, effectively funding any shortfall in the current account. These twin accounts must balance out over the long run—if one is in deficit, the other must show a corresponding surplus—ensuring the overall BOP is theoretically in equilibrium. Shifts in the balance of payments can thus impact foreign exchange rates, domestic interest rates, and even the perceived creditworthiness of the country, as global investors continually evaluate the sustainability of deficits and the attractiveness of U.S. assets. By monitoring patterns in the BOP, analysts can better understand the pressures on the U.S. dollar, gauge global demand for American exports and financial instruments, and anticipate changes in the broader economic climate.

Account	Focus	Illustrative Components
Current Account	Trade in goods/services, net income, transfers	Exports vs. imports, net wages/dividends, remittances
Capital and Financial Account	Cross-border capital flows	Foreign direct investment, portfolio investment, changes in central bank reserves

Such details underscore why the balance of payments is a cornerstone of international finance. A worsening trade imbalance, for instance, may push policymakers to consider tariffs or currency devaluations, while large capital inflows could lead to asset price inflation if foreign investors aggressively purchase real estate or corporate debt. Consequently, an accurate reading of the BOP helps market participants anticipate potential shifts in monetary policy, interest rates, and even diplomatic strategies tied to trade agreements. Over the long term, balance-of-payments trends can also reveal deeper structural features of the U.S. economy, from its reliance on specific import categories to the competitive advantages it maintains in key export industries.

2.3.3.2 GDP vs. GNP

Gross Domestic Product (GDP) measures the total value of all goods and services produced within a country's borders over a specific time period, regardless of who owns the means of production. In other words, if foreign companies operate factories on U.S. soil, the output of those factories contributes to U.S. GDP. This statistic is frequently regarded as a core barometer of an economy's overall size and health, as it reflects domestic production activities that generate income and employment within the nation. Policymakers, analysts, and investors track changes in GDP to infer whether an economy is expanding or contracting, often comparing it against previous quarters or years. When GDP grows consistently, it typically signals robust consumer demand, strong business investment, and possibly rising government revenues from higher tax collections. On the other hand, GDP contraction might reveal subdued economic conditions, prompting fiscal or monetary interventions to stimulate renewed growth.

Gross National Product (GNP), by contrast, focuses on the value of output produced by a country's residents and enterprises—regardless of where they are located geographically. Thus, GNP includes the earnings of U.S.-owned businesses or citizens working abroad, while excluding income earned within the U.S. by foreign residents or businesses. This distinction is most apparent in countries where a substantial portion of business activities, investments, or labor forces reside overseas. In such scenarios, GNP might significantly differ from GDP, providing a different lens on how citizens and companies are prospering through outward investments or expatriate workers. GNP can be especially relevant for assessing the global footprint of a nation's economic interests: a high GNP relative to GDP can indicate that a considerable amount of its wealth and production is generated externally. Ultimately, both GDP and GNP serve as valuable metrics for understanding the scale and sources of a country's economic output, but their nuances reflect different perspectives—one tied strictly to territorial boundaries, the other to the nationality of the entity producing goods or services.

Metric	Measures	Focus
GDP	Total value of goods/services produced **within** a country's borders	Territorial production (geographical)
GNP	Total value of goods/services produced by **a nation's residents** anywhere in the world	National ownership (where capital/labor is domiciled)

Analyzing both GDP and GNP can offer a more complete understanding of a nation's economic well-being and international engagements. A country with thriving domestic production but limited international investment might show a high GDP relative to GNP, while a nation with extensive overseas ventures could find its GNP surpassing domestic output. By examining these metrics side by side, economists and investors gain insights not just into how much is being produced, but also into who truly benefits from that production and how cross-border business activities shape the broader economic landscape.

2.3.3.3 Exchange Rates and Currency Impacts

Exchange rates serve as the linchpin of international trade and finance, dictating how one currency can be exchanged for another. These rates are sensitive to a variety of factors—including interest rates, inflation, and geopolitical stability—and can be determined through floating, fixed, or managed exchange-rate regimes. **Floating rates** fluctuate daily based on market supply and demand, reflecting immediate shifts in economic fundamentals and investor sentiment. **Fixed or pegged rates**, on the other hand, tie a currency's value to that of another (often the U.S. dollar) or a basket of currencies, imposing obligations on central banks to intervene when supply and demand deviate from the peg. A **managed float** lies in between, with central banks selectively stepping in to adjust rates and smooth volatility without strictly pegging them.

When the **domestic currency appreciates**—that is, strengthens relative to foreign currencies—imports generally become cheaper, potentially curbing local inflation if businesses can source goods at lower prices. However, a stronger currency may weigh on export competitiveness abroad, causing a trade deficit if domestic producers struggle to price goods attractively in foreign markets. Conversely, **depreciation** of a currency can spark export growth by making domestic goods more affordable overseas, though it also raises the cost of importing raw materials or consumer goods. Over time, these shifts can reshape trade balances, influence inflation, and even prompt central banks to adjust monetary policy. For instance, if a sudden depreciation stokes inflation by driving up import costs, policymakers might raise interest rates to support the currency, dampening economic growth. Similarly, currency movements can affect capital flows: a strengthening currency might attract foreign investment, driving up local asset prices and possibly leading to economic overheating, while a weakening currency could deter overseas investors or motivate them to withdraw funds.

Because foreign exchange (forex) markets are highly liquid and operate around the clock, currency values often respond rapidly to macroeconomic data releases or political events. A surprise interest-rate cut may spark an immediate sell-off in that country's currency, as yields on local investments become less attractive. Conversely, a hawkish monetary policy stance can draw in foreign capital seeking higher returns, pushing the currency upward. Multinational corporations hedge against such volatility through forward contracts or other financial instruments, aiming to lock in favorable exchange rates for future transactions. Likewise, investors might adjust portfolios to capitalize on (or protect against) exchange-rate swings, recognizing that currency fluctuations can amplify—or erode—the returns from international assets. By monitoring exchange-rate trends, policymakers, businesses, and market participants gain critical insight into global competitiveness, trade flows, and the overarching direction of economic cycles.

2.4 Offerings

2.4.1 Roles of Participants

Investment Bankers

Investment bankers are instrumental in helping issuers structure, price, and bring new securities to market. Often part of large financial institutions, these professionals assess the issuer's financial strength and recommend an appropriate offering size, timing, and distribution strategy. If the offering is a bond, an investment banker might conduct a thorough analysis of prevailing interest rates and comparable credit spreads to establish a coupon rate that appeals to investors while remaining cost-effective for the issuer. In equity offerings—such as an initial public offering (IPO) or follow-on issue—the investment banker typically advises on share pricing to balance the issuer's desire to raise capital at a favorable valuation with the market's capacity to absorb new shares.

In practice, investment bankers also coordinate due diligence, ensuring the issuer's disclosures align with regulatory requirements and investor expectations. They often organize "roadshows," where company executives and bankers present to prospective institutional investors, gathering feedback that can influence the final offer price or amount of securities sold. By carefully gauging demand and making adjustments during the marketing phase, investment bankers aim to promote a successful debut for the new issuance. This role requires a blend of analytical acumen—such as modeling cash flows and potential returns—and relationship management skills, as investment bankers must balance issuer objectives with market realities and regulatory constraints.

Underwriting Syndicate

An underwriting syndicate arises when multiple firms collaborate to underwrite a particularly large or complex securities offering. The lead underwriter—often referred to as the book-running manager—assembles the syndicate and oversees the offering's overall strategy, including pricing and distribution. Each member of the syndicate assumes a portion of the financial risk in purchasing the securities from the issuer before reselling them to investors. This shared risk model allows underwriters to tackle offerings that might be too sizable or specialized for any single firm to handle on its own. It also broadens the distribution network, enabling the offering to reach a wider pool of potential buyers.

Communication within the syndicate is critical. Firms must coordinate on marketing tactics, investor outreach, and real-time demand feedback. If demand lags, the lead underwriter might consider adjusting the price or the number of shares or bonds offered. Syndicate members may negotiate among themselves if strong demand arises, ensuring that each participant has an adequate share of the deal. Once the securities are sold, the syndicate dissolves, although certain post-offering obligations—like price stabilization or the publication of analyst research—may continue for a specified period. By pooling expertise and capital, an underwriting syndicate helps ensure that even the largest or most complex offerings proceed smoothly, balancing the issuer's objectives with the diverse expectations of institutional and retail investors.

Municipal Advisors

Municipal advisors specialize in guiding state and local governments, municipalities, and other public entities through the process of issuing debt securities. Their role in an offering centers on advocating for the municipality's interests—from initial structuring decisions to final bond pricing—ensuring that the community finances public projects at the lowest feasible cost and under terms that align with legal, budgetary, and political constraints. These advisors often conduct feasibility studies to project revenue streams for repayment, analyze the local tax base, and recommend appropriate debt structures (e.g., revenue vs. general obligation bonds). Because municipal finances can involve unique statutory requirements or voter approvals, municipal advisors must also navigate regulatory frameworks that differ significantly from those in the corporate sector.

During the underwriting phase, municipal advisors frequently collaborate with underwriters and bond counsel to finalize bond terms that resonate with investors while meeting the municipality's fiscal goals. They may also coordinate credit rating presentations or prepare offering documents that detail the locality's economic fundamentals, governance structure, and potential risks. In practice, municipal advisors serve as fiduciaries to their public clients, legally obligated to prioritize the municipality's best interests over any external considerations. Through careful stewardship of the offering process, they help public issuers raise funds for projects like schools, roads, or utilities, balancing community development needs with prudent debt management.

2.4.2 Types of Offerings

When a company, municipality, or other issuer decides to raise capital, they can typically choose between a **public securities offering** or a **private securities offering**. Public offerings are registered with the Securities and Exchange Commission (SEC), made available to the general investing public, and adhere to rigorous disclosure standards. In contrast, private offerings—often conducted under Regulation D—target accredited or institutional investors and require less extensive disclosure, though they generally come with restrictions on resale. This fundamental difference in distribution channels shapes both the scope of potential investors and the level of regulatory oversight each offering faces.

Within public offerings, further distinctions arise based on whether the issuer is selling securities for the first time or has already gone public. An **initial public offering (IPO)** represents the first sale of stock to the public and often garners significant market attention. Once a company is public, it can conduct a **secondary offering**, in which existing shareholders (like insiders) sell their shares, or a **follow-on offering**, where the company itself issues new shares to raise additional funds. Regardless of the offering type, issuers and underwriters typically select a **method of distribution**—such as best efforts or firm commitment—to structure the underwriting risk and the process for placing securities with investors. These choices collectively define how new securities move from the issuer's balance sheet into the hands of the investing public or private buyers.

2.4.2.1 Public vs. Private Securities Offering

In a **public offering**, the issuer sells securities to the general investing public under the regulatory framework established by the Securities Act of 1933. This means filing detailed registration statements with the Securities and Exchange Commission (SEC) and preparing a prospectus that discloses material information about the issuer's business, management, financial condition, and risks. These disclosures aim to give potential buyers a clear understanding of what they are investing in, fostering market transparency and investor protection. Since public offerings allow an unlimited number of investors—both retail and institutional—to participate, they can raise substantial amounts of capital. However, the process often involves significant underwriting expenses, legal fees, and ongoing reporting obligations once the company becomes publicly traded. Issuers also subject themselves to scrutiny from regulators and the broader market, which can bring benefits like enhanced credibility but also places pressures on corporate governance and quarterly earnings performance.

In a **private offering**, by contrast, an issuer takes advantage of exemptions under securities laws—commonly Regulation D—so the offering does not require the same level of public registration and disclosure. These exemptions allow issuers to market securities to a select pool of sophisticated or accredited investors (such as high-net-worth individuals, venture capitalists, or hedge funds) with minimal documentation compared to a public offering. Private offerings typically involve fewer investors, and while they can close more quickly than public deals, they often restrict how many non-accredited investors can participate and impose resale limitations to maintain exemption status. As a result, issuers that opt for private placements benefit from lower regulatory costs and faster execution but reach a narrower investor base. Consequently, private offerings can be ideal for early-stage companies or those that prefer not to disclose extensive details about operations and finances to the public, though this path may limit the total capital raised.

2.4.2.2 Initial Public Offering (IPO), Secondary Offering, Follow-on Offering

An **Initial Public Offering (IPO)** marks a company's transition from private to public ownership by selling shares to outside investors for the first time. In preparation, the issuer collaborates with investment bankers to conduct due diligence, finalize regulatory filings, and determine an appropriate share price based on anticipated demand, prevailing market conditions, and corporate valuation. The registration process before the Securities and Exchange Commission (SEC) involves compiling and disclosing detailed financial statements, risk factors, and business plans in a preliminary prospectus (often called a "red herring"), followed by a final prospectus once pricing is set. If the IPO is deemed successful—generating strong investor interest at or above the expected price—this can provide a significant infusion of capital to fund expansion, retire debt, or invest in research and development. However, going public also subjects the firm to ongoing reporting obligations and greater market scrutiny, requiring more transparency in areas such as executive compensation and strategic decision-making.

A **secondary offering** takes place when existing shareholders—often early investors, company insiders, or venture capitalists—opt to sell part of their stake after the company is already public. While the issuer itself does not receive proceeds from these transactions, secondary offerings can widen the shareholder base and improve liquidity by increasing the available float of shares on the market. The share price for a secondary offering is typically guided by current market conditions, and underwriters may offer these shares at a modest discount to encourage participation. Investors often perceive secondary offerings differently depending on the rationale: it can be positive if insiders are diversifying their holdings or if the offering clarifies share ownership structures, but it may raise red flags if major shareholders are exiting a large portion of their stake without transparent justification.

By contrast, a **follow-on offering** (sometimes called a seasoned equity offering) involves the company itself issuing additional shares to raise fresh capital. Though similar to an IPO in that new stock is placed into the public market, a follow-on generally involves a more streamlined regulatory process. Because the issuer has already filed disclosures and meets ongoing listing requirements, due diligence can focus on material changes or additional risks since the last offering. Companies might pursue a follow-on to fund strategic acquisitions, accelerate product development, or strengthen their balance sheet. While these offerings can boost liquidity, they can also dilute existing shareholders if the new shares represent a significant expansion of the total float. Therefore, investors tend to scrutinize the purpose and proposed uses of the proceeds, monitoring whether the expected returns justify potential dilution of their stake.

Offering Type	Shares Sold	Proceeds Recipient	Regulatory Disclosures
IPO	Newly created shares	Issuer (company)	Full SEC registration & prospectus (first time)
Secondary	Existing shares (from insiders/investors)	Selling shareholders (not the company)	Simplified updates to existing disclosures
Follow-on	Newly created shares	Issuer (company)	Updated disclosures, but less extensive than IPO

Collectively, IPOs, secondary offerings, and follow-on offerings form the backbone of equity capital formation, enabling companies to access public markets at different stages of growth or changing ownership dynamics. While each type involves distinct regulatory procedures, underwriting arrangements, and pricing considerations, they share a common theme: balancing the issuer's capital needs with investor demand and market sentiment. A well-executed offering—supported by transparent disclosures, effective marketing, and an appropriate price—can strengthen a company's financial position and appeal to a broader universe of investors.

2.4.2.3 Methods of Distribution (Best Efforts, Firm Commitment)

When a company issues new securities—such as common stock or bonds—investment bankers and underwriting syndicates use different contractual approaches to distribute these securities to investors. The two primary methods of distribution are **best efforts** and **firm commitment**. Each structure imposes distinct obligations and financial risks on underwriters while catering to different market conditions and issuer preferences.

Best Efforts

In a best efforts arrangement, underwriters agree to use their professional resources to market and sell the securities without guaranteeing the total amount will be sold. Essentially, they act as agents for the issuer, placing the securities with investors to the best of their ability, but they do not assume the risk of unsold shares or bonds remaining on the market. When an issuer opts for a best efforts offering—often because they have limited market visibility or higher perceived risks—investment bankers typically gauge investor appetite through preliminary marketing and adjust the number of securities or price range accordingly. If demand falls short, the issuer bears the primary risk: it may end up raising less capital than intended, or the deal might be canceled if certain thresholds aren't met (as can occur in a "minimum-maximum" best efforts structure).

In practice, best efforts underwriting can help reduce underwriting costs because the underwriters take on less financial exposure, which might lower fees or commissions relative to a firm commitment deal. However, the issuer must accept the possibility that the offering may not fully subscribe if market sentiment turns unfavorable. Small or emerging companies often adopt best efforts deals when market conditions appear uncertain or when they aim to mitigate the expense of a broader underwriting commitment. Investors evaluating best efforts deals may seek additional discounts or protective terms, recognizing that the underwriters have limited obligations if the sale does not go as planned.

Firm Commitment

Under a firm commitment arrangement, the underwriters purchase the entire offering from the issuer at an agreed-upon price—often a slight discount to the public offering price—and then resell those securities to investors. This approach shifts significant financial risk onto the underwriters: they become the owners of the shares or bonds at the moment they buy them, even if the market appetite later proves weaker than expected. From the issuer's perspective, a firm commitment offers greater certainty of raising the desired capital because the underwriters are contractually bound to buy the entire allotment. If the underwriters cannot place all of the securities with investors, they must hold any unsold portion on their balance sheet or reduce the offering price to stimulate demand.

Because of the higher exposure to losses, underwriters in a firm commitment deal typically receive more substantial fees or underwriting spreads. They also conduct more rigorous due diligence and market analysis to minimize the likelihood of an under-subscribed offering. For well-established issuers with solid financial track records and favorable market conditions, firm commitment deals present a reliable path to raising large sums of capital while signaling confidence to investors. By guaranteeing that the entire issue will be sold, the underwriters also provide an element of market stability, helping price the securities more precisely through book-building and investor feedback. Nonetheless, if broader market sentiment suddenly shifts—due to macroeconomic events or issuer-specific news—the underwriters can suffer notable losses, underscoring the inherent risk in guaranteeing an offering's success.

Method	Key Characteristic	Risk Allocation	Typical Use Case
Best Efforts	Underwriters sell securities as agents but do not purchase them outright	Issuer bears more risk if market demand is insufficient	Smaller or riskier offerings; uncertain market conditions
Firm Commitment	Underwriters purchase all securities, then resell to investors	Underwriters assume significant risk of unsold securities	Larger, well-established issuers seeking guaranteed capital raise

Ultimately, deciding between a best efforts and a firm commitment arrangement hinges on the issuer's risk tolerance, the strength of their market profile, and the confidence underwriters have in distributing the securities. Both methods serve legitimate roles in capital formation, ensuring flexibility in how new issues reach investors, whether the issuer is a startup testing the waters for the first time or a seasoned corporation aiming to tap public markets for significant funding.

2.4.3 Shelf Registrations and Distributions

Shelf registrations allow certain qualified issuers—often larger or well-established companies—to register securities with the SEC in advance and then "place them on the shelf" to be offered at a later time. By filing a shelf registration statement, the issuer secures approval for a specified amount of shares or bonds, but it does not have to sell them immediately. Once market conditions or strategic considerations become favorable, the issuer can tap into that pre-registered amount through incremental offerings without going through a full registration process each time. This flexibility can expedite capital-raising efforts and lower associated costs, as the company can respond quickly to emerging market opportunities.

The distributions themselves occur over time, allowing an issuer to access the market in tranches, as opposed to a single, large offering. This can also enable better pricing, since the company can wait for optimal market conditions before floating additional securities. Investors benefit because they have more timely information on the issuer's plans, and the issuer's disclosures are updated periodically to reflect material changes in its financial status or operations. Overall, shelf registrations streamline the path from registration to distribution, making it a valuable tool for issuers that anticipate multiple financing needs in the near future.

2.4.3.1 Definition and Purpose

Shelf registration is a regulatory framework under which qualifying companies register securities offerings with the Securities and Exchange Commission (SEC) ahead of time, retaining the flexibility to sell these securities in one or more tranches over an extended period—often up to three years. This procedure is commonly associated with Rule 415 of the Securities Act of 1933, which details how and when an issuer may file a shelf registration statement.

Unlike a traditional offering that must be sold in full immediately after registration, a shelf registration allows the issuer to wait until market conditions are optimal or capital needs arise, effectively "shelving" the securities until the moment is right. Because of this convenience, shelf registrations are most often utilized by established or well-known issuers that have already proven their market reputation and complied with rigorous ongoing reporting standards.

The primary benefit of this arrangement lies in its efficiency and cost-effectiveness. Rather than filing multiple registration statements every time the company needs to raise capital, an issuer can conduct one comprehensive registration and then sequentially offer small or large portions of the pre-approved securities as warranted. This reduces regulatory and underwriting expenses, shortens the time to market, and grants issuers a competitive edge by letting them strike quickly when market sentiment is favorable. From an investor's perspective, shelf registrations also heighten transparency: since the initial filing discloses key financial and operational information, any subsequent takedowns from the shelf must provide updated disclosures, ensuring potential buyers have current data when deciding whether to participate. This structured blend of preparedness and adaptability underpins the strategic appeal of shelf registrations for companies looking to maintain continuous access to capital while preserving flexibility in timing and volume.

2.4.3.2 Rule Requirements

Shelf registrations in the United States are primarily governed by **Rule 415** under the Securities Act of 1933, which establishes when and how an issuer may file a registration statement for delayed or continuous offerings. To be eligible, companies often must meet specific criteria, such as having a history of timely SEC filings and possessing a certain public float or market capitalization that meets the thresholds for using an abbreviated registration form—commonly Form S-3 for domestic issuers or Form F-3 for foreign private issuers. In addition, Rule 415 differentiates between "continuous" and "delayed" offerings: a continuous offering commences promptly and may continue for an extended period (e.g., a dividend reinvestment plan), whereas a delayed offering is placed "on the shelf" for possible future use. Many issuers file shelf registration statements for large debt or equity lines, disclosing a maximum aggregate amount that can be sold. As they tap the market over time, they issue prospectus supplements to update investors on crucial data, such as pricing and use of proceeds.

Because shelf-registered offerings involve multiple takedowns that could occur over months or years, regulators require that the issuer's disclosures remain accurate and current at all times. This maintenance typically involves periodically amending the registration statement or filing post-effective amendments to include new financial statements, business updates, or risk disclosures. If material events—such as mergers, significant legal actions, or changes to executive leadership—arise, the issuer must swiftly incorporate these details into the public record so prospective investors can make informed decisions. In some cases, an issuer designated as a "well-known seasoned issuer" (WKSI) benefits from streamlined shelf rules, such as automatic effectiveness of registration statements and fewer restrictions on communications before and during the offering. These relaxed rules reflect the assumption that such issuers already provide extensive, high-quality disclosures due to their size, market presence, and established reporting track record. Ultimately, by adhering to these rule requirements, issuers balance the convenience of raising capital on a flexible timeline with the regulatory mandate to keep investors well-informed throughout the shelf registration period.

2.4.4 Offering Documents and Delivery Requirements

When issuers or underwriters bring new securities to market, they must provide comprehensive disclosures to potential investors. The specific documents and delivery standards vary by offering type but share a common goal: to ensure purchasers receive enough information to make an informed decision. In municipal offerings, the **official statement** outlines crucial details regarding the issuer's financial health, the structure and security of the bond, and any associated risks. For certain structured or specialized products, such as those offered through a plan or program, a **program disclosure document** may offer similar insights into fees, investment objectives, and restrictions.

Corporate securities, on the other hand, often rely on a prospectus—either a **full statutory prospectus** or a **summary prospectus** designed to highlight key points in a more concise format. These documents must be delivered to investors by certain deadlines, often before or at the time of sale, to meet regulatory requirements set by the Securities and Exchange Commission (SEC) or, in the case of municipal issues, the Municipal Securities Rulemaking Board (MSRB). By enforcing robust delivery rules, regulators help maintain transparency and protect investors from misinformation or opaque practices, fostering greater confidence in the integrity of public offerings.

2.4.4.1 Official Statement (Municipal)

An official statement (OS) serves as the primary disclosure document for municipal securities offerings. Unlike corporate issuers that generally file a prospectus with the Securities and Exchange Commission (SEC), municipal issuers—such as state governments, cities, or other public entities—are exempt from SEC registration under federal securities laws. Instead, they adhere to standards set by the Municipal Securities Rulemaking Board (MSRB), whose rules emphasize that issuers and underwriters must provide all material information needed by investors to evaluate the features and risks of a municipal bond. In this context, an official statement becomes the key source of data on the issuer's fiscal health, the terms and security of the bond, and any economic or demographic factors that may influence the issuer's ability to repay the debt on time and in full.

Content and Scope

A well-structured official statement typically includes comprehensive details about the nature of the securities, such as their maturity schedule, coupon rates, redemption provisions, and any underlying security features (e.g., revenue pledges or tax-backed obligations). It also discloses relevant financial statements, budget projections, and an overview of the local economy or revenue streams supporting the bond. For general obligation bonds, the OS might highlight the municipality's taxation powers, debt limits, and credit ratings, so investors can judge whether local tax revenues are likely to remain sufficient. In the case of revenue bonds, the official statement would explain the flow of funds from the underlying project—such as a toll road or water system—and articulate how these revenues are expected to cover operating expenses and service the debt. Further sections may discuss ongoing litigation risks, outstanding debt obligations, and any recent legislative changes that might affect the issuer's revenue base or legal standing.

Because an official statement forms the bedrock of disclosure for municipal offerings, it is typically prepared with guidance from bond counsel and municipal advisors to ensure legal compliance and thorough financial transparency. Notably, while the MSRB and the SEC cannot directly mandate the content of the official statement (due to municipal securities' exempt status), Rule 15c2-12 under the

Securities Exchange Act of 1934 compels underwriters to ensure that investors receive accurate, timely disclosure. To fulfill these obligations, most issuers follow recognized industry practices that mirror the depth of detail found in registered corporate filings. Any material developments—such as a credit rating downgrade or major legal proceeding—must also be reported promptly, enabling investors to weigh new information before deciding to buy or sell the securities.

Delivery and Investor Protection

Upon finalization, underwriters and dealers are required to distribute the official statement to potential investors, often via electronic platforms like the MSRB's Electronic Municipal Market Access (EMMA) system. Early drafts, sometimes referred to as preliminary official statements, circulate before final pricing; the final OS is then updated with definitive terms once the bond sale concludes. The delivery of these documents is crucial: municipal bonds can carry a range of unique risks, including changes in local politics, infrastructure stresses, or shifts in demographic trends. An up-to-date official statement aims to arm prospective buyers with enough context to assess these uncertainties and compare the bond's yield and credit profile to other available investments.

From a broader perspective, the official statement bolsters transparency and confidence in the municipal market. By clarifying how proceeds will be used—whether for new school construction, highway repairs, or utility expansions—and outlining the municipality's capacity to meet its obligations, the OS reduces information asymmetry between local governments and the investing public. As a result, informed investors can better weigh the relative returns and risks of different municipal issuers, which in turn fosters a more efficient and liquid marketplace for tax-exempt and taxable municipal bonds alike.

2.4.4.2 Program Disclosure Document

A Program Disclosure Document (PDD) serves as a comprehensive guide for investors participating in certain specialized or "program" offerings, particularly municipal fund securities such as 529 college savings plans, ABLE accounts, or local government investment pools (LGIPs). Unlike a standard prospectus for corporate securities, the PDD focuses on the operational structure and benefits specific to the program, detailing everything from contribution limits and fee schedules to eligible participants, tax implications, and withdrawal rules. Because these municipal-based programs often involve unique regulatory considerations or state-specific guidelines, the PDD compiles crucial disclosures in one place, ensuring prospective investors fully grasp both the opportunities and constraints of the plan. By describing key features—such as matching grants, allowable investment options, or the scope of expenses covered—a well-crafted PDD helps investors discern how and when to utilize these programs effectively for their financial or educational goals.

Each PDD also outlines the ongoing administrative procedures and governance behind the fund. For instance, it may describe how the plan's managing authority selects, rotates, or discontinues certain underlying investment portfolios, including whether a state treasury or a contracted asset manager supervises those choices. Fee structures—covering enrollment fees, annual maintenance costs, or asset-based charges—are clarified, and the document may highlight any resident-specific tax deductions or credits. Since these programs typically aim to foster longer-term savings, the PDD often addresses potential penalties or recapture provisions for nonqualified withdrawals. To maintain transparency, updates or amendments to the PDD are disseminated as plan terms evolve (e.g., changes in federal tax laws or enhancements to state-based incentives). By centralizing all material details, a PDD fosters informed participation, allowing investors, families, or other eligible entities to weigh the plan's advantages, assess its fit for their particular circumstances, and clearly understand how the program complies with relevant municipal securities regulations.

2.4.4.3 Prospectus Requirements (Section 10, Summary Prospectus)

Under the Securities Act of 1933, **Section 10** establishes the core disclosure obligations for a statutory prospectus. This document is the issuer's principal vehicle for informing potential buyers about key aspects of the offering—such as the nature of the securities, the issuer's financial condition, risk factors, use of proceeds, and management structure. The prospectus must contain all information deemed necessary to provide a fair presentation of risks and rewards, enabling investors to make an informed decision before purchasing. Issuers and underwriters typically file a preliminary prospectus (also known as a "red herring") during the marketing phase, then finalize the statutory prospectus just prior to pricing and distribution. Because Section 10 requires extensive detail, including audited financial statements and material updates on corporate governance or pending litigation, the final prospectus is viewed as one of the most thorough regulatory disclosures an issuer will ever produce.

Recognizing that not all investors or institutions require the full statutory prospectus at first glance, the SEC also allows for a **summary prospectus**, which distills the most vital information into a more concise format. Aimed at reducing information overload and improving accessibility, the summary prospectus highlights items such as the investment strategy, fees and expenses, and principal risks in plain language. However, it must refer readers to the full statutory prospectus for additional detail and must be consistent with the comprehensive disclosures found therein. In many cases, mutual funds and other investment companies leverage the summary prospectus model, giving investors a streamlined view while still satisfying the statutory requirement that all material facts remain publicly available. By balancing the depth of Section 10's mandates with the summary document's brevity, regulators hope to foster a transparent environment in which both casual and sophisticated investors can readily understand their potential investments.

2.4.5 Regulatory Filing Requirements and Exemptions

Issuers selling securities are typically required to file various forms and disclosures with regulatory bodies such as the Securities and Exchange Commission (SEC). These **SEC filings** outline key financial and operational data, enabling prospective investors to assess a company's viability and risk profile. From the initial registration statement to periodic reports, these submissions ensure the ongoing availability of transparent, accurate information. However, certain exemptions—like those under Regulation D—allow issuers to bypass full registration when offering securities to accredited or sophisticated investors, provided the deal adheres to strict guidelines on advertising, investor limits, and resale restrictions.

In tandem with federal requirements, **blue-sky laws** come into play at the state level, mandating that securities be registered or qualify for an exemption in each jurisdiction where they are sold. The interplay between SEC regulation and state rules can influence how offerings are structured, especially for smaller issuers lacking the resources to file in multiple locations. While many states coordinate their regulations to reduce redundancies, diligent compliance is essential to ensure that issuers legally offer their securities and investors receive consistent levels of disclosure and protection.

2.4.5.1 SEC Filings

When companies or other issuers offer securities to the public, they typically must file registration statements and ongoing disclosures with the Securities and Exchange Commission (SEC). These documents serve the dual purpose of informing prospective investors and providing regulators with comprehensive data on the issuer's financial health, governance structures, and any risks inherent to the offering. In the initial stages, issuers often prepare a registration statement (such as Form S-1, S-3, or a similar form depending on eligibility) that contains detailed audited financials, descriptions of the securities being issued, and material information on corporate operations. This statement undergoes an SEC review process, during which the regulator may issue comment letters seeking clarification or additional disclosures. Upon resolving the SEC's concerns, the registration statement becomes effective, allowing the issuer to formally price and distribute the securities. Post-offering, issuers are generally subject to periodic reporting, including annual Form 10-Ks, quarterly Form 10-Qs, and current reports on Form 8-K for significant events—ensuring that investors continue to have access to updated information. These filings are publicly available through the SEC's Electronic Data Gathering, Analysis, and Retrieval (EDGAR) system, promoting transparency and leveling the playing field for the investing public.

Beyond these core registration and reporting obligations, certain specialized filings address unique circumstances. For example, Form S-4 is used for securities offered in mergers or exchange offers, while Form S-8 covers employee stock purchase or incentive plans. Additional disclosures may be required if the issuer pursues an exempt offering under Regulation D but later decides to "go public," or if significant shareholders choose to sell restricted stock under Rule 144. Regardless of the specific form, the common thread is that

SEC filings must present material facts accurately and in compliance with anti-fraud provisions. Any material misrepresentations or omissions can expose the issuer, its officers, and sometimes underwriters to legal liability. As a result, crafting SEC filings demands a high level of scrutiny and coordination among legal counsel, accounting professionals, and management teams—an effort that continues well after the offering completes, as companies keep the market informed through periodic and event-driven updates.

2.4.5.2 Blue-Sky Laws

Blue-sky laws are state-level securities regulations aimed at preventing fraud and protecting investors from unscrupulous issuers. The term originates from early 20th-century legislative efforts to stop speculators from selling "sham" securities with no more substance than "so many feet of blue sky." While federal statutes like the Securities Act of 1933 and the Securities Exchange Act of 1934 set nationwide standards, blue-sky laws empower individual states to impose their own registration, disclosure, and licensing requirements on issuers, broker-dealers, and investment advisers operating within their borders. In practice, this can mean a company planning a multi-state offering must not only register with the Securities and Exchange Commission (SEC) but also ensure compliance with each state's particular rules—or qualify for an exemption if available. For example, a firm raising capital might need to file specific forms, pay fees, and disclose pertinent information so that state regulators, often guided by the North American Securities Administrators Association (NASAA), can review and approve the offering.

The Uniform Securities Act serves as a model statute to harmonize provisions across states, though individual jurisdictions may adopt its clauses with slight variations. Typically, states recognize three main pathways to meet blue-sky registration: **notification (or filing), coordination, and qualification**. In a coordination scenario, the issuer's registration in a given state largely parallels its federal SEC filing, allowing state authorities to rely on the same documents for review. Qualification, by contrast, is more bespoke and often used by smaller issuers who may not be required to register federally; it demands a detailed submission tailored to the state's unique requirements. Many states also offer exemptions—such as a limited offering exemption for a small number of in-state investors—that can spare companies from the full rigors of registration. Despite these varied options, the overarching goal of blue-sky laws remains the same: protect local investors by ensuring that only legitimate, adequately disclosed securities can be sold within that state's jurisdiction. By adhering to these laws, issuers and financial professionals foster confidence in the capital markets and promote more transparent, accountable fundraising practices.

2.5 Key Rules and Regulations Affecting Capital Markets

2.5.1 FINRA Rules (2266, 2269, 5250, etc.)

The Financial Industry Regulatory Authority (FINRA) enforces a broad set of rules to maintain fair markets, protect investors, and uphold ethical conduct among broker-dealers. These requirements vary from customer communication obligations to prohibitions on particular compensation practices. In essence, FINRA's rules complement federal securities laws, ensuring that firms not only disclose essential information but also refrain from behaviors that could distort the market or exploit investors. By adhering to these guidelines, member firms demonstrate their commitment to transparency, investor protection, and the overall integrity of capital markets.

Among the key rules are **FINRA Rule 2266 (SIPC Information), FINRA Rule 2269**, and **FINRA Rule 5250**. **Rule 2266** mandates that broker-dealers disclose specific details regarding their membership in the Securities Investor Protection Corporation (SIPC). This includes providing clients, both at account opening and annually, with written statements indicating that SIPC protects customers against the loss of cash and securities in the event of a firm's insolvency (subject to SIPC's coverage limits). The rule also requires disclosure of SIPC's website and contact information, enabling investors to confirm coverage specifics or learn more about SIPC's role. Meanwhile, **Rule 2269** focuses on conflicts of interest in securities distributions. When a firm recommends or sells a security in a primary or secondary distribution where it has a financial interest—such as a participation in underwriting or other direct involvement—the firm must disclose this relationship to the customer before completing the transaction. This transparency ensures that clients are fully aware of the firm's stake and can assess whether the recommendation might be colored by any potential bias.

Rule 5250, on the other hand, addresses a different dimension of ethical behavior by prohibiting broker-dealers from accepting payments for market-making activities. Specifically, it bars a member firm from receiving compensation from an issuer or its affiliates as an inducement for maintaining a quote, publishing quotes, or making a market in that issuer's securities. This rule preserves the integrity of market-making, ensuring quotes reflect genuine supply and demand rather than paid promotion. Taken together, these regulations form a critical portion of FINRA's oversight, requiring clear disclosures and honest dealing in all aspects of securities sales, underwriting, and market-making. Firms that comply with these obligations not only mitigate legal risk but also cultivate trust in their client relationships and in the marketplace at large.

Rule	Focus	Key Requirements
2266	SIPC Information	Provide SIPC membership details, website, and coverage info at account opening and annually
2269	Disclosure of Participation or Interest	Disclose firm's financial interest in the primary or secondary distribution of recommended securities
5250	Payments for Market Making	Prohibits accepting payment from issuers/affiliates to quote or make a market in their securities

By enforcing these rules, FINRA upholds a standard of conduct that helps safeguard investors from hidden conflicts, misleading sales tactics, or manipulative market practices. Adherence to Rule 2266 promotes transparency about protective mechanisms like SIPC, while Rule 2269 tackles potential conflicts in underwriting and distribution. Meanwhile, Rule 5250 protects the pricing integrity of securities by banning pay-to-play arrangements in market-making. Each rule thus addresses a distinct dimension of broker-dealer interactions, collectively reinforcing the fundamental investor protections and ethical frameworks that shape U.S. capital markets.

2.5.2 MSRB Rules (G-11, G-32, G-34)

The Municipal Securities Rulemaking Board (MSRB) establishes rules specifically tailored to the municipal securities market, seeking to ensure fair dealing, transparent disclosures, and the orderly functioning of both primary and secondary trading. Unlike corporate markets overseen by the SEC and FINRA, municipal offerings present unique considerations—such as tax-exempt interest and state-level regulatory nuances—so MSRB rules are structured to address the particular obligations of underwriters, municipal advisors, and broker-dealers in these transactions. Three key MSRB rules that govern the primary issuance and immediate post-sale processes are **G-11 (Primary Offering Practices)**, **G-32 (Disclosures in Connection with Primary Offerings)**, and **G-34 (CUSIP Numbers, New Issue and Market Information Requirements)**.

G-11 (Primary Offering Practices)

Rule G-11 governs how underwriters coordinate and distribute new municipal issues, setting standardized procedures to ensure a level playing field for both underwriters and issuers. It addresses matters such as the formation of syndicates, priority provisions for allocating bonds, and procedures for handling orders submitted by various clients, including retail and institutional investors. Under G-11, managing underwriters must disseminate timely information on the structure of the issue, bond pricing, and distribution timetables to syndicate members. This standardized communication fosters transparency within the underwriting group so that orders can be accurately tracked and allocated according to the issuer's instructions or the syndicated agreement's stated hierarchy of order types (e.g., retail orders may receive priority). The rule also sets forth requirements for final settlement among syndicate members, specifying when and how net capital contributions and profit distributions should be reconciled.

From the issuer's perspective, G-11 ensures that competitive or negotiated sales proceed with consistency and fairness. In a negotiated underwriting, for example, the lead manager must disclose any changes that might affect the pricing or interest rates offered, reducing the risk of hidden fees or sudden adjustments that could surprise the issuer. Meanwhile, G-11's emphasis on clear records of syndicate communications supports regulatory oversight—if any irregularities or investor complaints emerge, these documents can verify whether the syndicate adhered to the issuer's goals and regulatory requirements.

G-32 (Disclosures in Connection with Primary Offerings)

Rule G-32 focuses on the obligations of underwriters and dealers to provide accurate and timely disclosure documents to investors in municipal offerings. When a new issue comes to market, the issuer or its municipal advisor typically prepares an official statement—a comprehensive document that outlines the bond's terms, security provisions, use of proceeds, and financial and demographic details regarding the municipality. G-32 mandates that underwriters deliver this official statement, or a preliminary version if one is available, to customers by the settlement date. If the final official statement is not yet ready, preliminary documents must still present core material facts, ensuring that investors can evaluate the offering's credit quality and risks before finalizing their purchase.

G-32 also outlines the time frames within which dealers must submit information about the offering to the MSRB's Electronic Municipal Market Access (EMMA) system, thereby making the official statement publicly accessible. Any amendments or addenda—such as changes in interest rates or credit rating updates—must be filed so that prospective and existing investors remain current on the bond's status. Violations of G-32 can arise if a dealer fails to provide official statements promptly or omits critical information, potentially leading to regulatory sanctions. Overall, by holding dealers accountable for delivering transparent and accurate disclosures, Rule G-32 underpins the principle of investor protection in the municipal bond market.

G-34 (CUSIP Numbers, New Issue and Market Information Requirements)

Rule G-34 deals with the assignment of CUSIP numbers—unique

identifiers for financial instruments—and the obligations of municipal underwriters or remarketing agents to obtain and disseminate these identifiers. When a new municipal offering is structured, the lead underwriter (or another obligated party) must apply for CUSIP numbers through designated services. This step ensures each maturity or subgroup of bonds can be tracked separately, simplifying trade clearance, settlement, and record-keeping. By assigning CUSIPs at the time of issuance, the market gains a standardized reference system that improves operational efficiency and reduces the risk of confusion among various bond series, especially when an issuer sells multiple tranches.

Beyond CUSIP assignment, G-34 covers the requirement to submit critical new issue information—such as interest rates, offering prices or yields, and initial trade data—to the MSRB in a timely manner. This information becomes part of the public domain via EMMA, enabling investors to view up-to-date pricing data and other transaction details. G-34 fosters transparency in the immediate post-sale environment, giving existing and prospective bondholders insight into the bond's initial distribution and overall market acceptance. It also aids regulators in monitoring compliance with primary offering practices, ensuring the transaction aligns with disclosures made to investors and the broader marketplace. By linking unique identification codes to real-time issue data, G-34 underpins the operational integrity of the municipal marketplace, supporting both regulatory oversight and efficient secondary trading.

Collectively, G-11, G-32, and G-34 form a pillar of the MSRB's regulatory framework for new municipal offerings. **G-11** ensures that underwriters collaborate in an orderly and fair manner when distributing new bonds, **G-32** enshrines robust disclosure duties so that investors can make informed decisions, and **G-34** standardizes how securities are identified and how key data is filed with public systems. Together, they reinforce transparency, protect investors, and provide issuers with consistent guidelines for selling bonds to the public.

2.5.3 SEC Rules and Regulations

At the federal level, the Securities and Exchange Commission (SEC) enforces a suite of rules and regulations that shape how businesses raise capital and how securities change hands in the marketplace. From the Securities Act of 1933—which lays out requirements for registering new offerings—to the Securities Exchange Act of 1934—addressing registration and regulation of broker-dealers and ongoing reporting—these foundational statutes set the tone for disclosure, antifraud measures, and market oversight. Rules like Regulation D permit companies to offer securities privately under certain exemptions, letting smaller or specialized issuers secure funding without going through full public registration.

Beyond these broad frameworks, specific SEC rules address scenarios such as the resale of restricted securities (Rule 144), disclosures for mergers or reclassifications (Rules 145, 147), and guidelines for delivering certain prospectus materials (Rule 164). Meanwhile, statutes like the Securities Investor Protection Act of 1970 (SIPA) safeguard investors against broker-dealer failures, providing coverage for lost securities or cash up to specified limits. Overall, these rules and regulations collectively reinforce a transparent, trustworthy environment by mandating that all market participants—issuers, intermediaries, and investors—adhere to consistent standards of disclosure and fair dealing.

2.5.3.1 Securities Act of 1933 (Sections 7, 8, 10, 23, 215, 431, etc.)

The Securities Act of 1933 is often described as the "truth in securities" law, setting the foundation for how new securities must be registered, disclosed, and sold to the investing public. Enacted in response to the market excesses and lack of transparency that contributed to the Great Depression, the Act's primary goals are to require issuers to **provide full and fair disclosure** of all material information and to **prevent fraudulent, deceptive, or manipulative acts and practices** in the offer and sale of securities. By mandating registration and disclosure of critical financial, operational, and risk-related data, the Act helps potential investors make more informed decisions about whether, and under what conditions, to invest in a given security. Certain sections within the Act—specifically Sections 7, 8, 10, 23, 215, and 431—clarify what exactly must be disclosed, how the registration statement takes effect, and what conduct is deemed unlawful in connection with an offering.

Section 7 – Information Required in a Registration Statement

Section 7 outlines the types of information that must appear in a registration statement filed with the Securities and Exchange Commission (SEC). This includes, among other things:

- Detailed financial statements, audited by an independent accountant
- A description of the issuer's business model, capital structure, and intended use of proceeds
- Relevant risk factors and pending legal proceedings
- Biographical and compensation details regarding officers, directors, and key shareholders

Section 7 ensures that investors have a robust understanding of the issuing entity, from its corporate governance practices to its balance sheet and the competitive environment in which it operates. By specifying the minimum data needed—rather than leaving it to the discretion of the issuer—Section 7 seeks to maintain consistency in registration disclosures across different offerings and industries.

Section 8 – Taking Effect of Registration Statements and Amendments

Section 8 governs how and when a registration statement becomes effective. After an issuer files an initial or amended registration statement, the SEC staff reviews the materials for compliance with the Act's disclosure requirements. If the SEC finds deficiencies—such as missing or unclear financial data—it may issue comment letters requesting clarification or revisions. The registration statement does not become effective until either:

1. The SEC declares it effective, indicating the disclosures satisfy the agency's standards, or

2. A specified time period elapses without the SEC objecting to the filing (often referred to as "automatic effectiveness" in certain circumstances).

In addition, Section 8 grants the SEC the power to issue a stop order if it believes that the registration statement contains false or misleading information or omits material facts. This enforcement mechanism underscores the Act's emphasis on accuracy and thoroughness. Until any such stop order is resolved, the issuer is prevented from selling or distributing the securities.

Section 10 – Information Required in Prospectus

Section 10 focuses on **prospectus requirements**, stipulating what must be included in the primary offering document given to prospective investors. The content specified in Section 10 typically parallels the disclosures found in the registration statement under

Section 7, but it is tailored for a more investor-focused presentation. Requirements can include:

- A summary of the issuer's business and financial condition
- Risk factors specific to the offering
- Terms of the securities being offered (e.g., share price, dividend policy, interest rates)
- Management's discussion and analysis of financial results

In effect, Section 10 ensures that the prospectus is both comprehensive and balanced, disclosing not just the issuer's potential strengths but also the possible risks. This requirement is central to the Act's mission, as it compels companies to lay bare all material facts in a way that retail and institutional investors can examine and compare against alternative investment opportunities.

Section 23 – Unlawful Representations

Section 23 prohibits **unlawful representations** connected with the registration process. Specifically, it makes it illegal for anyone—whether the issuer, an underwriter, or other associated persons—to suggest that the SEC's declaration of effectiveness is a guarantee of the offering's quality or a formal endorsement of the issuer's business. This clause is fundamental because the SEC's role is to ensure adequate disclosure, not to validate the investment's merit or profitability. If issuers or promoters were free to claim "SEC-approved" as a selling tactic, investors might be misled into thinking the government had vetted the offering's future success. Section 23 thus reinforces the principle that the burden is on investors to interpret the disclosed information, not on regulators to judge the viability of each offering.

Section 215 – Contrary Stipulations Void

Section 215 makes any contractual provision or clause that attempts to waive compliance with the Securities Act of 1933—or that seeks to disclaim liability for a violation—null and void. This rule effectively prevents issuers from forcing investors to sign away their legal rights to rely on the disclosures mandated by the Act. Without Section 215, issuers could potentially embed waivers in purchase agreements, disclaiming responsibility for incomplete or inaccurate statements, thereby undermining the Act's investor-protection framework. By invalidating such stipulations, Section 215 ensures that issuers remain accountable for the representations and disclosures they make, and that investors maintain the rights and remedies laid out by federal securities laws.

Section 431 – Summary Prospectuses

Section 431 authorizes the use of **summary prospectuses**, allowing issuers to present key information in a condensed, more accessible format. This strategy acknowledges that not all investors want or need to sift through the entire statutory prospectus. Instead, a well-crafted summary can highlight main selling points—like the security's financial metrics, management background, or risk profile—while pointing the reader to the full prospectus for further detail. Although the summary prospectus can enhance usability and reduce "information overload," Section 431 ensures it remains consistent with the more exhaustive disclosures. The summary cannot omit material information or contradict the full prospectus. This approach attempts to strike a balance between investor convenience and comprehensive disclosure, making the offering documents both more user-friendly and reliably informative.

Overall Significance of the 1933 Act Provisions

Sections 7, 8, 10, 23, 215, and 431 collectively reinforce the Securities Act of 1933's mission: promoting **transparency**, **truthful disclosure**, and **investor confidence** in newly issued securities. From the moment an issuer drafts its registration statement to the point at which shares are actually sold, these provisions shape every facet of the offering process. By ensuring accurate, timely, and non-misleading information, the Act seeks to reduce the incidence of fraudulent offerings and provide a level playing field for the public. In doing so, it sets a legal standard still upheld today, influencing how companies communicate with potential investors and shaping the regulatory philosophy that underlies U.S. capital markets.

2.5.3.2 Securities Exchange Act of 1934 (Section 3(a), 12, 15, 15A)

The Securities Exchange Act of 1934 marked a pivotal shift from the registration of new securities—covered by the Securities Act of 1933—to the **ongoing regulation of secondary markets** and broker-dealers. By establishing the Securities and Exchange Commission (SEC) and bestowing it with broad oversight powers, the 1934 Act aims to protect investors through continuous disclosure, antifraud provisions, and the registration of key market participants and trading venues. Several core sections—**3(a)**, **12**, **15**, and **15A**—offer the statutory backbone for defining crucial terms, mandating securities registrations, regulating broker-dealers, and setting forth the framework for national securities associations like FINRA. Collectively, these provisions ensure a marketplace where information flows freely and market professionals conduct business under uniform, transparent standards.

Section 3(a)

Section 3(a) of the 1934 Act supplies a suite of **definitions** critical to understanding its scope and application. It clarifies what constitutes a "security," "broker," "dealer," "exchange," and other fundamental terms, drawing distinctions that determine who must register and which transactions fall within the Act's purview. For instance, the Act's definition of "security" extends beyond common stock and bonds to include investment contracts and certain derivative products—anything that effectively represents an investment in a common enterprise with an expectation of profits from the efforts of others. This breadth ensures that emerging financial instruments remain subject to oversight if they share the economic reality of more conventional securities. By precisely articulating these definitions, Section 3(a) underpins the entire regulatory regime, preventing market participants from circumventing disclosure or registration requirements simply by labeling a product differently.

These definitions also guide how the SEC categorizes various market participants. A "broker," for example, is any person engaged in the business of effecting transactions in securities for the account of others, whereas a "dealer" purchases and sells securities for its own account as part of a regular business. Distinctions like these matter greatly when determining who must register with the SEC under Section 15 or who must adhere to exchange membership rules. Moreover, the definitional clarity fosters consistency across state and federal regulations, since many states model their own securities laws (blue-sky provisions) on the underlying definitions found in federal statutes. In sum, Section 3(a) cements the 1934 Act's foundational vocabulary, bridging the gap between the law's broad objectives and practical day-to-day enforcement.

Section 12

Whereas the Securities Act of 1933 focuses on registering new offerings, **Section 12** of the 1934 Act addresses **the ongoing registration of securities** listed on national exchanges or traded in broader over-the-counter markets (subject to certain thresholds).

This registration compels public companies to submit periodic financial reports (Forms 10-K, 10-Q) and event-driven disclosures (Form 8-K) to keep shareholders and potential investors informed about material developments. Notably, Section 12 covers two main avenues of registration:

1. **Section 12(a)** demands that securities be registered on a national exchange if they meet listing requirements and are publicly traded.

2. **Section 12(g)** requires registration for issuers that meet specific asset and shareholder thresholds, even if they do not list their securities on an exchange.

Through these stipulations, Section 12 aims to uphold transparency and accountability once a company has tapped the public markets. If a security becomes widely held, whether through exchange listing or a large base of record shareholders, the issuer must embrace the ongoing reporting and governance standards mandated by the SEC. Failure to maintain compliance—such as neglecting to file timely annual or quarterly reports—can lead to sanctions, delistings, or trading suspensions, thereby compromising the issuer's ability to raise capital or trade shares efficiently. Ultimately, Section 12 ensures that once a security has reached a certain scale of public ownership, the investing public has consistent and detailed information on the company's financial health and operational trajectory.

Section 15

Section 15 focuses on **the registration and regulation of broker-dealers**, positioning them under the SEC's purview to protect customers and maintain orderly markets. Anyone acting as a broker or dealer in U.S. securities markets typically must register under Section 15(b), unless they qualify for a specific exemption (e.g., certain foreign broker-dealers that limit interactions with U.S. clients). This registration obligates firms to abide by financial responsibility standards, recordkeeping rules, and operational controls that guard against fraud and safeguard customer assets. Moreover, Section 15 mandates that broker-dealers become members of a self-regulatory organization (SRO), usually FINRA, which imposes day-to-day supervisory rules and code-of-conduct obligations.

In addition, Section 15 grants the SEC disciplinary authority over broker-dealers. The Commission can revoke or suspend registration if it finds serious violations—such as repeated breaches of antifraud rules or inadequate compliance procedures that jeopardize market stability. Section 15(c) extends to limit certain forms of manipulative, deceptive, or otherwise unfair practices in connection with the sale or distribution of securities, reinforcing earlier antifraud provisions found in Section 10(b) and Rule 10b-5. Collectively, Section 15 ensures that firms entrusted with handling client orders and assets conduct business in alignment with statutory safeguards, thereby reinforcing investor confidence and market integrity.

Section 15A

Section 15A authorizes the creation and operation of **national securities associations**, with FINRA being the most prominent example. These associations regulate the conduct of member broker-dealers, subject to the SEC's overarching supervision. By establishing uniform rules, investigating potential infractions, and administering enforcement actions, an SRO like FINRA seeks to elevate ethical practices and investor protections in areas ranging from sales practices to net capital requirements. Under Section 15A, the SEC reviews the association's rule proposals and amendments to ensure they align with federal statutes and the public interest. If an SRO falls short—by failing to enforce its rules consistently, for instance—the SEC can step in to mandate reforms.

At the same time, Section 15A underscores the collaborative dimension of U.S. market regulation: the federal government entrusts certain frontline oversight duties to private entities familiar with industry structures, but retains final accountability. This public-private partnership allows for specialized expertise—FINRA's direct knowledge of broker-dealer operations, for instance—while reinforcing compliance through SEC oversight. The net effect is a layered regime in which broker-dealers answer to both statutory requirements under Section 15 and the day-to-day supervisory frameworks of a national securities association authorized by Section 15A. By creating a legally sanctioned space for self-regulation, the 1934 Act streamlines oversight and fosters industry best practices that are more agile than one-size-fits-all federal mandates alone.

Significance of Sections 3(a), 12, 15, and 15A

Together, **Sections 3(a), 12, 15, and 15A** form a robust infrastructure that underpins the U.S. securities markets beyond the initial offering phase. Section 3(a)'s definitions set the scope, Section 12 ensures publicly traded entities maintain current disclosures, Section 15 regulates and enforces broker-dealer behavior, and Section 15A empowers self-regulatory bodies to maintain ethical standards. Each provision addresses a different facet of market integrity, ensuring that once securities begin trading, the entire ecosystem—from corporate issuers to brokerage firms—meets a consistent level of oversight. This interplay is essential for promoting fair markets, mitigating systemic risks, and reinforcing confidence that all participants follow transparent rules under the vigilant eye of both the SEC and authorized SROs.

2.5.3.3 Regulation D (Private Placements)

Regulation D under the Securities Act of 1933 provides a framework for issuers to offer and sell securities without registering with the Securities and Exchange Commission (SEC), as long as they meet the specific conditions set forth in its rules. By establishing "safe harbors" for private placements, Regulation D allows companies—particularly startups, early-stage ventures, and smaller businesses—to secure funding from qualified or accredited investors without incurring the substantial costs and disclosures required in a public offering. While the exemptions available under Regulation D can streamline capital formation, they also place limits on factors such as the type and number of investors, the aggregate offering amount, and permissible solicitation methods. Each offering conducted under Regulation D must still comply with antifraud provisions and basic disclosure obligations, ensuring investors receive sufficient information to evaluate the risks and potential rewards.

Key Provisions of Regulation D

Regulation D encompasses several rules—most notably Rules 504, 506(b), and 506(c)—that define the terms under which an issuer can offer unregistered securities:

1. **Rule 504**

    - *Offering Limit:* Up to $10 million in any 12-month period.

    - *General Solicitation:* Generally prohibited unless the offering meets specific conditions (such as being registered in a state with substantive disclosure requirements).

    - *Investor Eligibility:* No explicit accreditation requirement; however, if the issuer uses general solicitation, sales may be limited to accredited investors under certain state law frameworks.

- *Key Attributes:* Often used by smaller issuers seeking modest amounts of capital. Rule 504 provides flexibility but comes with state-level compliance obligations if the issuer intends to advertise the offering openly.

2. **Rule 506(b)**

- *Offering Limit:* No maximum.
- *General Solicitation:* Prohibited; issuers cannot openly advertise the offering.
- *Investor Eligibility:* Unlimited number of accredited investors and up to 35 non-accredited but sophisticated investors.
- *Key Attributes:* Frequently utilized by private funds, venture capital groups, and small to mid-sized businesses. Many issuers favor 506(b) for the ability to raise unlimited funds while still including a limited cohort of non-accredited investors—provided they have adequate sophistication.

3. **Rule 506(c)**

- *Offering Limit:* No maximum.
- *General Solicitation:* Permitted, but *all* purchasers must be verified as accredited investors (i.e., the issuer must take "reasonable steps" to confirm accreditation status).
- *Investor Eligibility:* No non-accredited purchasers allowed.

- *Key Attributes:* Introduced as part of the JOBS Act reforms, 506(c) enables issuers to publicly market their offerings while restricting sales strictly to accredited investors. This provision aims to broaden the capital-raising reach of startups and growth companies by leveraging internet platforms, social media, and general advertisements without contravening securities laws.

Across all Reg D exemptions, the issuer typically files a Form D with the SEC within 15 days of the first sale, disclosing basic facts about the company, the offering, and the exemption relied upon. Although Reg D exempts companies from full registration, the antifraud provisions of the federal securities laws remain in effect, preventing issuers from making material misstatements or omissions in their offering materials. Moreover, resales of Reg D securities can be subject to restrictions, such as Rule 144 holding periods, unless structured otherwise through provisions like Rule 144A for qualified institutional buyers (QIBs).

Accredited Investor Concepts and Disclosure

A central pillar of Regulation D is the concept of the "accredited investor," which includes individuals or entities that meet certain net worth, income, or sophistication criteria, as well as institutional investors such as banks, insurance companies, or large retirement plans. The presumption behind focusing on accredited investors is that these market participants either possess the financial wherewithal to absorb losses or have specialized knowledge to assess the risks presented by early-stage or privately placed securities.

Issuers often tailor their disclosure packages—ranging from private placement memoranda (PPMs) to financial statements—to suit their investor pool. While the SEC does not mandate a uniform format akin to a public offering prospectus, the underlying principle holds that enough material information be provided so that potential investors can make an informed decision. For instance, offerings under Rule 506(b) that involve non-accredited investors may require more detailed disclosures, mirroring certain elements of a registered offering. By contrast, 506(c) offerings can restrict themselves to accredited purchasers, placing somewhat less emphasis on mandatory disclosure (though the antifraud standard remains). In all cases, investors can request more data or ask questions to verify the company's representations, reinforcing the due diligence process inherent to private placements.

Advantages and Limitations of Regulation D

Reg D exemptions offer a streamlined avenue to raise capital without meeting the substantial expense and time commitment of registering under the Securities Act. This benefits smaller issuers, entrepreneurial ventures, and private funds that rely on alternative financing methods (e.g., angel investors, private equity) to launch or expand operations. Meanwhile, accredited investors gain access to potentially high-growth opportunities not typically available in the public markets.

However, Regulation D offerings come with trade-offs. General solicitation constraints (especially under 506(b)) can limit how widely an issuer can market the securities, forcing reliance on pre-existing networks or intermediaries. Even under 506(c), where solicitation is permitted, issuers face an affirmative obligation to verify that each purchaser meets accreditation standards—a process that may introduce friction and costs in verifying income or net worth. Additionally, these securities often carry liquidity restrictions; investors must understand that they could be locked into their positions for extended periods, unlike stocks trading on national exchanges. Nonetheless, the success and prevalence of Reg D offerings over recent years underscore the exemption's critical role in fostering early-stage innovation, supporting specialized funds, and maintaining robust private capital markets.

Overall Impact on the Market

By balancing eligibility requirements, solicitation rules, and disclosure standards, **Regulation D** promotes a **flexible yet regulated** environment for private capital formation. Its safe harbors encourage investment in emerging enterprises—many of which contribute significantly to innovation and job creation—while striving to protect less sophisticated investors from the risks inherent in unregistered offerings. Although the approach differs from the highly transparent realm of publicly listed securities, Regulation D's nuanced rules remain integral to the U.S. capital ecosystem, offering a viable capital-raising avenue for companies that might otherwise struggle to bear the compliance burdens and scrutiny of a full SEC-registered public offering.

2.5.3.4 Rules 144, 144A, 145, 147, 164

The Securities Act of 1933 grants the Securities and Exchange Commission (SEC) authority to promulgate specific rules that refine how new and outstanding securities can be offered, sold, or resold. Among these, **Rules 144, 144A, 145, 147, and 164** each address distinct scenarios under which companies and investors can navigate federal securities laws with varying degrees of flexibility. Whether it involves reselling restricted shares to the public, transacting large blocks of private securities among qualified institutions, structuring mergers with shareholder approval, conducting intrastate offerings, or deploying free writing prospectuses in registered deals, these rules function as targeted carve-outs or procedures aligned with the broader objective of safeguarding investors while promoting an efficient flow of capital.

Rule 144 – Resales of Restricted and Control Securities

Rule 144 sets forth a "safe harbor" under which holders of restricted or "control" securities (i.e., stock owned by insiders or affiliates of the issuer) can publicly sell them without registering the transaction under the Securities Act of 1933. Restricted securities are often acquired through private placements, employee stock benefit plans, or other exempt offerings. Control securities refer to holdings by individuals who have the power to direct or influence the issuer, such as officers, directors, or major shareholders. By requiring adherence to specific holding periods, volume limitations, current public information requirements, and, in some cases, the filing of a Form 144, the rule ensures the market is protected from insider overhang and potential manipulation while still allowing legitimate holders to monetize their investments.

From a timing perspective, **non-affiliate holders** of restricted securities may resell them free of most conditions under Rule 144 after a six-month holding period if the issuer is a reporting company that is up to date with filings, or after one year if the issuer is non-reporting. Affiliate holders face additional restrictions, including caps on the percentage of outstanding shares they can sell within any three-month window and mandatory Form 144 filings for significant trades. These disclosures inform the market of insiders' intent to sell and enable investors to gauge whether large blocks might soon enter the market. By balancing the needs of private investors, founders, and early employees against the investing public's desire for transparency, Rule 144 creates a regulated pathway for distributing unregistered shares into public markets over time.

Rule 144A – Private Resales to Qualified Institutional Buyers (QIBs)

Rule 144A addresses a different segment of the market, permitting the resale of restricted securities—often high-yield debt, private equity placements, or structured products—to **qualified institutional buyers (QIBs)** without triggering full registration. QIBs typically include large institutions, such as banks, insurance companies, and pension funds, that manage a minimum of $100 million in securities. The presumption is that these sophisticated parties can adequately analyze risk without the same level of mandated disclosures required in a public offering.

Transactions under Rule 144A may take place through broker-dealers that specialize in matching institutional counterparties or via proprietary trading platforms. Many issuers, particularly foreign corporations or specialized entities, rely on 144A placements to access deep institutional pools of capital in the United States without subjecting themselves to the rigorous disclosure obligations of public registration. While these securities can eventually find their way into the mainstream market (often through Rule 144 conversions after holding periods), the initial distribution under 144A remains confined to QIBs, underscoring the rationale that large, knowledgeable investors require fewer regulatory guardrails than the general public.

Rule 145 – Reclassification of Securities, Mergers, Consolidations, and Asset Transfers

Rule 145 governs the registration requirements for certain corporate reorganization events—such as mergers, consolidations, or asset transfers—that effectively result in one class of security being exchanged for another. In a typical scenario, if Company A merges with Company B and shareholders receive new shares of the combined entity, the transaction can resemble a public offering, thus implicating the registration obligations under the Securities Act. Rule

145 clarifies when and how these transactions must be registered, ensuring shareholders receive full disclosure about the newly formed or restructured company's financial and operational landscape.

Additionally, the rule addresses scenarios like reclassifications (changing a security's rights or designations) or asset transfers in which shareholders receive new securities as compensation. Because these events can significantly alter an investor's original position, the SEC regards them as material changes warranting prospectus-level disclosure. The rule also includes provisions concerning the resale of any newly created or issued shares, intending to prevent affiliates or controlling persons from exploiting corporate reorganizations to bypass normal registration or resale restrictions. In this way, Rule 145 protects shareholders by mandating transparency and reaffirming the principle that significant corporate changes should not be executed at the expense of informed shareholder decision-making.

Rule 147 – Intrastate Offerings

Rule 147 focuses on **intrastate offerings**, providing an exemption for issuers that offer and sell securities exclusively within their home state to resident investors. The goal is to facilitate local capital formation by relieving purely in-state financing activities from the burdens of federal registration—on the assumption that states themselves have adequate jurisdiction and interest in regulating offerings made solely to their residents. Issuers must meet stringent tests demonstrating that their principal place of business and a significant portion of their operations (e.g., assets, revenue, or employees) are located in the same state as the buyers of the securities. Additionally, investors must agree not to resell the shares to non-residents for a designated period, typically six months, preserving the in-state character of the offering.

While Rule 147 fosters localized entrepreneurship and community investments, it also requires compliance with state securities laws (blue-sky laws), which can be intricate. Issuers often find themselves navigating both local registration or exemption processes and the rule's residency and operational requirements. If the issuer or any investor violates these stipulations—such as by selling the securities to an out-of-state buyer too soon—the entire offering may lose its intrastate exemption. As a result, successful reliance on Rule 147 demands careful attention to distribution logistics and robust investor screening procedures, ensuring no cross-border transaction undercuts the rule's purely intrastate premise.

Rule 164 – Post-filing Free Writing Prospectuses

Rule 164 permits the use of **free writing prospectuses** (FWPs) after an issuer has filed a registration statement, expanding the ways companies can communicate with potential investors during the "waiting period" prior to the offering's effective date. A free writing prospectus is any written communication—including electronic or graphic materials—that goes beyond the statutory prospectus content. Under Rule 164, issuers can supplement the main registration documents with timely updates, interactive features, or marketing materials, provided they contain necessary legends and references to the SEC-filed prospectus. This added flexibility aids in marketing and educational efforts, allowing issuers to adapt rapidly to investor questions or market conditions.

However, the rule imposes important safeguards: the FWP must not contradict the statutory prospectus and must be filed promptly with the SEC if used broadly. Issuers still bear responsibility for ensuring the information is accurate and that no material facts are omitted. If an FWP inadvertently introduces misleading statements or fails to align with previously filed disclosures, it could create liability under the antifraud provisions of federal securities laws. Rule 164 thus strikes a balance between modern communication practices—like online presentations or social media outreach—and the investor-protection tenet that prospective buyers deserve carefully vetted information, consistent with the official registration materials.

Overall Impact on Capital Formation

Rules 144, 144A, 145, 147, and 164 expand the pathways by which securities can be offered, exchanged, or resold under the federal regulatory umbrella. Whether smoothing the route for insiders to unload restricted stock (Rule 144), enabling large institutional investors to trade private securities efficiently (Rule 144A), mandating disclosures in corporate reorganizations (Rule 145), fostering local capital markets (Rule 147), or modernizing how issuers communicate with investors (Rule 164), these provisions each address specific circumstances that standard public registration may not accommodate. Combined, they nurture a more nuanced marketplace—one that upholds transparency and fairness while accommodating the diverse strategies and needs of issuers, investors, and intermediaries.

2.5.3.5 Securities Investor Protection Act of 1970 (SIPA)

Enacted in the wake of numerous broker-dealer insolvencies in the late 1960s, the **Securities Investor Protection Act of 1970 (SIPA)** created a federally mandated safety net for investors whose broker-dealers fail financially. Key to this framework is the Securities Investor Protection Corporation (**SIPC**), a nonprofit membership organization funded by broker-dealers that are required by law to join. Unlike federal deposit insurance, which covers bank depositors, SIPA's scope is narrower: it protects customers' cash and securities held in their brokerage accounts up to certain limits, stepping in primarily to return those assets if the broker-dealer becomes insolvent or goes through liquidation. Under SIPA, coverage for cash and securities in a customer's account typically extends to a combined total of $500,000, which includes up to $250,000 of cash. Although SIPC coverage cannot compensate customers for market losses, it ensures that shares and other assets remain intact and are returned to customers to the fullest extent possible, even if the failed brokerage's own financial reserves are depleted.

When a SIPC-member firm enters liquidation due to insolvency or other severe financial distress, a court-appointed trustee is generally assigned to administer the process. This trustee works closely with SIPC to identify valid customer claims, differentiate customer property from the firm's own assets, and either transfer the accounts to a solvent broker-dealer or return the assets directly to customers. SIPC's primary role is to oversee and fund any shortfall in assets attributable to customer accounts, within the specified coverage limits. Once customers are made whole—assuming no excessive shortfalls remain—any leftover claims effectively become unsecured debts against the firm's remaining estate. Notably, SIPC's involvement in protecting customer assets has no bearing on a security's underlying market value; if a customer's holdings drop in worth due to fluctuations in price, SIPC does not insure that loss. Instead, the organization focuses solely on ensuring that the securities (or equivalent cash value if those securities cannot be located) are restored to the rightful owner.

Structure and Oversight of SIPA

Under SIPA, broker-dealers must conspicuously inform their clients about SIPC membership and the basics of coverage, often providing this disclosure at account opening and through annual notifications. These statements reinforce that SIPC acts as a backstop in the event of a member's failure, giving investors confidence that their shares and funds won't be commingled with or lost among a firm's own liabilities. While the SEC supervises and enforces compliance with SIPA, SIPC itself is not a government agency. Instead, it operates similarly to an industry-sponsored insurance cooperative. By pooling assessments from all member broker-dealers—scaled according to each firm's volume and risk profile—SIPC sustains a reserve fund from which claims are paid when insolvencies occur.

When a member firm collapses, the trustee's liquidation process typically involves a detailed forensic accounting to track each customer's holdings. If securities are missing (for example, if the broker-dealer unlawfully used them as collateral or outright misappropriated them), SIPC can authorize the trustee to replace those securities up to the coverage limit. Should multiple parties claim ownership of the same assets, the trustee resolves disputes through a verified claims procedure. This ensures that legitimate customers with documented ownership receive priority over unsecured creditors, reinforcing the Act's customer-protection ethos.

Significance for Investors and Markets

By guaranteeing customer property remains separate from a broker-dealer's own obligations, **SIPA** bolsters trust in the U.S. securities markets. Investors are more likely to place funds and securities with brokerage firms—especially smaller or boutique firms—when they know their accounts receive a base level of protection should the firm fail. SIPA therefore contributes to market stability by reducing the likelihood of runs on brokerages in times of panic. Although SIPC coverage may not encompass every situation—nor does it mitigate market losses or fraudulent investment schemes outside of broker insolvencies—it remains a cornerstone of investor confidence, ensuring that the failure of one member firm does not cascade into widespread losses for retail and institutional clients.

Over the decades, **SIPA** has evolved through amendments that reflect changing market structures and the complexities of modern brokerage operations. Yet the core principle persists: clients' assets are sacrosanct, shielded from the firm's corporate liabilities, and supplemented by an industry-based reserve if a shortfall arises. By requiring membership and mandating specific disclosures, SIPA tightly integrates into the broader regulatory network overseen by the SEC and self-regulatory organizations like FINRA. The result is a multi-layered safety mechanism whereby firms remain cognizant of their custody obligations, regulators have clear standards to enforce, and investors gain practical reassurance that their securities or uninvested cash remain protected in the face of unforeseen broker-dealer distress.

Chapter 3 Understanding Products and Their Risks

3.1 Products

3.1.1 Equity Securities

Equity securities, commonly referred to as stocks, represent an ownership stake in a corporation. When an investor purchases shares, they gain rights proportional to their shareholdings—such as the potential to receive dividends if the company distributes profits, and the possibility of capital appreciation if market sentiment drives share prices higher. *Common stock* is the most familiar type of equity, conferring voting rights on significant corporate matters and offering the potential for unlimited upside, although its value can fluctuate widely. *Preferred stock*, by contrast, typically grants priority over common shareholders in terms of dividend payments and liquidation proceeds, though it generally lacks or restricts voting privileges. In addition, certain companies use *American Depositary Receipts (ADRs)* to enable U.S. investors to trade the shares of foreign corporations through U.S. exchanges, simplifying cross-border investing.

Because equity ownership exposes investors to the company's fortunes, shareholders assume a higher degree of risk relative to bondholders—if the business falters or dissolves, equity holders may lose part or all of their invested capital. Yet for those willing to accept volatility and market swings, equities can provide long-term growth and a potential hedge against inflation, especially when reinvesting dividends. Company fundamentals, economic conditions, and broader market sentiment all shape stock performance, underscoring why investors often diversify among different issuers and sectors to moderate the inevitable risks that come with equity ownership.

3.1.1.1 Types of Equities (Common, Preferred, ADRs)

Equity securities come in various forms, each offering distinct rights and risk-return profiles. The most widely held is **common stock**, which provides shareholders with voting privileges on matters such as the election of board members and major corporate actions like mergers or acquisitions. Common stockholders also benefit from potential capital appreciation if market conditions drive the share price higher. However, should the company encounter financial trouble, common shareholders rank behind creditors and preferred shareholders in liquidation, meaning they risk losing their entire investment if the firm becomes insolvent. Dividends on common stock are never guaranteed; they are declared at the board's discretion based on earnings and cash flow considerations. For investors seeking growth and the possibility of dividend income without fixed obligations, common stock can be an attractive vehicle, though it demands tolerance for price volatility tied to company performance and broader market sentiment.

Preferred stock, in contrast, typically guarantees a fixed dividend and places holders ahead of common shareholders in terms of claim on assets or earnings. This prioritization means that a company must pay its preferred dividends—in most cases—before distributing any profits to common shareholders. While preferred stock often lacks voting rights, certain classes may allow votes if dividends remain unpaid for a specified period. Variations like *cumulative preferred* require missed dividends to accrue and be paid retroactively, *participating preferred* allows holders to receive additional distributions if common shareholders get above-average dividends, and *convertible preferred* grants the option to exchange shares into a designated number of common shares under predetermined terms. Because of its more predictable income stream and partial insulation from common stock volatility, preferred stock appeals to investors balancing higher dividend yields with reduced potential for capital gains.

American Depositary Receipts (ADRs) represent a third significant category, allowing U.S. investors to purchase shares of foreign corporations without navigating overseas exchanges or currency conversions directly. A U.S. bank acts as a depositary by holding the underlying foreign shares and issuing ADRs in return. These instruments list on domestic exchanges or trade over the counter (OTC), with dividends usually paid in U.S. dollars. ADRs come in several "levels," reflecting how extensively the foreign company adheres to U.S. regulatory standards and reporting requirements. *Sponsored ADRs* typically involve direct cooperation between the foreign issuer and the depositary bank, while *unsponsored ADRs* may be established without the issuer's active participation. Although ADRs simplify international investing, holders remain exposed to global economic shifts, foreign corporate governance standards, and currency fluctuations that can influence the translated dividend amounts and the underlying share value.

3.1.1.2 Rights and Warrants

Rights and warrants are specialized equity-related instruments that offer existing or prospective shareholders the opportunity to buy additional stock—often at a specified price and within a defined timeframe. Although both confer an option to acquire shares, they differ significantly in their typical life spans, exercise prices, and underlying strategic uses. *Rights* are generally short-term privileges granted to existing shareholders, allowing them to maintain their proportional ownership in the event of a new stock issuance. *Warrants*, by contrast, tend to be longer-term and can be attached to other securities—such as bonds or preferred stock—to enhance those offerings' attractiveness. When properly understood and used, these instruments provide flexibility for both issuers and investors, although they also introduce unique complexities in terms of pricing, dilution, and potential speculation.

Rights typically accompany a pre-emptive rights offering, through which existing shareholders can purchase newly issued shares at a discount to the market price. This arrangement helps shareholders avoid dilution of their ownership percentage and also provides the issuer with a reliable path to raise capital. Each shareholder receives a certain number of rights—often one per share owned—and a predefined ratio of how many rights are needed to buy one new share. Because rights tend to expire within a few weeks, investors must act quickly to exercise them (subscribing to the new shares) or sell them in the open market if such a facility exists. If shareholders forgo participating, their ownership stake may be diluted when the newly minted shares enter the market. Despite the short fuse, rights are relatively straightforward to value based on the discount to market price and the time left until expiration, and they may trade at a small premium if the discount is sufficiently attractive.

Warrants, on the other hand, are often bundled with other securities—such as corporate bonds—to sweeten the deal for investors. A warrant grants the holder the right to buy a certain number of shares at a set *exercise price*, typically above the market price at issuance. The exercise price and expiration date can span years, allowing the company's stock price ample time to appreciate and making the warrant valuable. Because they enable a purchase of shares at a potentially advantageous price later on, warrants can exhibit high leverage if the stock climbs above the exercise price. Conversely, if the stock remains below that threshold, the warrant may expire worthless. Issuers benefit by attracting a broader pool of investors, while warrant holders aim for long-term stock appreciation. However, any exercise of warrants expands the total share count, creating potential dilution for existing shareholders.

Hence, understanding how rights and warrants fit into the broader capital structure—along with each instrument's expiration, pricing model, and potential for dilution—helps investors gauge when these tools serve as beneficial opportunities and when they may pose heightened risk

3.1.1.3 Ownership Concepts (Liquidation Order, Limited Liability)

In the corporate hierarchy of claims, equity holders stand behind creditors and bondholders if a firm must dissolve or liquidate. Typically, the proceeds from selling the company's assets first pay off secured creditors who hold specific collateral backing their loans. Next in line are unsecured creditors, ranging from suppliers owed money to holders of unsecured bonds. If additional debts exist—such as subordinated debentures—they follow. Only after all these obligations have been satisfied do preferred shareholders receive any remaining funds, reflecting their priority in liquidation. Common shareholders, while they have unlimited growth potential if the company thrives, are last in line should the business fail. This ordering underscores the inherent risk in common equity: while it can outperform other instruments during prosperous times, it also offers the lowest claim on assets when a firm faces bankruptcy or dissolution. Shareholders who accept this risk do so under the assumption that the firm's growth prospects and dividend potential justify the possibility of recovering little or nothing in a worst-case scenario.

At the same time, corporate stock typically grants the advantage of **limited liability**. Under this principle, shareholders can lose only what they've invested in the shares, and their personal assets remain protected from the company's creditors. Even if the issuer goes into severe financial distress, shareholders are not compelled to contribute additional capital beyond their initial purchase price. This contrasts sharply with other legal structures, such as certain partnerships, where participants may be personally liable for debts incurred by the business. Limited liability thus encourages broader public participation in the equity markets, enabling investors to place funds into ventures they deem promising without risking more than their initial stake. By accepting the residual claim on assets, shareholders position themselves for potentially greater returns, fully aware that the corporate form shields their personal wealth if fortunes turn.

3.1.1.4 Voting Rights and Control Restrictions (Rule 144)

Shareholders who own **common stock** typically possess the right to vote on major corporate decisions, a power that can shape board composition, authorize mergers or acquisitions, and approve changes in the corporate charter. In most cases, this involves *statutory voting*, meaning each share entitles the holder to one vote per board seat up for election; alternatively, some corporations adopt *cumulative voting*, allowing investors to concentrate all votes on fewer candidates, which can benefit minority shareholders seeking board representation. Although these basic rights are central to the concept of shareholder democracy, companies sometimes issue **non-voting** or **limited-voting** shares, especially in dual-class structures where founders or insiders retain tighter control. Investors exploring such stock categories should scrutinize the specific voting privileges and limitations spelled out in corporate charters or prospectuses, as these can materially influence their say in governance and strategy.

In parallel with voting rights, regulators impose **control restrictions** on shareholders deemed *affiliates* or *insiders*, typically including officers, directors, or individuals holding a substantial ownership stake. **Rule 144**, promulgated under the Securities Act of 1933, defines the conditions under which these affiliates—and holders of restricted (unregistered) stock—may sell their shares into the public market. Control shares come with strict constraints: affiliates must observe volume limits (capping how many shares can be sold within a three-month window), ensure the issuer complies with ongoing reporting requirements, and file Form 144 if sales exceed certain thresholds. Meanwhile, restricted securities acquired in private placements or through certain benefit plans require a specified holding period—usually six months for a fully reporting issuer—before public resale. By enforcing these conditions, Rule 144 balances the legitimate need of insiders and early investors to monetize their positions with the broader objective of preventing excessive insider selling, which might disrupt market liquidity or unfairly disadvantage outside investors. Ultimately, these provisions acknowledge that while voting rights form a key part of share ownership, shareholders with substantial influence must navigate extra obligations to safeguard market integrity.

3.1.1.5 Convertible Features

Convertible features enable certain equity holders—most commonly those holding **convertible preferred stock**—to exchange their shares for a predetermined number of common shares. This conversion ratio is typically set at issuance and reflects how many common shares one preferred share can command. For example, if the ratio is 1:5, a holder of one convertible preferred share may convert it into five shares of common stock. Because convertible preferred often pays a fixed dividend that ranks above common dividends, investors receive regular income while retaining the opportunity to participate in equity upside if the company's prospects significantly improve. To decide whether to convert, holders compare the conversion value (i.e., the number of common shares multiplied by the common share price) against the market value of the preferred itself. If the conversion value exceeds the price of the preferred, converting could lock in immediate gains and potentially grant more long-term growth potential.

Still, the presence of convertible features can impact both issuers and investors in various ways. From the issuer's perspective, convertible securities may carry lower dividend or coupon rates at issuance, since the possibility of capital appreciation attracts investors to accept lower yields. Over time, however, large-scale conversions may dilute existing shareholders if considerable numbers of new common shares enter the market. To minimize sudden or unplanned dilutions, some issuers include protective provisions (such as "forced conversion" triggers or antidilution clauses) that either limit the circumstances under which conversion can occur or adjust the conversion ratio if the company issues additional common shares at prices below a certain threshold. Meanwhile, investors must weigh both the steady stream of dividends from the preferred and the potential capital gains from conversion, noting that once they convert to common shares, they forfeit their priority claims on dividends and liquidation proceeds. By offering this dual character—part fixed-income, part equity upside—convertible features can appeal to investors seeking a balanced approach between income stability and long-term stock appreciation.

3.1.2 Debt Instruments

Debt instruments represent a broad category of securities in which the investor lends funds to an issuer—such as a corporation, municipality, or government entity—in exchange for interest payments and the return of principal at maturity. Unlike equity investors, bondholders do not own a stake in the entity; instead, they rank higher in claim on assets if the issuer faces financial distress. Common examples include U.S. Treasury bills, notes, and bonds, which the federal government sells to fund operations, and corporate bonds, where businesses borrow to finance growth or manage capital structures. Agency securities—such as mortgage-backed (MBS) or asset-backed (ABS)—pool loans like home mortgages or credit card receivables, passing interest and principal payments through to investors. Because each type of debt instrument carries unique credit, duration, and market risks, investors often select bonds based on interest-rate environment forecasts, issuer creditworthiness, and their own income or diversification goals.

Within this category, **municipal securities** stand out for their potential tax advantages. Issued by state and local governments, these bonds often offer interest that is exempt from federal—and sometimes state—taxes, making them attractive to investors in higher tax brackets. Meanwhile, **short-term money market instruments**, such as certificates of deposit (CDs), bankers' acceptances (BAs), and commercial paper, provide a lower-risk, highly liquid option for managing short-term cash needs. Interest payments and market prices for all debt instruments hinge on prevailing rates, credit spreads, and broader economic conditions, underscoring why bond valuations move inversely to interest-rate shifts. By understanding how factors like coupon, maturity, and ratings affect yield, investors can choose from a range of debt vehicles aligned with their specific return objectives and tolerance for market volatility.

3.1.2.1 Treasury Securities (Bills, Notes, Bonds, T-Receipts)

Treasury securities constitute a foundational element of the U.S. government's debt issuance strategy, appealing to investors for their historically low default risk and high liquidity. In broad terms, the government uses these instruments to fund daily operations and finance public projects, and they are backed by the full faith and credit of the U.S. Department of the Treasury. *Treasury bills (T-bills)* are short-term obligations typically issued at a discount and maturing within one year—common intervals include 4, 13, 26, or 52 weeks. Investors purchase T-bills below par value and receive the par amount at maturity, with the difference representing their implied interest. *Treasury notes (T-notes)* occupy a middle ground, offering maturities of 2 to 10 years and paying a fixed coupon semi-annually. Meanwhile, *Treasury bonds (T-bonds)* represent longer-term commitments, featuring maturities of 20 or 30 years, and also distribute interest semi-annually. Because these instruments trade actively in the secondary market, their yields fluctuate in response to shifts in interest rates, economic data, and geopolitical developments. Still, given their reputation for stability, Treasuries often serve as a benchmark for other fixed-income securities, influencing everything from corporate bond spreads to mortgage rates.

Beyond these conventional forms, the Treasury market includes variations like *Treasury receipts*—unofficially created zero-coupon bonds stripped from the interest and principal payments of Treasury notes or bonds. Brokerage firms or other financial institutions pool Treasury securities and separate their coupon payments from the underlying principal, selling each component as a standalone "receipt." Investors in these stripped receipts receive no periodic interest, instead buying them at a steep discount and realizing a return when the principal amount is paid at maturity. While the yields can be more attractive due to the discount, holders accept heightened price sensitivity to interest-rate changes compared to coupon-bearing bonds. Such instruments can be beneficial for those seeking a predictable lump sum at a future date, like funding a college tuition payment or retirement goal. However, the tax treatment can be more complex because investors owe taxes on the "imputed" interest each year, even though they do not actually receive cash interest until maturity or sale. Consequently, Treasury securities, in their many forms, offer a spectrum of durations, payment structures, and tax considerations—empowering market participants to tailor their holdings to meet specific investment objectives and risk profiles.

3.1.2.2 Agency Securities (MBS, ABS)

Agency securities commonly refer to debt instruments issued or guaranteed by government-sponsored enterprises (GSEs) or certain federal agencies. Within this sphere, **mortgage-backed securities (MBS)** and **asset-backed securities (ABS)** stand out for their role in connecting investors with pools of loans, ranging from residential mortgages to consumer credit obligations. In an MBS structure, the interest and principal payments from multiple home loans flow through to investors, while an ABS pools other forms of receivables, such as auto loans or credit card debt. Because these securities transform illiquid individual loans into standardized, tradable bonds, they help to broaden access to capital for borrowers and offer investors a way to diversify into an array of income-producing assets. However, the complexity of MBS and ABS can make them particularly sensitive to interest-rate fluctuations, prepayment behavior, and the credit quality of the underlying borrowers.

In the MBS arena, GSEs like Fannie Mae (Federal National Mortgage Association) and Freddie Mac (Federal Home Loan Mortgage Corporation) purchase conforming mortgages from originating lenders, package them, and issue pass-through certificates. These certificates entitle holders to proportional shares in each month's mortgage payments. Securities backed by Ginnie Mae (Government National Mortgage Association) differ in that they carry a direct guarantee from the U.S. government, providing a higher level of credit protection. Regardless of which agency backs them, MBS investors must consider **prepayment risk**—the likelihood that homeowners refinance or pay off their loans early—since unexpected cash flows can change yield projections and reinvestment options. In an environment of falling interest rates, higher refinancing activity can return principal sooner, leading to reinvestment at lower yields. Conversely, if rates rise, slower prepayments can lock investors into older, lower-interest-rate securities.

By contrast, **asset-backed securities** typically bundle non-mortgage debt, including auto loans, student loans, and credit card receivables. Each ABS class features unique repayment schedules and risk considerations tied to consumer behavior, default rates, and the underlying collateral. For instance, auto loan ABS may incorporate a predictable depreciation factor for vehicles, while credit card ABS depends heavily on monthly payment patterns and the revolving nature of credit balances. Issuers often slice these receivables into **tranches**—layers offering varying priorities of payment or different maturities—allowing investors to choose risk-reward profiles best suited to their investment goals. Like MBS, ABS can carry complexities around cash flow modeling, prepayment rates, and default assumptions. Agency involvement or credit enhancements (like insurance wraps or senior/subordinate structures) can mitigate certain credit risks, but investors remain exposed to broader economic conditions that might alter consumer repayment behavior.

Over time, MBS and ABS have evolved with shifting regulations and market demands. They can provide relatively higher yields compared to Treasury or agency debt, compensating for added uncertainties about loan performance and interest-rate movements. These instruments also play a pivotal role in expanding credit availability, as issuers transfer risk from originators to a broader base of capital market participants. Nonetheless, the financial crisis of 2008 illustrated how misaligned incentives or overly complex securitizations in mortgage markets can amplify systemic vulnerabilities. Consequently, both MBS and ABS now come under stricter oversight, reinforced disclosure requirements, and more rigorous credit rating practices. By understanding how each type of security structures cash flows, addresses default risk, and responds to interest-rate shifts, informed investors can evaluate where agency MBS or ABS might fit within a diversified income portfolio.

3.1.2.3 Corporate Bonds

Corporate bonds are debt securities issued by publicly traded or privately held companies as a means of raising capital for operational needs, expansion projects, or restructuring existing debt. Unlike U.S. Treasury or agency securities, corporate bonds carry **credit risk** specific to the issuing firm's financial strength, and their yields typically surpass those of comparable government obligations to compensate for this added risk. Maturities can range from short-term notes to 30-year (or longer) debentures, with periodic coupon payments often made semiannually. Interest rates, pricing, and bond features hinge on a variety of factors, including the issuer's creditworthiness, prevailing market rates, and the specific structure or covenants embedded in the bond's indenture.

One fundamental distinction within corporate bonds is **secured vs. unsecured debt**. *Secured bonds*—often referred to as mortgage bonds or equipment trust certificates—are backed by tangible corporate assets pledged as collateral, effectively reducing default risk for investors. In contrast, *unsecured (debenture) bonds* rely solely on the issuer's general credit. If the company defaults, secured creditors can claim pledged assets first, leaving debenture holders in line behind them. Issuers may also craft subordinate or junior debentures, which rank behind other unsecured obligations, making them riskier but often higher-yielding. *High-yield (or "junk") bonds* sit near the speculative end of the credit spectrum, offering elevated coupons but with a pronounced risk of default. In contrast, *investment-grade* corporate bonds—those rated BBB/Baa or above by agencies such as S&P or Moody's—represent companies with stronger financials, albeit with lower yields than riskier counterparts.

Beyond these distinctions, corporate bonds can feature **callable or puttable provisions**. A *callable bond* grants the issuer the right to redeem the debt prematurely, usually at a premium, if market interest rates drop or the firm prefers to restructure obligations. While the call feature benefits issuers, it introduces **reinvestment risk** for bondholders if their higher-yielding bond is retired early. Conversely, *puttable bonds* let investors demand early redemption under specific conditions (e.g., a downgrade or a predefined date), offering a measure of downside protection. Some corporates also incorporate *sinking fund* provisions mandating that issuers retire a portion of the bond issue gradually, reducing the risk of a large, lump-sum payment at maturity. Across all these variations, careful reading of the indenture and rating agency reports is vital for investors to comprehend the covenant protections, call schedules, and event triggers that might influence yield and principal safety.

Because corporations file *registration statements* with the Securities and Exchange Commission (SEC) when issuing public bonds, investors can assess official disclosures such as recent financial statements, debt covenants, and management's discussion of risk factors. This transparency, combined with ongoing credit rating surveillance, helps the market price corporate bonds in line with their perceived default likelihood. Ultimately, corporate bonds occupy a broad continuum of risk and reward, from highly rated, secured debentures with relatively modest yields to highly speculative, unsecured "junk" bonds that can produce strong returns or major losses. By diligently evaluating an issuer's credit profile, bond structures, and call or put provisions, investors can align corporate bond selections with their target duration, liquidity needs, and risk tolerance.

3.1.2.4 Municipal Securities (GO Bonds, Revenue Bonds, Short-Term Obligations)

Municipal securities are issued by states, cities, counties, or other local government entities to fund public projects and services—from building schools to updating water systems. The two primary long-term categories are **general obligation (GO) bonds** and **revenue bonds**, each offering distinct sources of repayment and risk profiles. **GO bonds** rely on the issuer's taxing power—often property taxes (ad valorem), sales taxes, or income taxes—to meet principal and interest payments. Because investors can look to the full breadth of the municipality's taxable resources for repayment, GO bonds typically feature higher credit quality and lower yields than many other debt instruments, assuming the municipality has a stable tax base and sound fiscal management. Before issuing GO bonds, local governments often require voter approval, ensuring the taxpayers who will ultimately bear the burden of debt service have consented to the new liability. Despite their relatively strong backing, GO bonds remain sensitive to economic downturns that weaken tax revenues, regional demographic shifts, or legal ceilings on tax rates that cap how much revenue the issuer can collect.

By contrast, **revenue bonds** are secured by a specific stream of income generated by a project or enterprise—such as tolls from a highway, fees from a hospital, or charges from a water authority. The success of the project, therefore, stands central to bondholders' potential returns: if user fees or occupancy rates fall short of projections, the issuer may struggle to meet scheduled payments. This structure often translates into higher yields due to the added uncertainty surrounding revenue performance, as well as the absence of a broad tax pledge. To mitigate risk, many revenue issues incorporate bond covenants that require the borrower to meet certain operational targets—like maintaining a debt-service coverage ratio above a specified threshold—or to set aside a portion of revenues in a reserve fund. While these provisions can provide some reassurance, investors are still betting on the financial viability of the underlying project and local economic conditions. If the pledged source falters, revenue bondholders may find themselves holding a bond with limited recourse beyond the project's operating revenue.

Many municipalities also issue **short-term obligations**, commonly referred to as **notes**, to manage cash flow gaps or address interim funding needs while awaiting longer-term financing. *Tax anticipation notes (TANs)*, for instance, allow a city or county to bridge the interval until property or sales taxes are collected. *Revenue anticipation notes (RANs)* function similarly but are tied to expected incoming funds from a dedicated source, such as federal subsidies or enterprise revenues. Additionally, there are *bond anticipation notes (BANs)*, which provide temporary financing in advance of a future bond sale. These notes typically mature within three months to a year, often aligning with the estimated arrival of the anticipated revenue stream. Because these instruments are short term, interest rates may be relatively lower than those on long-term debt; however, their credit quality still depends on the issuer's capacity to collect the projected tax or revenue flows in a timely manner. Investors find these notes appealing for short-term diversification or as a parking place for liquidity, especially in stable municipalities with predictable revenue cycles.

From a taxation perspective, interest on most municipal bonds is exempt from federal income tax—and, in certain cases, from state and local taxes as well—if the investor resides within the issuing state. This tax advantage can create a strong incentive for high-income investors seeking to reduce taxable income. Nonetheless, considerations around the alternative minimum tax (AMT) can apply if the bond finances projects deemed "private activity," underscoring the importance of thorough due diligence on each issuance's tax status. Regardless of whether an investor is drawn to the relative safety of a GO bond, the potentially higher yield (and more specialized risk) of a revenue bond, or the short-term flexibility of notes, understanding the specific revenue pledge, debt covenants, and broader economic backdrop is critical to evaluating both yield potential and risk exposure.

3.1.2.5 Other Money Market Instruments (CDs, BAs, Commercial Paper)

Money market instruments encompass short-term debt obligations that typically mature within one year, emphasizing liquidity and minimal credit risk for investors with immediate capital preservation needs. Beyond Treasury bills, agency securities, or municipal notes, three prominent examples are **certificates of deposit (CDs)**, **bankers' acceptances (BAs)**, and **commercial paper (CP)**. Each offers its own combination of maturity, issuer, and yield characteristics, making these instruments valuable tools in a corporate treasury or individual investor's short-term allocation strategy. While they generally yield more than comparable Treasury bills because of their issuer's credit risk, they remain popular for short-term investing due to predictable principal repayment and ready secondary market liquidity for higher-quality issuances.

A **certificate of deposit** is a time deposit typically offered by banks and thrift institutions. *Negotiable CDs*—those exceeding $100,000, sometimes called "jumbo CDs"—can be traded in the secondary market, allowing investors to realize liquidity before maturity if necessary. These negotiable instruments usually bear a fixed interest rate, paid at maturity, though some may distribute interest periodically. Issuers are incentivized to offer higher rates than standard savings or short-term deposits to attract larger institutional funds. The FDIC insures bank-issued CDs up to statutory limits if the issuing bank is FDIC-insured, though corporate and institutional investors often exceed these limits. Investors must monitor any potential credit concerns if the CD is not fully insured, especially if the issuing bank's financial health is uncertain. In many cases, the combination of an attractive yield, straightforward structure, and FDIC coverage (within insurance limits) makes CDs a mainstay for short-term, low-risk allocations.

Bankers' acceptances (BAs) arise from commercial transactions where a bank guarantees payment on a draft drawn by an importer or exporter, usually involving the shipment of goods. By "accepting" the draft, the bank adds its credit backing to the underlying commercial transaction, transforming the draft into a negotiable money market instrument. Traders in commodities and import-export businesses often rely on BAs for short-term financing, as the bank effectively assures the exporter they will be paid. Once accepted, the draft can be sold in the secondary market—sometimes at a discount—where short-term investors can buy them for a set return upon maturity. While BAs often yield more than T-bills due to the bank's credit exposure and the commercial nature of the transaction, they remain relatively secure if the accepting bank has high credit quality. Liquidity stems from their role in facilitating global commerce: many institutional portfolios or corporate treasurers purchase BAs to capture slightly higher yields than government issues, confident that the bank's commitment underwrites the repayment.

Commercial paper (CP) is an unsecured promissory note issued by corporations, typically to cover short-term liabilities such as payroll or inventory expenses. Because it is unsecured, only companies with high credit ratings—often those classified as investment-grade—can issue commercial paper at competitive rates. Maturities usually range up to 270 days to avoid SEC registration requirements, with many issues circulating at 30- to 90-day tenors. Commercial paper is often sold at a discount to face value, much like T-bills, although interest-bearing versions exist. Large financial institutions, industrial companies, or other well-established issuers leverage CP for cost-effective short-term funding. For investors, commercial paper can deliver higher returns than similarly dated government bills, but it introduces credit risk tied to the issuer's creditworthiness and any external economic pressures. Rating agencies like Moody's, S&P, or Fitch provide CP ratings, and investors typically restrict their purchases to top-tier paper (e.g., A-1/P-1/F1), underscoring the importance of credit evaluation in capturing incremental yield without undue risk.

Taken together, CDs, BAs, and commercial paper represent key segments of the broader money market ecosystem, each serving issuers' short-term financing needs while offering institutional and retail investors reliable interest income with a near-term maturity horizon. Their structures facilitate secondary market trading or discount-based pricing, enabling efficient cash management. Although credit risk and liquidity considerations vary—particularly in times of market stress—these instruments generally fill the role of low-volatility, short-duration allocations in an investor's fixed-income lineup, bridging the gap between longer-dated bonds and overnight instruments like repurchase agreements or money market mutual funds.

3.1.2.6 Coupon, Par Value, Yield, Ratings, Callable/Convertible Features

Bonds carry several defining characteristics that shape their risk-return profiles and market behavior. Understanding terms such as *coupon rate*, *par value*, *yield*, *credit ratings*, and *callable/convertible structures* is critical for evaluating how a bond aligns with an investor's objectives and risk tolerance. By clarifying how interest payments are set, how principal is repaid, and under what conditions the bond's features might change over time, these attributes collectively govern both the issuer's cost of capital and the investor's potential returns.

Coupon Rate and Par Value

When an issuer first sells a bond, it typically quotes an annual *coupon rate*—the percentage of the bond's *par value* (also called *face value*) that will be paid in interest each year. For instance, a par value of $1,000 and a 5% coupon rate equate to $50 in annual interest, often delivered semi-annually ($25 every six months) until maturity. The par value also represents the principal amount investors expect to recover upon the bond's maturity date. Bonds can trade above or below par in the secondary market, but their coupon remains fixed based on the original issuance terms. As a result, an investor purchasing a bond at a premium or discount will see their effective yield differ from the coupon rate. In an environment of declining interest rates, bonds issued with higher coupons are likely to trade at premiums; conversely, higher-rate environments may push bond prices below par.

Yield Metrics and Credit Ratings

A bond's *yield* can be examined in multiple ways. *Current yield* compares the bond's annual interest to its current market price, offering a snapshot of income relative to cost. *Yield to maturity (YTM)* captures the total return expected if the investor holds the bond until it matures, factoring in coupon payments, capital gains or losses, and the time value of money. *Yield to call (YTC)* performs a similar calculation but assumes the bond is redeemed on its earliest call date. Because yield computations incorporate price adjustments, changes in interest rates, or the likelihood of a call, the metrics can shift as market conditions evolve. Meanwhile, *credit ratings*—assigned by agencies such as Moody's, S&P, or Fitch—offer a distilled assessment of the issuer's creditworthiness. Higher ratings (e.g., AAA or AA) indicate a low risk of default but typically come with more modest yields, whereas lower ratings (e.g., BB or below) signify higher default risk and command higher coupon rates or yields as compensation. While these ratings can help guide investment decisions, bondholders should conduct additional due diligence, since rating agencies may revise their outlooks if issuer fundamentals deteriorate or the macroeconomic climate shifts.

Callable and Convertible Features

Two additional attributes can significantly shape a bond's value and price dynamics: callability and convertibility. A *callable bond* grants the issuer the right to redeem the bond before its scheduled maturity, often at a *call price* above par. Issuers typically invoke this option if interest rates fall below the coupon rate on their existing debt, allowing them to refinance at a lower cost. This scenario presents *reinvestment risk* for investors, who must reinvest the returned principal at prevailing lower interest rates. Callable structures usually come with a "call protection" period, during which the issuer cannot call the bond. The coupon on callable debt often starts higher than on non-callable equivalents, acknowledging the uncertainty and potential early redemption faced by bondholders.

A *convertible bond*, by contrast, can be exchanged for a specified number of the issuer's common shares, usually at a predetermined conversion price or ratio. This feature blends the steady income and seniority of a bond with the potential upside of equity if the issuer's stock appreciates significantly. Issuers benefit by offering relatively lower coupon rates, since investors value the embedded equity option. However, upon conversion, the debt effectively disappears, replaced by newly issued stock, which can dilute existing shareholders. Investors in convertibles must weigh the trade-off between locking in fixed interest versus switching to equity if the conversion value surpasses the bond's price. In volatile or growth-oriented sectors—like technology or biotech—convertible structures may prove particularly attractive, offering downside protection through the bond component while preserving equity potential.

Overall, these attributes—coupon, par value, yield metrics, credit ratings, and callable/convertible provisions—interact to define a bond's cash flow profile and risk exposure. In an environment of shifting interest rates or changing corporate fortunes, an investor's willingness to accept reinvestment risk, credit risk, or equity-linked volatility influences which combination of features is most suitable. A keen grasp of each feature's implications can thus guide portfolio construction, ensuring that bond selections align with an investor's overarching income, risk, and liquidity objectives.

3.1.2.7 Price–Interest Rate Relationship

A defining characteristic of fixed-income instruments—whether they are Treasuries, corporate bonds, or municipal securities—is that their market prices adjust inversely to changes in prevailing interest rates. When rates rise, newly issued bonds offer higher coupons, making older ones with lower coupons relatively less attractive. As a result, the secondary-market prices of outstanding bonds must drop to align their yields with the new interest-rate environment. Conversely, if rates fall, existing bonds with higher coupons become more valuable, driving their prices upward. This fundamental inverse relationship stems from the notion that a bond's coupon payments and face-value redemption are contractually fixed, so its market value fluctuates to ensure that new buyers receive a yield consistent with current market benchmarks.

Two key measures illuminate how drastically a bond's price might move in response to a shift in interest rates. **Duration** reflects the bond's sensitivity by estimating the weighted average time it takes to recover the bond's cost through all scheduled interest payments and final principal redemption. A higher duration implies greater price volatility for any given rate change, making long-maturity or low-coupon bonds especially vulnerable to rate hikes. Conversely, shorter-term or higher-coupon bonds tend to be less reactive. **Convexity** refines this analysis by recognizing that price changes at different interest-rate levels are not perfectly linear—a point particularly important when interest rates move substantially or for bonds with embedded features like calls or puts. By monitoring these metrics, fixed-income investors can tailor portfolios to their rate expectations: those anticipating rising rates may favor shorter durations or floating-rate notes, while those expecting steady or falling rates might pursue longer durations to potentially capture capital gains. Regardless of the strategy, understanding the inverse relationship between bond prices and rates is central to managing interest-rate risk in a fixed-income portfolio.

3.1.3 Options

An option is a financial contract that grants the holder the right, but not the obligation, to buy or sell an underlying asset at a specified strike price before (or sometimes on) a specific date. *Call options* offer the right to purchase, while *put options* grant the right to sell. Many investors use options for hedging—protecting against adverse movements in a stock or index—while others employ them for speculative gains, aiming to profit from anticipated price swings with limited initial capital outlay. Because option premiums reflect factors such as the underlying's volatility, time to expiration, and prevailing interest rates, their pricing can fluctuate significantly as market conditions evolve.

In addition to these fundamentals, options vary in style—*American* options can be exercised at any point until expiration, whereas *European* options permit exercise only at maturity. Coverage status also matters: a "covered" call, for instance, involves an investor who owns the underlying shares, reducing risk compared to an "uncovered" position that might require purchasing shares at higher market prices if assigned. Each approach carries unique risk-return trade-offs, making a clear grasp of option mechanics vital for employing these derivatives effectively.

3.1.3.1 Types of Options (Puts, Calls; Equity vs. Index)

Options are derivative contracts that give buyers the right—but not the obligation—to trade an underlying asset at a specific price on or before a defined date. The two fundamental varieties are **calls**, which confer the right to buy, and **puts**, which confer the right to sell. Although options can be structured around many underlying assets—ranging from individual stocks to indexes or even commodities—this section focuses on **equity** options (tied to individual stocks) and **index** options (tied to broad market benchmarks). Each instrument addresses different hedging, income, and speculative strategies, making it critical for market participants to understand the differences in settlement, pricing variables, and potential risk profiles.

Call vs. Put Options

A **call option** grants its holder the right to purchase the underlying asset at the stated **strike price** any time (for American-style) or only at expiration (for European-style). Buyers of calls typically expect the asset's price to rise above the strike before expiration, allowing them to either exercise the option at a favorable price or sell the contract at a profit. If the market price remains below the strike, the call can expire worthless, limiting the buyer's losses to the option **premium** paid. Sellers (or writers) of calls adopt the opposite stance: they earn the premium upfront but assume the obligation to deliver the underlying shares if assigned. Depending on whether the call is "covered" (meaning the writer already owns the shares) or "uncovered/naked" (no shares on hand), the potential for loss varies significantly—uncovered call writers face theoretically unlimited risk if the stock rallies far above the strike.

Conversely, a **put option** gives its holder the right to sell the underlying at the strike price, functioning as a defensive position if the investor anticipates a decline. Put buyers might purchase such contracts to protect an existing portfolio against downside risk (akin to buying insurance) or to speculate on price drops with limited capital outlay. If the underlying asset's market price falls below the strike, exercising the put or selling it in the secondary market can yield a profit. Conversely, if the asset's price stays above the strike, the put could expire worthless, again limiting the buyer's downside to the premium. Put writers (sellers) collect the premium but must stand ready to buy shares at the strike if assigned. A "covered" put situation is less common since it involves other offsetting positions, but "naked" put writers face the risk of a falling stock price that compels them to purchase shares at a higher strike.

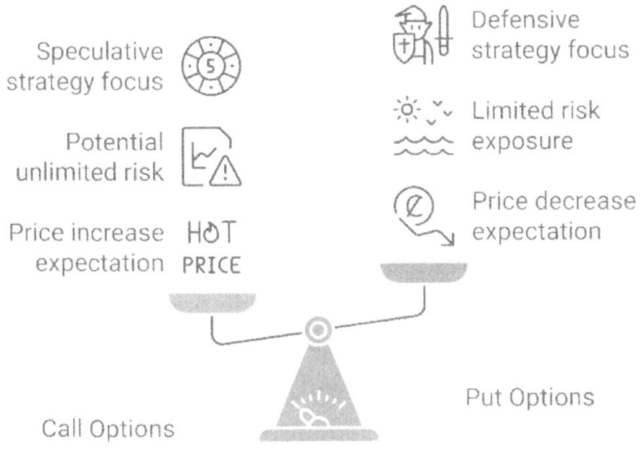

Equity vs. Index Options

Whereas **equity options** are tied to a specific company's stock, **index options** settle on the value of a market benchmark, such as the S&P 500 (SPX) or the Dow Jones Industrial Average (DJX). This distinction affects both settlement and typical use cases. Equity options usually settle by physical delivery—if a call is exercised, the writer must deliver the actual shares to the call buyer (for puts, the shares are handed over by the put buyer to the put writer in exchange for the strike-price payment). By contrast, many index options settle in **cash** due to the impracticality of delivering all the component stocks of a broad index. Upon exercise or expiration, the net difference between the index's value and the option's strike determines the cash to be paid.

From an investor's perspective, **equity options** often target single-name exposure—either to speculate on a firm's outlook or to hedge a position in a particular stock. Meanwhile, **index options** serve broader portfolio-level strategies. Fund managers might buy index puts to protect a diversified portfolio against a market downturn or write index calls to generate premium income against overall market exposure. Pricing dynamics differ subtly too: equity option premiums can be heavily influenced by individual corporate events (earnings announcements, product launches), while index option prices hinge on macroeconomic data, sector rotations, and overall market volatility as measured by metrics like the VIX. The total risk-reward profile also depends on the style of the option—American index options allow early exercise, whereas many index options listed on U.S. exchanges are European style, limiting exercise to expiration.

Comparative Overview

Feature	Equity Options	Index Options
Underlying Asset	Specific company stock	Market index (e.g., S&P 500)
Settlement	Primarily physical delivery (shares), though some cash-settled	Typically cash-settled
Exercise Style	Can be American or European	Often European (e.g., SPX), though variations exist
Major Influences	Company-specific news, dividends, earnings	Macro factors: economic data, sector performance, overall volatility

Whether investors opt for single-stock calls or broad-market puts, options can be tailored to a range of strategic goals—from speculation on imminent price swings to hedging longer-term holdings or generating extra income via premium writing. Mastery of the nuances—like how time decay erodes extrinsic value or how implied volatility drives premiums—is indispensable for responsible options trading. Proper risk management (setting stop-loss thresholds or balancing option positions with offsetting holdings) is equally crucial, as the leverage inherent in options can magnify both gains and losses.

3.1.3.2 Basic Terminology (Strike Price, Premium, In/Out-of-the-Money)

The **strike price** is the agreed-upon level at which the holder of an option can buy or sell the underlying security. For a call option, it represents the price per share at which the holder may purchase the underlying asset; for a put option, it is the price at which the holder can sell. Because this figure is locked in when the option contract is created, the strike price becomes the focal point for comparing the option's intrinsic value (if any) to the underlying market price as expiration nears. An option buyer will exercise the contract only if it proves advantageous relative to current market conditions: a call holder benefits when the market price exceeds the strike, while a put holder profits if the market price falls below the strike.

The **premium** is the cost paid by the option buyer (or received by the option seller) to acquire (or write) the contract. This price reflects two key components. First, there is *intrinsic value*, which, for calls, is how far the market price lies above the strike, and for puts, how far the market price is below the strike. Any additional amount above that intrinsic portion is called *time value*, encompassing variables such as the time left to expiration, volatility of the underlying security, prevailing interest rates, and investor sentiment. As expiration approaches, time value decays, often accelerating in the final weeks or days. Meanwhile, the full premium amount constitutes the maximum possible loss for buyers of options, while it forms the maximum immediate gain for writers—although writers then face potentially open-ended exposure should the underlying price move unfavorably.

An option is said to be **in-the-money (ITM)** if exercising it would yield a profit based on the current underlying price. A call sits in-the-money when the market price is above the strike, whereas a put is ITM if the market price is below the strike. **Out-of-the-money (OTM)** describes the opposite condition: a call is OTM when the market price remains below the strike, and a put is OTM when the market price stands above the strike. **At-the-money (ATM)** occurs when the market price precisely matches the strike. Although an at-the-money option may hold considerable time value if there is ample time to expiration, it has no intrinsic value. Understanding these relationships—strike price, premiums comprising intrinsic and time value, and whether an option is ITM, OTM, or ATM—lets traders more accurately assess the contract's potential payoff, enabling them to structure strategies that align with their market outlook and risk preferences.

3.1.3.3 Covered vs. Uncovered, American vs. European Style

In options markets, two important distinctions arise when a trader sells (writes) an option: whether the position is **covered** or **uncovered**, and whether the option itself follows an **American** or **European** exercise style. The first distinction impacts how much risk a writer faces in meeting exercise obligations, while the second governs the holder's timing of potential exercise. Understanding how each factor influences payoff profiles and risk management is crucial for anyone structuring an options strategy.

Covered vs. Uncovered (Naked)

A **covered option**—most commonly seen with calls—occurs when the option writer already holds the underlying asset or another offsetting position. For instance, a covered call writer owns the shares on which the call is written, ensuring that if the call is exercised, the writer can deliver the shares without purchasing them at potentially higher market prices. This setup reduces risk considerably: the writer's maximum loss is partially hedged by the fact that they hold the underlying stock, although they still forfeit any additional upside in the stock beyond the strike price. The covered call strategy often seeks incremental income—writers collect the premium—and may potentially offset slight downward movements in the stock through that premium income. Still, covered writers remain exposed to the stock's inherent price risk: if shares drop sharply, the losses on the equity holding might exceed the premium gains.

An **uncovered** (or **naked**) option has no underlying offset. Writing a naked call is particularly risky because if the market rallies well above the strike, the writer must purchase shares at escalating prices to fulfill the exercise obligation. Theoretically, a naked call writer faces unlimited losses. Naked put writers, while exposed to potentially large losses if the stock plummets, face a maximum risk corresponding to the strike price minus the collected premium (since the worst-case scenario would be buying shares at the strike if they fall near zero). Despite these risks, some sophisticated traders employ uncovered strategies, believing market conditions or time decay favor their positions. However, brokerage firms typically impose higher margin requirements for naked positions and often restrict these trades to accounts with advanced option approval levels.

American vs. European Style

Separately, **American-style** options can be exercised at any point up to and including expiration. This flexibility tends to favor the buyer if circumstances change—such as the underlying stock paying an unexpected dividend, or interest rates shifting—making early exercise advantageous for a call or put holder. Equity options listed on U.S. exchanges are predominantly American-style; holders might exercise early if the time value remaining in the option is less valuable than capturing a dividend (for calls) or locking in a profit based on a quick stock price move (for puts).

By contrast, **European-style** options permit exercise only at the official expiration date. As a result, the holder cannot capitalize on mid-contract swings by exercising prematurely, although they can still trade (buy or sell) the contract in the secondary market. Many index options—such as those on the S&P 500—use a European format to simplify cash settlement; the final exercise settlement value is determined at expiration based on the index's closing price or a special opening print. While European options limit early exercise, some issuers or traders appreciate the reduced administrative complexity. Additionally, the pricing models differ slightly in how they incorporate early-exercise risk for American vs. European contracts, sometimes leading to variations in time premiums for otherwise comparable options.

Taken together, these distinctions underscore how options strategies can vary widely in both structure and risk. A covered call writer might accept capped gains for limited downside protection, while a naked call seller faces open-ended risk if the market surges. Meanwhile, American-style exercise imbues option holders with a strategic choice throughout the life of the option, whereas European-style locks the decision until final expiration. Mastering these nuances enables traders and portfolio managers to fine-tune their approach to market outlook, desired timeframe, and risk tolerance.

3.1.3.4 Hedging and Speculative Strategies

Investors and traders often turn to options for **hedging**—the process of protecting an existing portfolio or position from adverse price movements. One of the most common hedges is a *protective put*, in which a shareholder purchases put options on the same underlying stock. By doing so, they lock in a minimum sale price (the strike) for the shares. If the stock price drops below this strike, the gain on the put contract can help offset losses on the shares themselves. Another frequently used hedge, particularly by those holding short positions, is a *protective call*. In this case, a short seller buys call options to cap potential losses if the stock rallies beyond the call's strike. Both forms of protection help limit downside (or upside) risk while still permitting upside (or downside) participation to a degree. Another defensive strategy is the *collar*, wherein an investor simultaneously writes a call and buys a put, thereby trading potential gains above the call's strike for partial protection below the put's strike. All hedging strategies involve a trade-off: while they mitigate exposure, they also increase costs through option premiums or they reduce potential profit if the position moves favorably.

On the other side of the spectrum are **speculative strategies**, where options serve primarily to profit from expected short-term price swings without direct ownership of the underlying asset. Buying a call reflects a bullish outlook: if the underlying asset's price exceeds the strike by more than the paid premium, the call buyer may either exercise at a profit (for American-style) or sell the contract on the open market. This approach offers significant leverage, as an option premium is typically far smaller than the cost of purchasing shares outright, though it remains time-sensitive—if the market does not move as anticipated before expiration, the premium can be lost in full. Conversely, buying a put is a speculative bet on price declines; the more the underlying falls below the strike, the more intrinsic value the put can build. Sellers of options also speculate, but in a contrarian manner: a call writer may believe the underlying will remain flat or decline (making calls expire worthless), whereas a put writer expects the underlying to stay above the put's strike. These positions can generate consistent premium income but involve higher risk if the market defies the writer's outlook.

Complex spread positions—such as *vertical spreads*, *calendar spreads*, or *straddles/strangles*—further refine the speculative or hedging approach, enabling traders to shape a more nuanced risk-reward profile. For instance, a *bull call spread* pairs a long call with a simultaneous short call at a higher strike, lowering the net premium while capping potential gains. A *straddle* involves buying both a call and a put at the same strike, anticipating a sharp price move in either direction. Such strategies help manage cost outlays and define maximum losses, yet they demand careful attention to implied volatility, time decay, and strike selection to ensure that expected market moves—or the lack thereof—are captured profitably. Whether the motive is to buffer existing holdings from adverse shifts or to seek targeted opportunities for profit, options provide a versatile toolkit—though success hinges on understanding the intricate interplay of premiums, strike selections, expiration dates, and potential assignment obligations.

3.1.3.5 Options Disclosure Document (ODD) and the OCC

In the U.S. options market, two critical pillars underpin investor protection and market integrity: the **Options Disclosure Document (ODD)**, also known as the Characteristics and Risks of Standardized Options, and the **Options Clearing Corporation (OCC)**. Together, they provide a framework of transparency and operational safeguards, enabling market participants to understand the nature of options trading and to conduct trades with confidence that all contract obligations will be met.

Options Disclosure Document (ODD) The ODD is a comprehensive publication that details the characteristics, potential risks, and mechanics associated with standardized options listed on exchanges such as the Chicago Board Options Exchange (CBOE). Before an investor can trade options for the first time, brokerage rules—often influenced by self-regulatory organizations (SROs) and SEC mandates—require the firm to furnish the ODD to the client. This ensures the investor has baseline knowledge about how calls and puts function, what factors drive their pricing, and what scenarios could result in losses greater than the initial premium paid (as in certain uncovered positions). In addition to describing the contract specifications (e.g., strike price, expiration, and exercise style), the

ODD spells out how events like stock splits, mergers, or dividend announcements might alter the terms of an outstanding option contract (for instance, adjusting strike prices or contract size).

Moreover, the ODD carefully outlines the responsibilities of both buyers and sellers, touching on issues such as early exercise possibilities, assignment procedures, and the potential for large or unlimited losses in the case of certain uncovered strategies. Because the market evolves over time, updated versions or supplements to the ODD may be issued as new products come to market, as regulatory rules shift, or when novel exercise and settlement mechanisms appear. Investors, therefore, rely on this document to keep pace with changes, gaining crucial insights into how margin requirements, capital rules, or shifts in market volatility can impact their option positions.

Options Clearing Corporation (OCC) As the central clearinghouse for all listed equity, index, and some commodity options in the U.S., the OCC operates as a financial intermediary between buyers and sellers. Once an option trade is executed on an exchange, the OCC steps in—becoming the buyer to every seller and the seller to every buyer—to ensure the fulfillment of contract terms. By **guaranteeing** each side of the transaction, the OCC eliminates the need for traders to evaluate the creditworthiness of individual counterparties. Instead, members must meet robust capital and margin requirements. This "novation" process means that if a call buyer decides to exercise, the OCC assigns the obligation to a writer in a fair, randomized process, ensuring no bias in who must deliver the underlying shares or provide cash settlement.

Part of the OCC's risk management includes monitoring member firm exposures daily. If volatile market swings or changes in interest rates elevate the risk of potential defaults, the OCC can require additional margin deposits from clearing members, thereby reinforcing systemic stability. Furthermore, the OCC enforces uniform contract specifications—standardizing strikes, expirations, and contract sizes for exchange-traded options—and oversees the option symbol assignment process. Through this uniformity, the markets become more transparent and liquid, as investors can easily identify and trade the same standardized contracts. In conjunction with the ODD, the OCC's role ensures that participants understand their responsibilities (whether as buyer or seller) and can rely on a central guarantor that backstops obligations. This dual structure of disclosure (via the ODD) and centralized clearing (via the OCC) has been instrumental in building and maintaining confidence in the listed options markets.

3.1.4 Packaged Products

Packaged products are pooled investments designed to offer diversified exposure without requiring investors to assemble individual positions themselves. They typically include **investment companies**—such as mutual funds (open-end), closed-end funds, and unit investment trusts (UITs)—all of which allow participants to buy shares or units representing fractional ownership of a professionally managed portfolio. These structures can provide instant diversification across numerous securities, lowering the overall impact of a single company's performance on the investor's holdings. Operating under regulatory frameworks (e.g., the Investment Company Act of 1940), these entities must adhere to rules on disclosure, governance, and fees, which help investors understand exactly how their money is being invested and what costs they incur.

Beyond traditional funds, **variable annuities** also fall under the packaged products umbrella. Offered by insurance companies, these products let policyholders choose from various investment subaccounts—often resembling mutual fund portfolios—and potentially accrue tax-deferred growth. However, variable annuities introduce insurance-related features (like death benefits or income guarantees) that can add layers of complexity and expense. Across all these vehicles, investors generally benefit from centralized professional management, simplified recordkeeping, and built-in diversification—albeit at the expense of ongoing fees and certain liquidity constraints. The selection of the right packaged product typically hinges on factors like risk tolerance, time horizon, fee structure, and the desired level of active involvement in portfolio construction.

3.1.4.1 Investment Companies (Open-End, Closed-End, UITs)

Investment companies pool money from multiple investors and invest those funds according to a defined strategy, leveraging professional management to diversify across different asset classes. They must adhere to regulations under the Investment Company Act of 1940, ensuring consistent disclosures, oversight, and standardized practices. Among the primary forms of investment companies are **open-end funds (mutual funds)**, **closed-end funds**, and **unit investment trusts (UITs)**. Each structure offers a different approach to managing and distributing shares, balancing liquidity, pricing, and investment objectives.

Open-End Funds (Mutual Funds)

Open-end funds issue new shares to investors on demand and redeem existing shares at the fund's net asset value (NAV). Because they stand ready to create or retire shares in response to capital inflows or outflows, their total shares outstanding fluctuate daily. NAV calculation typically occurs once at the close of each trading day, taking the total market value of the fund's portfolio minus liabilities, then dividing by the number of shares. This pricing mechanism ensures that purchases and redemptions occur at a fair proportion of the fund's underlying assets. In addition, open-end funds are often classified by investment style or asset category (e.g., equity growth, fixed income, balanced), enabling investors to select funds in line with their risk tolerance or market outlook. A key attribute is *redeemability*: shareholders can generally sell their shares back to the fund at NAV without having to seek buyers on the secondary market. However, some mutual funds impose short-term redemption fees or maintain minimum holding periods to discourage excessive trading that might inflate costs for other fund shareholders. The potential downside for managers is having to keep sufficient cash on hand to meet redemption requests, sometimes compelling them to sell holdings at inopportune times or maintain higher liquidity than an equivalent closed-end fund.

Closed-End Funds

Unlike open-end funds, closed-end funds issue a fixed number of shares through an initial public offering (IPO). After launch, these shares trade on an exchange or in the over-the-counter market, akin to a stock. Market forces of supply and demand dictate the share price, which can diverge—sometimes significantly—from the fund's NAV. A closed-end fund might trade at a premium if investors are especially bullish on its strategy or at a discount if negative sentiment or market uncertainty prevails. In contrast to open-end mutual funds, closed-end fund managers need not worry about daily share redemptions, allowing them to invest in less liquid or longer-term assets. This structure can be advantageous for portfolios that focus on specialized or less liquid markets (e.g., emerging markets, private credit), yet an investor holding these shares must typically accept price fluctuations not only from changes in underlying asset values but also from shifts in market perception of the fund.

Unit Investment Trusts (UITs)

A UIT generally offers a static, fixed portfolio of bonds, stocks, or other securities for a set term. Unlike actively managed funds, UITs do not adjust holdings frequently; instead, they often "buy and hold" until maturity (in the case of bond UITs) or a set termination date, providing a clearer view of expected cash flows or dividend income. Investors purchase units from the trust—originally established under an indenture—and the trust dissolves or redeems outstanding units upon reaching its maturity or termination date. Because UITs lack ongoing portfolio management, their annual expenses are often lower than those for actively managed funds, but they also lack the ability to respond dynamically to market changes. This structure appeals to certain buy-and-hold investors seeking predictable distributions or wanting to lock in a particular strategy from inception to termination without later intervention by a portfolio manager.

Overall, the choice among open-end funds, closed-end funds, or UITs reflects each investor's preference for share liquidity, management style, and the desired level of control over the underlying portfolio. Mutual funds typically suit those seeking daily pricing and ease of redemption, while closed-end funds can potentially offer specialized strategies and leverage without constant inflows and outflows. UITs, in turn, provide a more static structure that appeals to investors wanting a defined life cycle and predictable holdings. All three fall under regulatory frameworks aiming to ensure transparency, fair pricing, and investor protections—attributes that support investment companies' longstanding popularity among a broad swath of market participants.

3.1.4.2 Variable Annuities (Types, Subaccounts, Expenses)

Variable annuities are insurance contracts that combine investment features with the potential for tax-deferred growth. In contrast to fixed annuities, which credit a guaranteed interest rate, variable annuities channel the owner's premium into a selection of **subaccounts**—each resembling a mutual fund that invests in stocks, bonds, or money market instruments. As the values of these subaccounts fluctuate, so does the annuity's overall account value. Once the contract reaches annuitization (or during partial withdrawals before that), the payouts can shift upward or downward based on market performance, granting a measure of inflation protection and growth opportunity over long time horizons. Insurers often structure variable annuities with optional riders—such as guaranteed minimum withdrawal benefits or death benefits—that can soften the impact of market volatility, although these add an extra layer of cost.

Within variable annuities, two broad categories typically emerge: **deferred** and **immediate**. *Deferred variable annuities* let investors accumulate assets in subaccounts over years before converting (or annuitizing) to an income stream, whereas *immediate variable annuities* start payouts soon after the initial lump-sum contribution. Subaccounts themselves might track specific investment objectives—like aggressive equity growth, conservative fixed income, or balanced allocation—giving the owner flexibility to adjust allocations in line with shifting market conditions or personal risk tolerance. However, any reallocation across subaccounts can be subject to the insurer's rules on frequency and timing, though no immediate tax consequence arises unless the assets are withdrawn from the annuity entirely.

A key consideration for variable annuities lies in their **expense structure**, which is more multifaceted than the straightforward expense ratio of a typical mutual fund. Common charges include a *mortality and expense (M&E) risk fee*, covering the insurance company's promises, such as a guaranteed death benefit or living benefits. These typically hover around a certain percentage of the annuity's daily net assets. Additional administration or contract fees, subaccount operating expenses, and rider charges (for optional guaranteed income or principal-protection features) can accumulate. Investors who exit the contract prematurely may also face **surrender charges**—a declining penalty applied if the contract is liquidated within a set number of years after purchase. Over time, these ongoing fees can significantly erode returns if the underlying investments do not perform strongly enough to offset them. Consequently, analyzing the annuity's total expense burden, along with the subaccounts' track records and the insurer's credit quality, is essential before committing to a variable annuity for long-term retirement or wealth-management objectives.

3.1.4.3 Share Classes, Loads, NAV, 12b-1 Fees

When investors enter a mutual fund, they often encounter multiple **share classes**, each with varying cost structures and associated time horizons. Although the underlying pool of assets and investment strategy typically remain the same across share classes, the distinct fee or load arrangements can significantly affect both short-term and long-term returns. By selecting a share class that aligns with their investment horizon and trading frequency, individuals can optimize fees and reduce needless expense erosion.

Loads and Share Classes

Many mutual funds impose a **sales load**, a commission paid either when shares are bought (*front-end load*), when shares are sold (*back-end load* or *contingent deferred sales charge, CDSC*), or sometimes not at all (in "no-load" funds). A typical classification includes:

- **Class A shares** often carry a front-end load, charging a percentage of the initial investment (e.g., 4% or 5%) as a sales commission. Because of that upfront cost, the ongoing expenses may be comparatively lower, making Class A preferable for investors with a longer time horizon who can spread the initial load cost over many years.

- **Class B shares** frequently carry a back-end load or CDSC, which diminishes gradually, usually over six to eight years. If an investor redeems shares before that period ends, the load is assessed. Over time, Class B shares might convert to Class A, dropping to the lower cost structure after the CDSC schedule expires.

- **Class C shares** typically have no front-end load but carry higher ongoing expenses and, in some cases, a modest or short-term CDSC (like 1% if sold within the first year). Because the higher expense ratio remains in place indefinitely, Class C may benefit shorter-term holders who don't intend to keep the fund for a lengthy period.

Beyond these standard categories, some funds may create specialized share classes (e.g., Class I or Class R) intended for institutional buyers, retirement plans, or other specific investor segments. Regardless of the class, investors must evaluate the total effect of loads and recurring expenses over their projected holding period to gauge which approach produces the most favorable cost profile.

Net Asset Value (NAV)

A mutual fund's **NAV** per share equals the current market value of its portfolio minus liabilities, divided by the total shares outstanding. This figure is generally calculated once per trading day at market close, dictating the price at which new investors buy shares (for open-end funds) and existing shareholders redeem them. For funds carrying a front-end load, investors pay the public offering price

(POP), which is NAV plus any sales charge. Conversely, redemptions involving a back-end load can see a deduction from the shareholder's proceeds if they redeem earlier than a certain threshold. Monitoring NAV is essential for investors, as it directly reflects the fund's underlying portfolio performance—if the assets in the fund appreciate, the NAV rises, even if the number of shares in circulation changes due to purchases and redemptions.

12b-1 Fees

In addition to load charges, some mutual funds assess **12b-1 fees**, named after the SEC rule permitting their existence, which help defray marketing, distribution, and sometimes shareholder service expenses. Calculated as a percentage of fund assets (e.g., 0.25% to 1.00% annually), these fees reduce the fund's net return. Although 12b-1 fees are a form of operating cost, they focus specifically on compensating brokers or financial intermediaries who help distribute the fund. Not all share classes levy 12b-1 fees at the same rate: certain classes, especially in the no-load category, may carry minimal or zero 12b-1 fees, while others rely heavily on these fees to compensate selling agents in lieu of front-end loads.

Careful review of a fund's prospectus or summary prospectus reveals the detailed breakdown of these costs, enabling comparisons across different funds or share classes. Over time, high 12b-1 fees can drag on returns, particularly if the fund's investment strategy yields only moderate performance. Investors, therefore, weigh the potential benefits of advisor guidance or broker services—possibly funded through 12b-1 fees—against lower-cost alternatives that skip the intermediary. By understanding precisely how sales loads, NAV, and 12b-1 fees interact, individuals can better align their mutual fund choices with personal preferences, expected holding periods, and desired service levels.

3.1.4.4 Breakpoints, ROA, LOI, Redemption/Surrender Charges

When purchasing mutual funds with a front-end sales load (often Class A shares), investors may qualify for **breakpoints**—discounted sales charge levels that kick in once they invest enough to surpass specified dollar thresholds. For example, a fund might reduce its front-end load from 5.00% to 4.00% when an investor's cumulative purchase hits $50,000, and then to 3.00% at $100,000. These breakpoints reward larger total investments in the same fund family, lowering the overall cost of ownership. An investor approaching a breakpoint might time additional purchases or consolidate funds to cross the relevant threshold and secure a beneficial load reduction. It's important for customers to know and document all eligible holdings, including retirement accounts or investments in a spouse's or child's name, since many fund families allow aggregated ownership for meeting breakpoint levels. Failure to inform the broker or fund company of potential breakpoint eligibility can lead to higher sales charges—a compliance issue known as a "breakpoint sale" violation, which regulators scrutinize closely to protect investors from overpaying.

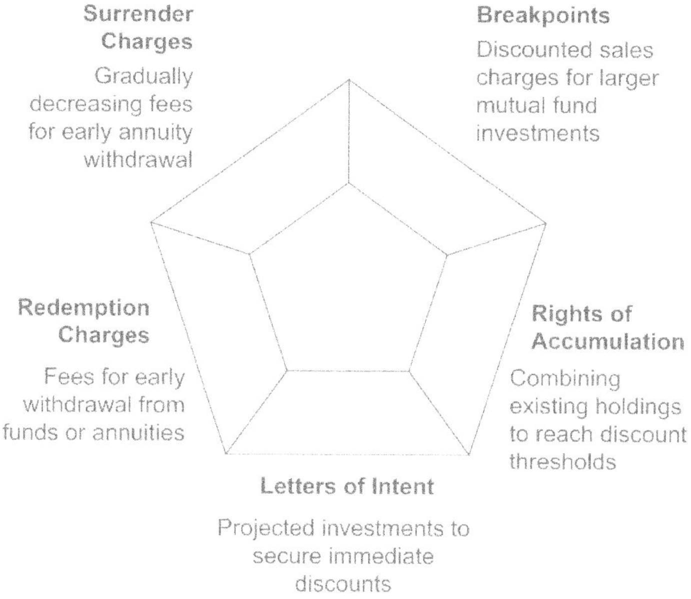

Beyond breakpoints, some funds permit **Rights of Accumulation (ROA)**, enabling investors to combine the current purchase with the value of existing holdings in that same fund family to reach a breakpoint. The investor simply references the account balance total—often verified by statements—so the fund calculates whether the new purchase qualifies for a reduced load. Similarly, the **Letter of Intent (LOI)** allows an investor to project new investments over a specified window (commonly 13 months) to secure an immediate breakpoint reduction. Essentially, the fund treats the investor as though they have already reached the future investment total. If the investor fails to complete the intended purchases, the fund retroactively adjusts the sales charge to what would have applied absent the LOI. Both ROA and LOI thus enable systematic or periodic investors to secure fee savings even if they can't invest a lump sum immediately.

In addition to sales loads, mutual funds or variable annuities may impose **redemption fees** (sometimes called "short-term trading fees"), which differ from contingent deferred sales charges (CDSC) in that the fee goes back into the fund to defray costs inflicted on other shareholders by frequent trading. Especially for funds that invest in less liquid holdings, a redemption fee deters quick in-and-out speculation. Variable annuities, meanwhile, often enforce **surrender charges** if investors withdraw funds during the early years of the contract. These charges decline gradually over a set schedule—say, 7% the first year, then 6% the second, and so on—compensating the insurer for the sales commissions and marketing expenses they incur at issuance. While a surrender charge can be waived for certain life events, such as disability or medical emergencies, it remains a notable liquidity constraint for individuals who might need to tap the annuity prematurely. Awareness of these fee structures—and selecting the best share class or annuity design—ensures that investors align their time horizon with the product's cost model, preventing unpleasant surprises if they change course or redeem assets earlier than initially planned.

3.1.5 Municipal Fund Securities

Municipal fund securities generally refer to investment products offered by state or local governments. Unlike traditional municipal bonds, these vehicles often feature structures more akin to mutual funds, with proceeds dedicated to specific public initiatives, such as education or disability support. A notable example is **529 plans**, which help families save for future college expenses in either a prepaid tuition or savings format. The latter typically invests contributions in portfolios managed by professional firms, growing on a tax-advantaged basis if used for qualifying education costs.

Other municipal fund securities include **local government investment pools (LGIPs)**, intended for the short-term investing of public funds, and **ABLE accounts**—tax-advantaged accounts designed for individuals with disabilities to cover allowable expenses. While each type targets distinct policy objectives, they share similar investment traits: professional oversight, potential tax benefits (depending on the plan and residence), and varying degrees of market risk. Investors should carefully weigh plan guidelines, fees, and any residency requirements to fully leverage the intended benefits.

3.1.5.1 529 Plans (Prepaid Tuition, Savings Plans)

529 plans are tax-advantaged vehicles designed to help families save for education expenses. Each state (and in some cases certain educational institutions) sponsors these plans under Section 529 of the Internal Revenue Code. While features vary from state to state, the plans fall broadly into two categories: **prepaid tuition** and **college savings**. Both typically offer federal income tax-free withdrawals if the funds are used for qualified education costs, and many states also provide tax incentives to residents who invest in their home state's plan. It's crucial for potential contributors to understand each plan's structure, allowable uses, fees, and residency implications before selecting a sponsor.

Prepaid Tuition Plans

Prepaid tuition plans let families lock in today's tuition rates for a future student, effectively shielding them from rising tuition costs. Typically, a contributor can purchase "units" or "credits" that correspond to the cost of tuition at an in-state public university. If the beneficiary later decides to attend a participating institution, the plan credits cover the designated tuition (and sometimes required fees) without additional payments, regardless of any tuition inflation during the intervening years. Some states also allow the prepaid credits to be applied toward private or out-of-state colleges, although the plan may limit coverage to the average in-state public tuition cost, requiring the beneficiary to pay any difference.

Prepaid tuition plans reduce future tuition uncertainty but can be restrictive. Many stipulate that the beneficiary must reside in the sponsoring state or use the funds at specific in-state institutions to realize full value, and if the beneficiary changes schools or moves out of state, the plan's coverage might provide less generous benefits. Additionally, some plans freeze or limit new enrollments when actuarial assessments project a funding deficit. While contributions are not guaranteed from loss by the federal government, certain states may back the plan's obligations. Nonetheless, liquidity and flexibility can be less than ideal: if the beneficiary does not attend a participating institution, the plan may refund only the principal contributions or offer a limited growth adjustment rather than the full tuition benefit.

Savings Plans

Savings-type 529 plans function more like tax-advantaged investment accounts, allowing contributors to invest in various portfolios—often comprising mutual funds or similar instruments—designed by the plan sponsor or a financial institution. Account owners can typically select from multiple asset allocations or age-based "glide path" portfolios that become more conservative as the beneficiary nears college. Earnings grow federal (and often state) tax-free, and withdrawals remain tax-free if used for qualified education expenses: tuition, fees, books, supplies, and sometimes room and board or even certain K–12 costs under recent legislative updates.

Compared to prepaid tuition plans, college savings plans are more flexible in institution choice—beneficiaries can apply the funds to virtually any accredited college or university across the United States (and sometimes abroad), public or private. The main trade-off, however, is market exposure: if the chosen investments perform poorly, the account balance could be insufficient to cover anticipated tuition. Similarly, if tuition inflates faster than investment returns, the account might not keep pace. Contributors who prefer direct control over asset allocation or who value portability typically favor savings plans, acknowledging the need to manage or monitor risk, costs, and the account's overall performance to align with the student's anticipated enrollment date.

Regardless of the 529 plan type—prepaid or savings—annual contribution limits can be high, but large contributions may trigger gift-tax considerations unless spread over multiple years. Some states provide partial or full tax deductions for contributions; others do not. Plans differ in fee structures and the underlying investment menu, so comparing expense ratios, administrative charges, and performance track records can lead to substantial cost savings over the lifetime of the account. Moreover, account owners retain control of the plan assets and can change beneficiaries if the original beneficiary decides not to attend college or receives scholarships. If withdrawals are made for nonqualified expenses, any earnings portion is typically subject to ordinary income tax plus a 10% federal penalty. These attributes make 529 plans one of the most popular approaches to saving for higher education, especially when contributors seek a balance of tax efficiency, potential investment growth, and a degree of flexibility regarding usage and beneficiary assignment.

3.1.5.2 Local Government Investment Pools (LGIPs)

Local Government Investment Pools (LGIPs) offer a collective investment mechanism for municipal entities—counties, cities, school districts, or other public bodies—seeking short-term, highly liquid instruments. Rather than each entity managing idle funds individually, LGIPs consolidate public money in a central pool, leveraging economies of scale to access favorable yields, professional management, and streamlined administration. Although they often resemble money-market funds in their overarching goals of stability and liquidity, LGIPs typically do not register under the Investment Company Act of 1940 and may be exempt from SEC registration, depending on how they are structured at the state level. Instead, these pools frequently adhere to separate statutes, investment guidelines, and oversight provided by the sponsoring state agency or a designated governing board.

In practice, LGIPs invest primarily in conservative, short-duration instruments, such as U.S. Treasuries, agency debt, high-quality commercial paper, or certificates of deposit. This ensures the principal remains relatively stable and that participating governments can readily withdraw funds as cash flow needs arise. Rates of return and risk tolerance vary by pool; some LGIPs maintain a stable net asset value (NAV) with daily liquidity, while others float NAV in response to market conditions. Fee structures—often minimal due to the public-service orientation—may include administrative costs and portfolio management expenses. Transparency also varies: certain states require robust disclosure and regular reporting of holdings, yield, and performance, while others rely more on internal oversight and board governance. Given their policy function, LGIPs typically emphasize capital preservation, consistent yield, and ease of withdrawals over maximizing returns. As such, they can serve as a dependable liquidity tool for municipalities, letting local governments focus on budget priorities rather than day-to-day portfolio management.

3.1.5.3 ABLE Accounts (Owner vs. Beneficiary, Tax Advantages)

ABLE accounts—formally established under the Achieving a Better Life Experience (ABLE) Act—offer a specialized way for individuals with disabilities to save and invest for qualified expenses without forfeiting access to certain government benefits. By design, these accounts resemble 529 college savings plans, carrying tax advantages if funds are used appropriately. The key distinction is that an ABLE account benefits someone whose disability onset occurred before age 26, and who meets specified criteria. Many states sponsor ABLE programs, often with slightly varying rules or investment choices, but any eligible individual may typically open an account in a state's plan, regardless of residency. Contributions can come from the beneficiary, family members, or other supporters, but annual limits often mirror federal gift-tax thresholds. Accumulated earnings grow tax-deferred, and withdrawals remain tax-free if used for qualified disability expenses—such as housing, education, transportation, or healthcare needs related to the beneficiary's disability.

Owner vs. Beneficiary Structures

In practice, the individual with the disability is usually both the beneficiary and the account owner, granting them direct control. However, an authorized person—like a parent, guardian, or power of attorney—may manage the account if the beneficiary cannot do so independently. This arrangement allows for seamless integration with existing financial support systems while preserving the beneficiary's personal autonomy wherever possible. Crucially, the beneficiary can hold funds in an ABLE account (up to certain thresholds) without jeopardizing eligibility for programs like Supplemental Security Income (SSI) or Medicaid. Generally, SSI disregards up to $100,000 in the ABLE account balance, though amounts exceeding that can trigger a suspension of benefits until the balance falls back below the threshold. Medicaid eligibility, in many cases, continues regardless of account size, though states can potentially file claims against the account after the beneficiary's death to recover certain expenses.

Tax and Benefit Implications

From a tax perspective, all principal contributions to an ABLE account are made on an after-tax basis, but the account's growth is federally tax-free if withdrawals go toward qualified disability expenses. Many states also extend favorable state-tax treatment, though the specifics vary. Furthermore, the contributions do not count toward the beneficiary's income, protecting them from breaching strict asset or resource limits for government benefits. Nonetheless, if withdrawals finance non-qualified expenses—those not directly related to the beneficiary's disability—the distributed earnings become subject to income taxes and a 10% penalty, akin to the rules for 529 college savings. This penalty regime, plus annual contribution caps, discourages misapplication of the funds. By channeling financial resources in a tax-advantaged, carefully regulated environment, ABLE accounts aim to empower individuals with disabilities to accumulate savings for essential services, assistive technology, continuing education, or broader life needs without sacrificing crucial public support programs.

3.1.6 Direct Participation Programs (DPPs)

Direct Participation Programs (DPPs) allow investors to participate in the cash flows and tax benefits of specific business ventures—frequently in sectors like real estate, energy (oil and gas), or equipment leasing—without acquiring a traditional corporate equity interest. These programs often take the legal form of limited partnerships or tenants-in-common (TIC) structures, wherein investors contribute capital in exchange for a proportional claim on income and tax deductions. Because the entity typically pays no corporate tax—i.e., "pass-through" treatment—investors may receive deductions for depreciation, depletion, or operating losses, which can potentially reduce their personal tax liability.

However, DPPs also carry unique risks. Limited partnership interests can be highly illiquid, with no active secondary market, making it difficult to exit the investment prior to the program's conclusion. The success of a DPP often hinges on the operational performance of the underlying project (e.g., finding oil, leasing property, or collecting rental payments). Additionally, changes in tax law or project cost overruns can erode anticipated returns. Consequently, DPPs generally suit accredited or high-net-worth investors who are comfortable with long holding periods, higher levels of project-specific risk, and the complexities of pass-through taxation.

3.1.6.1 Limited Partnerships, Tenants in Common (TIC)

Limited Partnerships

A **limited partnership (LP)** is a legal structure that commonly underpins direct participation programs. It consists of at least one *general partner (GP)*—who manages the day-to-day operations and bears unlimited liability—and one or more *limited partners (LPs)*, whose liabilities are capped at the amount of their initial investment. In exchange for this limited liability, LPs typically relinquish direct managerial control, allowing the GP to make business decisions. These partnerships often appear in real estate development, energy exploration (oil and gas programs), and equipment leasing. The motivation behind investing in a limited partnership stems from the potential for direct exposure to the project's economic returns (such as rental income or revenue from commodity extraction), combined with pass-through taxation. Because the entity itself generally does not pay corporate tax, the partnership's gains, losses, deductions, and credits flow through to the individual partners, who report them on their personal returns. This approach can yield substantial tax benefits—for instance, depreciation or depletion deductions—though it also entails considerable complexity, given the possibility of passive loss limitations and the requirement for K-1 tax forms.

Moreover, LP shares can be highly illiquid: investors often cannot easily sell or transfer their interests, and must rely on the GP's execution of the venture and eventual liquidation or buyout to recover principal and any profits.

General partners maintain fiduciary duties to protect the partnership's interests, but also shoulder risks if project outcomes disappoint. Should the partnership's debts or lawsuits exceed its assets, GPs could face unlimited personal liability. Meanwhile, limited partners may lose only their initial stake, but they risk not having a say if they disagree with the GP's strategies—excess involvement can even endanger their limited-liability status. Consequently, the LP structure hinges on selecting a competent general partner with proven expertise, as the business's success or failure often rests on the GP's planning and execution. In many DPPs, GPs market the offering to accredited or high-net-worth investors who understand the inherent illiquidity, operational risks, and potential for capital calls if additional funding is required mid-project. Given these constraints, LPs typically appeal to those seeking potentially high returns, specialized tax write-offs, or sector-specific exposure, provided they can commit to a multi-year horizon and accept hands-off involvement.

Tenants in Common (TIC)

Another ownership form sometimes employed in DPP-style arrangements is **tenants in common (TIC)**, particularly in real estate ventures. Under a TIC agreement, multiple individuals each hold an undivided fractional interest in a property, meaning each owner has the right to access and use the entire property, rather than being restricted to specific physical portions. Investors often rely on TIC for 1031 exchange transactions, where they seek to defer capital gains tax by reinvesting sale proceeds from one property into a portion of a larger replacement property. Because each tenant in common is recognized as a direct owner, the arrangement can facilitate these tax-deferred exchanges more easily than other investment vehicles.

While a TIC structure maintains tax advantages and direct property ownership, it also introduces logistical and legal complexities. Each tenant in common must share decisions regarding maintenance, refinancing, or property disposition. If the group conflicts—say, some owners want to sell while others prefer to hold—resolving disagreements can be cumbersome. Additionally, lending criteria can be more stringent: a lender may require each tenant in common to qualify, complicating financing. Unlike many LPs, however, TICs do not centralize power under a single general partner; major actions often necessitate unanimous or majority consent, balancing control among co-owners. Despite potential administrative challenges, a TIC can provide an avenue for smaller investors to hold interests in high-value commercial real estate, harness partial ownership benefits (rental income, appreciation), and preserve certain tax efficiencies, all while reducing the per-investor capital outlay compared to purchasing the entire property outright.

3.1.6.2 Pass-Through Tax Treatment, Liquidity Considerations

Pass-Through Tax Treatment

Direct Participation Programs (DPPs)—whether structured as limited partnerships, tenants in common, or other pass-through entities—are designed to avoid corporate-level taxation. Instead, the partnership or ownership structure passes income, losses, credits, and deductions directly through to individual investors, who then report them on their personal tax returns. This setup can be especially appealing in sectors such as real estate or oil and gas, where large depreciation or depletion deductions may accrue. If a DPP realizes a taxable profit, each investor's share flows through on a pro rata basis; similarly, if the project posts a loss, investors can potentially offset other income (subject to passive loss limitations).

In practice, DPPs typically provide investors with **Schedule K-1** documents indicating each investor's share of the entity's net income or loss and other relevant tax items. While these advantages can substantially reduce individual tax liability, DPP investors must be prepared for potentially complex tax filings and rules that distinguish "passive losses" from "active" or "portfolio" income. Certain depreciation or depletion write-offs can also alter an investor's cost basis, influencing capital gains tax calculations upon eventual disposition of the DPP interest.

However, pass-through treatment does not always guarantee immediate tax benefits. Passive loss rules can restrict an investor's ability to use DPP-generated losses if they lack sufficient passive income from other sources. Additionally, some states impose their own partnership filing and tax requirements, adding administrative layers for investors with multi-state exposure. Another aspect to remember is the "phantom income" scenario, where a DPP secures a loan restructuring or experiences a partial forgiveness of debt—generating deemed income that flows to investors even if no cash distributions occurred. Investors contemplating a DPP often confer with tax professionals to gauge how partnership earnings and losses might interplay with their broader financial picture, ensuring the pass-through concept truly aligns with their planning objectives.

Liquidity Considerations

Although the promise of direct tax advantages or asset-linked income can be enticing, DPPs are by nature **illiquid** investments. Most lack a formal secondary market, making it difficult for investors to exit before the project's maturity or liquidation event. In a limited partnership, for instance, transferring ownership typically requires permission from the general partner or other limited partners, and a pre-established buy-sell mechanism might not exist. Similarly, tenants in common structures do not lend themselves easily to partial sales, unless the co-ownership agreement expressly allows it—and even then, finding a buyer for an undivided interest in real property can prove challenging. Investors may thus remain locked into the DPP's life cycle—ranging from a few years to over a decade—unless the sponsor arranges an asset sale, merger, or buyout.

This illiquidity can expose participants to prolonged market and operational risks. Should the DPP face unplanned cash calls (e.g., for well repairs in an oil drilling partnership or capital improvements in a real estate venture), investors might be compelled to contribute further capital rather than dilute or lose their share. Distributions, if any, typically hinge on the underlying venture's performance: real estate might distribute rental income after expenses, while oil and gas projects rely on production revenue. If the project underperforms or requires reinvestment, payouts can be minimal or suspended, adding to liquidity challenges. Consequently, prospective DPP investors should thoroughly assess their capacity for a long-term commitment, the stability of projected cash flows, and the sponsor's track record before committing capital. Despite the potential for steady income and significant tax benefits, the inherent lack of liquidity demands careful planning so that essential cash reserves and shorter-term goals remain separate from funds devoted to DPP ventures.

3.1.7 Real Estate Investment Trusts (REITs)

Real Estate Investment Trusts (REITs) are companies that own, operate, or finance income-producing real estate. By law, most REITs distribute at least 90% of their taxable income as dividends to shareholders, allowing them to avoid corporate income tax and pass through most earnings directly to investors. Because of this requirement, REITs can provide a steady stream of dividends, often backed by rent payments from shopping centers, apartment buildings, office complexes, or mortgages. Yet their share prices still move in response to overall real estate values and broader market trends, blending elements of both equity and property exposure.

REITs are generally categorized as **equity REITs**, **mortgage REITs**, or **hybrid REITs**. Equity REITs invest in physical properties and derive revenue primarily from rental income, whereas mortgage REITs focus on the financing side—buying or originating real estate loans and earning interest. Hybrid REITs combine both approaches. Like stocks, many REITs trade on major exchanges, offering a comparatively liquid avenue for real estate investment. However, some structures are private or registered but non-listed, potentially limiting share redemption options and transparency. Investors must weigh factors like management expertise, property type, geographic diversification, and interest-rate sensitivity when including REITs in a portfolio.

3.1.7.1 Private, Registered Non-Listed, Listed

A key distinction among Real Estate Investment Trusts (REITs) lies in how they are offered to investors and the extent of their regulatory compliance and liquidity. **Private REITs** are typically sold via private placements and do not register with the Securities and Exchange Commission (SEC). This framework often restricts offerings to accredited or institutional investors. Because private REITs are exempt from some disclosure mandates, they can be more flexible in their real estate strategies, but they also carry higher risks tied to minimal public transparency and limited liquidity—buyers may face lock-up periods or lack any secondary market for share redemption. In addition, the sponsor's track record and the specific property portfolio become pivotal in evaluating the likelihood of steady income or eventual capital gains. Private REIT shares might be valued internally and updated less frequently, so investors must rely heavily on sponsor-provided performance data.

Registered non-listed REITs, also called unlisted or non-traded REITs, are SEC-registered but do not trade on an exchange. They comply with filing and disclosure requirements, providing more public insight into operations and financials than private REITs. However, they remain relatively illiquid because no active secondary market exists; redemptions often occur through share repurchase programs that may impose monthly or quarterly limits, fees, or gating mechanisms. This structure allows the REIT's managers to focus on acquiring and stabilizing properties without the short-term trading pressures associated with exchange-listed entities. Yet an investor may need to hold these shares for years, awaiting a liquidity event such as a merger, listing, or property liquidation. Non-listed REITs often aim for higher dividend yields, supported by rental income from real estate holdings. Over time, they may transition to a listed REIT if their asset base and strategy align with public-market expectations.

By contrast, **listed REITs** are fully publicly traded on major exchanges (e.g., NYSE), thus providing daily share pricing and robust liquidity. This arrangement typically mandates regular SEC filings—Forms 10-K, 10-Q, and proxy statements—helping investors gauge the REIT's financial health, portfolio composition, and risk profile. Listed REITs can rapidly raise capital through secondary offerings, which may fund further acquisitions or property development. Their share prices fluctuate in real time with market sentiment and real estate sector trends, sometimes deviating from net asset value (NAV). While this volatility can unnerve conservative investors, it also opens up opportunities to buy at discounts or to exit positions readily if circumstances change. For many, listed REITs combine real estate's income potential with the flexibility of traditional stock ownership, but with higher correlation to broader equity markets than private or non-traded counterparts.

3.1.7.2 Real Estate Equity vs. Debt REITs, Tax Advantages

REITs can broadly be divided into two main categories—**equity** and **debt**—based on the types of real estate assets they hold and how they generate income. **Equity REITs** concentrate on owning and managing physical properties, such as office towers, shopping centers, apartments, or warehouse facilities. These trusts typically earn revenue through rents and pass on the majority of their rental income to shareholders in the form of dividends. The performance of an equity REIT often hinges on occupancy levels, rental rate trends, property appreciation, and the management's competence in acquiring or developing properties at attractive yields. Because their holdings consist of tangible real estate, equity REITs exhibit sensitivity to property-market fundamentals, local supply-demand dynamics, and broader economic conditions influencing tenants' ability to pay rent. Over time, capital gains may accrue if property values rise, creating potential asset-based gains in addition to dividend income.

By contrast, **debt REITs** (often referred to as mortgage REITs) focus on the financing side of real estate, investing primarily in mortgages, mortgage-backed securities, or related loans. Their revenue flows mainly from interest payments on these debt instruments, meaning their fortunes are more closely linked to credit risk, interest-rate spreads, and prepayment patterns than direct rent collection. Mortgage REITs can either originate loans or acquire them on the secondary market, profiting from the difference between the interest they receive on mortgage assets and the interest they must pay on borrowed funds. If interest rates rise sharply or if borrowers default, a mortgage REIT's net income and dividends can be pressured. Similarly, accelerated prepayments—e.g., when borrowers refinance in lower-rate environments—can erode the REIT's portfolio yields sooner than expected. As a result, mortgage REITs often have higher volatility and sometimes offer larger dividends than equity REITs, compensating shareholders for the additional credit and interest-rate risks.

Tax Advantages

A principal appeal of REITs—whether equity or debt—stems from the structure's tax benefits. Under the REIT rules, a real estate investment trust generally pays no corporate federal income tax if it distributes at least 90% of its taxable income to shareholders each year. This pass-through mechanism ensures that most income from rent or interest flows directly to shareholders without being diminished by a corporate tax layer. The REIT itself, however, remains responsible for taxes on retained earnings not paid out as dividends or on any prohibited transactions. Although the elimination of double taxation typically boosts dividend yields, shareholders face ordinary income tax rates on these distributions (unless the dividends qualify under specific rules, such as those for capital-gain distributions or return of capital). Still, many REIT dividends do not count as "qualified dividends" at lower rates, meaning that individuals may incur higher ordinary tax rates on that portion of income.

Recent legislative changes, including those introduced by the Tax Cuts and Jobs Act, allow for a *qualified business income (QBI) deduction* of up to 20% on certain pass-through income, which can include REIT dividends. This deduction effectively lowers the tax cost on REIT distributions if the investor meets the relevant criteria. Additionally, return of capital components distributed to shareholders reduce their cost basis in the REIT shares, deferring some taxes until the shares are sold. From a strategic perspective, investors seeking steady income might accept REIT dividends taxed as ordinary income, particularly if they hold the shares in tax-advantaged accounts such as IRAs. Meanwhile, others may capitalize on the potential for long-term appreciation in an equity REIT's property portfolio or look for higher yields and distinctive interest-rate sensitivity in mortgage REITs. By carefully evaluating the interplay of rents vs. interest income, distribution policies, and the personal tax situation, investors can integrate REITs into a broader portfolio strategy that balances risk, liquidity, and potential tax efficiency.

3.1.8 Hedge Funds

Hedge funds are private investment vehicles open primarily to accredited or high-net-worth investors. These pools often pursue unconventional or opportunistic strategies—such as long/short equity, global macro, event-driven, or relative value arbitrage—aimed at absolute returns regardless of broader market conditions. Operating with fewer regulatory constraints than mutual funds, hedge funds can employ leverage, short selling, derivatives, and concentrated positions, potentially amplifying both gains and losses. Because of the specialized nature of these strategies, hedge fund managers typically charge higher fees, including a management fee (e.g., 2% of assets) and a performance fee (e.g., 20% of profits), aligning their compensation with fund success but also incentivizing risk-taking.

Most hedge funds prohibit daily redemptions, imposing "lock-up" periods or quarterly or annual liquidity windows to give portfolio managers leeway in executing longer-term or more complex trades. As a result, investors need sufficient risk tolerance and a multi-year investment horizon. While hedge funds can produce significant upside if the chosen strategies pay off, they also bring higher volatility and greater opacity—some strategies or holdings remain private, and the fund's periodic reporting may reveal less detail than a registered mutual fund. In exchange for these constraints, participants hope the hedge fund model can capitalize on market inefficiencies or protect capital in downturns more nimbly than a traditional long-only approach.

3.1.8.1 Partnership Structure, Minimum Investment

Hedge funds commonly organize as private partnerships, with the **general partner (GP)** serving as the fund's manager and the **limited partners (LPs)** contributing the majority of capital. The GP often invests personal funds to align interests with those of the LPs, and exercises day-to-day control over investment decisions, risk management, and fund operations. Because hedge funds rely on exemptions from the Investment Company Act of 1940 and often operate under Regulation D of the Securities Act of 1933, they can admit only certain qualified or accredited investors (e.g., individuals with high net worth or substantial annual income, or institutions meeting regulatory thresholds). This framework bypasses some of the more stringent SEC mandates that apply to retail funds, granting hedge funds flexibility in deploying tactics such as short selling, derivatives, or leverage.

Structurally, domestic hedge funds typically form limited partnerships under state law, ensuring pass-through taxation (i.e., no entity-level tax at the partnership level). Each LP's share of profits and losses flows onto their personal or corporate returns via **Schedule K-1**. For international or institutional investors seeking U.S. tax advantages, hedge fund managers might set up an offshore entity in tandem with the onshore master fund—commonly referred to as a *master-feeder* structure—enabling a uniform strategy while tailoring tax treatment to different investor profiles. In all cases, the partnership agreement details provisions such as management and performance fees, lock-up periods, withdrawal constraints, and the manager's discretion in gating or suspending redemptions under volatile market conditions.

Another defining trait of hedge funds is their **minimum investment requirements**, which can range from $250,000 to several million dollars, depending on the fund's strategy, cachet, and target clientele. In part, these high entry points reflect legal constraints that limit hedge fund participation to sophisticated entities or individuals with significant capital. The manager also seeks to maintain a more stable investor base, preventing frequent in-and-out trading that might interfere with the fund's long-term or opportunistic trades. For investors prepared to meet the threshold, hedge funds may offer access to specialized strategies, potential absolute returns, and dynamic risk management; however, these come with elevated risks, restricted liquidity, and minimal regulatory oversight compared to standard retail investment vehicles. Investors need to review each partnership's private placement memorandum (PPM) and consult advisors to ensure that the fund's complexity, lock-up terms, and fees align with their tolerance for risk and investment horizon.

3.1.8.2 Private Equity Features, Liquidity Considerations

Many hedge funds adopt **private equity–like features** in their pursuit of long-term capital appreciation, especially when venturing into illiquid or control-oriented investments. In such scenarios, hedge fund managers may allocate a portion of the fund's capital to private companies, distressed assets, or special situations where the holding period typically extends well beyond a year. This approach enables the fund to pursue higher returns through strategic influence—negotiating restructurings, guiding portfolio companies toward public listings or sales, or bundling assets for eventual exit at favorable valuations. As with traditional private equity funds, these investments can hinge on operational turnarounds, management expertise, or industry-specific synergies that take time to materialize.

To support these deeper, longer-term strategies, hedge funds with private equity components often institute "side pockets," segregating illiquid holdings from the main portfolio. While side pockets aim to treat investors equitably—preventing quick redeemers from taking full advantage of illiquid gains—they also entail more complex valuation protocols and restricted redemption policies for those specific assets.

Because of such extended horizons and the unpredictability of exit events, **liquidity considerations** can prove more restrictive than those in a typical long-short hedge fund. In addition to the lock-up periods and infrequent redemption windows common in standard hedge funds, private equity–style hedge funds may impose multi-year commitments, capital calls, and partial distributions rather than regular dividends. Investors are generally unable to withdraw capital allocated to illiquid holdings until an exit (sale, IPO, or other liquidity event) occurs, which can take several years. Moreover, if additional funds are required to safeguard or optimize a private investment—say, bridging a financing gap or capitalizing on an opportunistic acquisition—the fund may request or mandate further capital from existing investors. These constraints underscore the importance of thorough due diligence: investors must assess both their own time frames and the fund manager's track record in shepherding private, long-duration projects to profitable conclusions. While the potential payoff can be significant—reflecting the manager's capacity to unlock value in niche or undervalued assets—it demands a degree of patience and tolerance for opaque valuations that exceed what most short-term hedge fund strategies entail.

3.1.9 Exchange-Traded Products (ETPs)

Exchange-Traded Products are securities that trade on an exchange and can be bought or sold throughout the trading day at market-determined prices. Most commonly, they track an index, commodity, or basket of assets, offering diversification and immediate transparency in pricing. Investors appreciate ETPs' intraday liquidity, as well as their generally lower operating expenses compared to many actively managed funds. Because they are priced continuously, ETP share values can fluctuate with real-time market sentiment and supply-demand conditions.

Within ETPs, **Exchange-Traded Funds (ETFs)** and **Exchange-Traded Notes (ETNs)** are the two main categories. ETFs typically hold the underlying assets they track—such as a replica portfolio matching a specific benchmark—while ETNs function as unsecured debt instruments issued by financial institutions, returning a performance-based payout at maturity. Although both trade like stocks, their risk profiles differ: an ETN's value may hinge partly on the issuer's creditworthiness, whereas an ETF's price often reflects the net asset value of its holdings. Overall, ETPs can serve as flexible tools for asset allocation, enabling quick shifts across various sectors or markets without incurring the higher transaction costs or redemption constraints of many traditional funds.

3.1.9.1 ETFs vs. ETNs

Exchange-Traded Funds (ETFs)

ETFs typically hold a basket of underlying assets such as stocks, bonds, or commodities that mirror a specific index or strategy. This direct ownership gives an ETF tangible holdings: for instance, an equity ETF might own every stock in the S&P 500 in proportion to that index's composition. Investors benefit from continuous pricing during trading hours, relatively tight bid-ask spreads for larger, more liquid funds, and the ability to execute intraday trades—features shared with individual stocks. The creation/redemption mechanism, in which authorized participants exchange "creation units" of underlying securities for ETF shares, helps maintain the ETF's market price close to net asset value (NAV). If the market price drifts above or below the NAV, arbitrageurs can step in to buy or sell the underlying basket, thereby bringing the ETF price back into line. Because of this structure, tracking error—how closely an ETF follows its benchmark—remains a critical metric; well-managed funds keep slippage minimal by rebalancing holdings whenever the index changes. Expense ratios for ETFs often prove more competitive than those for actively managed mutual funds, reflecting the generally passive nature of index replication.

Another appeal of ETFs is tax efficiency: capital gains distributions can be minimized if underlying securities are moved in and out through in-kind transactions instead of being sold for cash. In many cases, shareholders realize taxable events only when they sell their ETF shares, rather than encountering yearly capital gains distributions. Nonetheless, some specialized or actively managed ETFs may generate more frequent rebalancings or hold illiquid instruments, potentially increasing tracking error or expenses. Liquidity in the secondary market depends on both the liquidity of the underlying portfolio and investor demand for the ETF itself. For broad equity or bond indexes, trading volumes can be high, with spreads that narrow further as the fund gathers assets and more market participants enter the fray.

Exchange-Traded Notes (ETNs)

ETNs, in contrast, are unsecured debt obligations issued by financial institutions, promising to deliver returns based on the performance of a reference index or asset. They do not hold the actual underlying securities—no direct portfolio of stocks or bonds underpins the ETN. Instead, the issuer tracks the index's performance using its own internal hedging strategies and commits to paying out an amount at maturity that reflects the index's gains or losses, minus fees. Because ETNs rely on the issuer's creditworthiness, holders assume an added layer of counterparty risk absent from ETFs. If the issuing bank faces default or severe credit downgrades, ETN prices can deviate significantly from the reference asset's value.

On the positive side, ETNs can offer more precise tracking of a benchmark because they do not incur the trading costs or rebalancing frictions of an ETF holding physical assets. Conceptually, an ETN's return exactly matches the index (minus fees) as long as the issuer remains solvent. Moreover, ETNs can be structured to follow obscure or complex strategies that might be impractical for an ETF, such as thinly traded commodities, foreign exchange baskets, or leveraged/inverse exposures. However, these same unique strategies may create intricate pricing dynamics—spreads can widen if the reference assets or currency markets are volatile or illiquid, and early redemption features can be restrictive or associated with higher fees. Thus, investors weighing ETNs against ETFs must weigh the straightforward collateral backing of an ETF's portfolio against an ETN's credit reliance on the issuing institution. Depending on portfolio objectives and risk tolerance, the convenience of near-perfect index replication with an ETN can be overshadowed by solvency concerns, whereas an ETF's partial tracking error might be more acceptable if it eliminates counterparty risk.

3.1.9.2 Active vs. Passive Strategies

Within the universe of Exchange-Traded Products (ETPs), an essential distinction arises between **active** and **passive** approaches. Both varieties trade on exchanges throughout the day, offering investors continuous pricing and generally low transaction costs compared to many traditional mutual funds. The difference lies in the managerial philosophy and objectives behind constructing the underlying portfolio—and by extension, the potential risk-return outcomes, fee structures, and performance drivers.

Passive (Index-Tracking) Strategies

Passive ETPs, which encompass most popular Exchange-Traded Funds (ETFs), seek to **replicate** the performance of a specified index or benchmark, such as the S&P 500, a particular bond index, or a niche sector/industry. These funds hold a basket of securities (or, in some cases, a representative sample) to mirror that benchmark's composition. Their primary goal is **minimizing tracking error**—the divergence between the ETP's returns and those of the index—while keeping operational costs low. The creation/redemption mechanism, wherein authorized participants swap large blocks of the underlying holdings (called "creation units") for shares of the ETF, aids in maintaining the fund's price close to its net asset value (NAV). Since passive managers rarely engage in discretionary trading—mostly adjusting holdings only when the index changes constituents or weighting—the fund's turnover remains modest, leading to reduced transaction costs and typically fewer taxable events. For this reason, many passive ETFs come with **some of the lowest expense ratios** in the ETP space, making them attractive for buy-and-hold investors seeking broad market exposure without paying the higher fees of active management.

Despite these advantages, purely passive funds face certain limitations. They cannot respond to market anomalies, corporate news, or macroeconomic shifts beyond what index rules prescribe. If an index experiences prolonged underperformance relative to other benchmarks, a passive ETP tracking that index will mirror such results. Additionally, niche or thinly traded indexes can introduce higher tracking error, as replicating illiquid components or adjusting for daily fluctuations is harder. Nonetheless, for investors content with the risk-reward profile of a given benchmark—and confident in the merits of a low-cost, rules-based approach—passive ETPs often form the cornerstone of an efficient, diversified portfolio.

Active (Discretionary) Strategies

Active ETPs, though fewer in number and often smaller in asset size compared to passive peers, are managed by investment teams or portfolio managers with the freedom to **select securities** and time trades in pursuit of returns exceeding a benchmark or meeting specific objectives (e.g., maximizing income, exploiting momentum). Unlike passive index trackers, active managers may rotate among sectors, overweight or underweight particular positions, and incorporate market outlook or company-specific research. This discretionary decision-making can allow the fund to hedge or capitalize on perceived inefficiencies—potentially outperforming if the manager's assessments prove accurate. However, the capacity for alpha (excess returns) often comes alongside higher expense ratios. Portfolio turnover may be more frequent, incurring trading costs and tax consequences that trickle down to shareholders.

From an operational standpoint, active ETPs maintain the same intraday tradability as passive funds, but they can be more opaque if the manager refrains from full daily disclosure of holdings—some adopt **semi-transparent or non-transparent** models to protect proprietary strategies. As a result, market-makers might encounter more challenge in consistently arbitraging the fund's share price to NAV, potentially widening bid-ask spreads or introducing greater pricing variance. On the investor side, active ETPs can appeal to those seeking a specialized focus—whether sector rotation, alternative assets, or a conviction in a particular manager's skill—yet they must weigh whether the higher fees and the possibility of underperformance (versus a simpler passive benchmark) justify the risk. The manager's track record and the ETP's liquidity profile are thus key considerations when evaluating an actively managed product.

Overall, the choice between an active or passive ETP reflects each investor's preference for cost control, desired market exposure, and confidence in human expertise versus systematic replication. Passive ETPs excel at cost efficiency, transparency, and consistent index-based returns, whereas active ETPs strive to add value through skilled security selection or timing. By understanding how each style structures its portfolio, manages risk, and aligns fees with outcomes, investors can match the appropriate ETP approach to their broader strategy and risk tolerance.

3.1.9.3 Fees, Advantages, Risks

Exchange-Traded Products (ETPs) frequently come with relatively low **expense ratios** compared to many traditional mutual funds, especially for passive index-tracking varieties. These fees encompass management, administrative, and, in some cases, licensing costs associated with replicating or maintaining the fund's underlying basket or index. While passive ETPs often boast some of the lowest annual expenses in the industry, actively managed ETPs may charge higher expense ratios to cover the cost of research, trading, and portfolio management decisions. Beyond the stated expense ratio, investors face secondary costs whenever they transact in ETP shares, including bid-ask spreads and brokerage commissions. For large investors creating or redeeming shares in bulk, there can also be creation/redemption fees to offset the cost of delivering the underlying securities. Although these charges seldom impact retail traders directly, they can indirectly influence liquidity and overall pricing efficiency. By scrutinizing the expense ratio and understanding a product's trading mechanics, investors can better assess the all-in cost of owning a given ETP.

Among the **principal advantages** of ETPs is intraday tradability. Shares can be bought and sold at market-determined prices throughout the trading session, allowing real-time portfolio rebalancing, short selling, or hedging strategies not readily available with once-daily-priced mutual funds. This intraday liquidity often appeals to active traders, though even long-term investors value the transparent pricing and flexibility to respond quickly to market events. Many ETPs also offer broad diversification in a single trade—covering entire equity indexes, specific market sectors, or baskets of bonds, commodities, or currencies. Because ETPs generally provide daily holdings disclosures, investors can closely monitor the underlying assets. Tax efficiency is another frequently cited benefit, especially for ETFs structured with in-kind redemptions that reduce taxable events inside the fund. Overall, ETPs strike a balance between accessibility and cost control, catering to a wide range of portfolio objectives, from short-term tactical plays to long-term core holdings.

Nonetheless, **risks** vary significantly depending on the ETP's structure and underlying market exposure. Traditional index-based ETFs typically face "market risk" in line with their benchmark, whereas more specialized funds—like leveraged or inverse ETPs—introduce compounding risk and potential for large tracking deviations if held longer than their designed rebalancing window (often just one day). In commodity or currency-linked ETPs, rolling futures contracts can generate "roll yield" complexities that influence returns beyond simple spot-price movements. Credit risk also arises for ETNs, since holders depend on the issuing institution's solvency to receive promised returns. Moreover, any ETP can experience **tracking error**, where its performance lags or surpasses the benchmark due to transaction costs, imperfect replication, or liquidity constraints in the underlying market. Intraday pricing, while beneficial, can briefly diverge from net asset value if trading imbalances occur. By examining how each ETP addresses these structural and market hazards—evaluating turnover, rebalancing methodology, and sponsor creditworthiness—investors can better weigh the suitability and reliability of a product within their broader portfolio strategy.

3.2 Investment Risks

3.2.1 Definitions and Identification of Risk Types

Investors face a variety of risks that can erode returns or jeopardize capital, depending on economic conditions, market sentiment, or specific characteristics of the instruments they hold. **Capital risk** refers to the possibility of losing the entire invested principal—a stock going to zero, for example, leaves little or nothing for shareholders to recover. **Credit (default) risk** emerges primarily in debt instruments, where an issuer (such as a corporation or municipality) could fail to make timely interest or principal payments. Bonds with lower credit ratings typically offer higher yields to compensate for this heightened chance of default, but if the issuer's financial state worsens, bondholders may suffer partial or total losses. Similarly, **currency risk** arises when assets denominated in a foreign currency fluctuate in value relative to the investor's home currency, potentially negating gains even if the asset's price appreciates in its local market.

Another key threat is **inflation,** also termed purchasing-power risk, which erodes the real value of investment returns. Even if a fixed-income security generates steady interest, rising costs of goods and services can outpace its coupon rate, meaning the investor's purchasing power declines over time. Alongside inflationary concerns, **interest-rate risk** looms large, especially for fixed-income investors. As market interest rates rise, newly issued bonds with higher coupons become more attractive, prompting existing bond prices to drop to maintain competitive yields. This risk is further compounded by **reinvestment risk**—the challenge of reinvesting coupon payments or maturing principals at prevailing rates if yields have fallen. In a prolonged low-rate environment, fixed-income investors can find it hard to maintain prior income levels, whereas a high-rate shift can depress bond prices for those seeking to sell before maturity.

Beyond these rate-driven and credit-driven perils, securities may carry **liquidity risk**, reflecting the potential difficulty of unloading a position promptly at or near a fair market price. Thinly traded stocks, complex structured products, or funds with lock-up periods can leave investors stranded if they urgently need cash or if market conditions shift unfavorably. Additionally, **market or systematic risk** stems from overall economic or market-wide downturns. Even well-managed companies can see their stock prices tumble if recessionary fears or global crises prompt broad sell-offs. By contrast, **non-systematic (company-specific) risk** focuses on factors unique to an individual firm—like management scandals or product failures—that can be mitigated via diversification. Another external risk factor is **political or geopolitical risk**, wherein regulatory upheavals, regime changes, or trade tensions disrupt investment strategies, especially in emerging markets. Lastly, **prepayment risk** mainly affects mortgage-backed securities and other asset-backed instruments: if borrowers repay loans ahead of schedule—often in falling-rate environments—investors must reinvest returned principal at lower yields, curtailing total returns.

In practice, these risks often intersect. A bondholder, for instance, might see credit risk intensify in tandem with liquidity risk if the issuer's financial troubles cause fewer buyers to remain interested. Similarly, currency movements can amplify inflation or interest-rate pressures in multinational portfolios. Identifying and understanding each risk dimension—capital, credit, currency, inflation/purchasing power, interest rate, reinvestment, liquidity, market/systematic, non-systematic, political, and prepayment—forms the backbone of prudent portfolio management. By calibrating exposure to each risk according to goals and time horizon, investors can better insulate themselves from unpredictable market events while still positioning for meaningful

3.2.2 Strategies for Mitigation of Risk

Diversification

Diversification reduces exposure to the unique risks of any single asset or sector by spreading an investor's capital across different types of securities, industries, and possibly geographic regions. The rationale is straightforward: if one stock or bond underperforms, other holdings may offset those losses. Typically, portfolios incorporate a mix of equities, fixed income, and sometimes alternative assets (e.g., commodities, real estate, private equity) that do not move perfectly in tandem. In a well-designed diversified portfolio, securities often have low or negative correlations with each other, meaning they respond differently to economic shifts, interest-rate changes, or investor sentiment. This helps smooth overall returns and moderates volatility. Over time, modest allocations to less-traditional categories (like emerging-market bonds or hedge-fund strategies) can further broaden diversification, though these may bring added complexity and higher due-diligence requirements.

Crucially, diversification is no guarantee against market-wide declines—systematic risk can still affect nearly all asset classes in a global downturn. Nonetheless, it cushions against company-specific or sector-specific events that would hurt a heavily concentrated portfolio. Selection of distinct investment styles—value vs. growth stocks, short-term vs. long-term bonds—also aids diversification, as each style thrives under different market conditions. One practical approach is using index-tracking funds or exchange-traded funds

(ETFs) that offer immediate exposure to wide swaths of equities or fixed income. Periodically, investors reassess their allocations to ensure that evolving market correlations and personal circumstances have not undermined the strategy's overall balance.

Portfolio Rebalancing

Rebalancing involves realigning a portfolio back to its intended asset mix whenever market performance causes significant drift from the original allocation targets. For instance, if rising stock prices swell the equity portion from 60% to 70% of total assets, rebalancing might entail selling some equities and redeploying capital into bonds or other asset classes, restoring the 60/40 balance. This practice aims to maintain the portfolio's desired risk-return profile and can instill discipline by prompting investors to lock in gains on outperforming assets and reinvest in underperforming (often less expensive) ones. Over long horizons, systematic rebalancing can reduce volatility and, in certain market conditions, enhance returns because it encourages a contrarian mindset—buying assets when they have become temporarily cheaper.

The frequency and triggers for rebalancing vary. Some investors choose a time-based model—e.g., annually or semiannually—while others set threshold bands (like a 5% deviation from target) that automatically trigger adjustments. Because frequent trading can incur transaction costs or tax consequences, investors must weigh the benefits of precise alignment against the costs. In tax-advantaged accounts (like IRAs or 401(k)s), rebalancing is simpler due to the absence of immediate capital gains taxes. By contrast, rebalancing in taxable accounts may involve carefully selecting which positions to trim or deciding whether to harvest losses to offset gains. Successful rebalancing ensures a portfolio's risk exposures remain steady over market cycles and helps investors avoid emotional "chasing" of hot sectors at potentially inopportune times.

Hedging (e.g., Using Options)

Hedging deploys financial instruments—commonly options, but also futures or swaps—to counterbalance potential losses in an existing investment. For example, a stock investor might purchase put options to shield their position from a sudden drop. If the stock's price falls below the put's strike, gains on the option can offset the declines in the shares. This approach, often called a protective put, essentially acts like an insurance policy and can suit risk-averse investors seeking to lock in a floor value for their equity holdings. Likewise, covered call writing involves selling call options on owned shares, generating premium income that can cushion minor dips in the stock but caps upside potential if the shares surge. Although these techniques can preserve capital and reduce volatility, they also involve costs—the option premiums or margin requirements—and can limit gains if the underlying asset performs better than anticipated.

Other hedging tactics exist for interest-rate, currency, or commodity exposures. A bondholder might short interest-rate futures or purchase interest-rate swaptions to mitigate the impact of rising rates on bond valuations. Meanwhile, currency hedges—through forward contracts or currency options—address exchange-rate fluctuations in global portfolios. Regardless of the vehicle, effective hedging depends on matching the hedge's size and duration to the underlying exposure, while remaining mindful of the costs and complexity. Over-hedging can undermine returns if the market moves in the predicted direction anyway, and partial hedges may still expose an investor to residual risk. As a result, the hedge's purpose must be clearly defined—whether it is short-term downside protection, long-term volatility dampening, or a tactical overlay. By blending hedging with diversification and rebalancing, investors can shape a more stable return profile without sacrificing growth opportunities entirely.

3.3 Key Rules and Regulations for Products

3.3.1 FINRA Rules (2261, 2262, 2310, 2330, 2342, 2360, etc.)

FINRA rules establish uniform standards of conduct for broker-dealers and registered representatives, ensuring ethical practices and investor protection throughout the securities industry. **FINRA Rule 2261 (Disclosure of Financial Condition)** requires member firms to furnish their most recent balance sheet (or a summary) to any bona fide customer or investor who requests it. This transparency fosters confidence by letting clients assess the firm's financial stability. **FINRA Rule 2262 (Disclosure of Control Relationship with Issuer)** obliges firms to disclose any control relationship they maintain with the issuer of a recommended security—such as ownership stakes or shared personnel—so customers can evaluate potential conflicts of interest.

When it comes to **suitability, FINRA Rule 2310** compels members and associated persons to ensure recommendations align with the client's financial situation, investment experience, and objectives. Before suggesting a transaction or investment strategy, representatives must gather and analyze relevant customer information—e.g., risk tolerance, liquidity needs, and time horizon—to determine that the product is appropriate. Beyond just a single recommendation, the rule emphasizes a "reasonable-basis" component (understanding the product in general) and a "customer-specific" component (matching it to the investor's profile). While the 2012 update to FINRA's suitability standards has since merged with Regulation Best Interest obligations, the core principle remains: protect customers from recommendations that are unsuitable or excessively risky for their profile.

Variable annuities fall under specialized requirements set forth in **FINRA Rule 2330**, which instructs brokers to perform heightened due diligence before recommending these insurance-linked products. Representatives must note the prospective annuity's potential surrender period, fees, living or death benefits, and market risk inside the subaccounts. Additional scrutiny applies to exchanges of existing annuities—if a client already holds one, switching to a new contract may trigger surrender charges or reset expensive riders. As a result, 2330 requires a thorough cost-benefit analysis and documentation, ensuring that any recommended exchange or purchase is truly beneficial given the customer's goals.

Another area prone to confusion involves **breakpoints** for front-end sales charges in mutual funds. **FINRA Rule 2342** addresses a closely related concern: ensuring that customers receive information on breakpoint discounts, which can substantially reduce sales loads for larger-scale fund purchases. Representatives who fail to apply an available breakpoint discount risk overcharging investors. Thus, the rule obliges firms to provide educational materials about breakpoints, including details on how to aggregate purchases across accounts or rely on letters of intent (LOIs) to lock in lower loads.

In **options trading**, **FINRA Rule 2360** outlines a comprehensive framework covering account approvals, disclosures, supervision, and recordkeeping. Customers contemplating options trades must receive a copy of the Options Disclosure Document (ODD), detailing risks and mechanics of calls, puts, or spread strategies. Additionally, the firm designates a registered options principal to oversee approvals, ensure trades align with the client's experience and net worth, and confirm the account type (e.g., covered options vs. uncovered options) is suitable. The firm's supervisory system must also manage margin requirements—particularly relevant for short options positions that can entail open-ended risk. By prescribing these steps, Rule 2360 attempts to safeguard investors from misusing options' leverage and to maintain robust oversight so that trades remain within the client's capacity and risk tolerance.

Taken together, these FINRA rules serve as crucial guardrails for investor protection, product suitability, and market integrity. Firms must train their representatives to adhere to best practices—disclosing conflicts, evaluating the nuances of annuities or mutual funds, and vetting more complex products like options. Through ongoing supervision and compliance monitoring, broker-dealers aim to fulfill both the technical requirements of these regulations and their broader fiduciary-like duty to place customers' interests first.

3.3.2 MSRB Rules (D-12, G-17, G-30, G-45)

D-12 (Municipal Fund Securities)

Under MSRB Rule D-12, "municipal fund securities" refer to interests in a trust or similar investment vehicle established by states or local governments, typically including 529 college savings plans, ABLE programs, or local government investment pools. Because these are not traditional municipal bonds but still fall under the broader category of municipal securities, D-12 clarifies that sales and marketing practices for these offerings must comply with MSRB oversight. This designation ensures that brokers and other intermediaries selling or advising on municipal fund securities adhere to the same fair dealing and disclosure standards applicable to underwriters of conventional municipal debt. In practice, the rule compels firms to provide key information—such as plan features, fees, and investment risks—so that investors understand the tax and policy context of the product.

Unlike typical municipal bonds, municipal fund securities can exhibit features more akin to mutual funds, such as daily net asset values, multiple share classes, and redemption restrictions. Firms need to carefully distinguish between these products and standard municipal notes when training representatives and disclosing terms to clients. D-12 thus ensures that the industry addresses their unique structure—often involving state agency sponsors or trustees—by applying MSRB rules on suitability, transaction reporting, and customer-first conduct. This framework helps protect investors venturing into educational or disability-related savings vehicles by guaranteeing robust transparency and consistent regulatory treatment.

G-17 (Conduct of Municipal Securities and Municipal Advisory Activities)

Rule G-17 serves as the ethical cornerstone of the MSRB's rulebook, requiring dealers and municipal advisors to treat counterparties fairly and without deceptive or manipulative practices. It mandates not only honesty but also underscores an affirmative duty to disclose all material facts about a transaction. That can include explicit risk factors, call features, or potential conflicts of interest relevant to the security or the role the dealer plays. Firms must ensure that any marketing materials, official statements, or hypothetical illustrations present accurate and balanced information, so investors can form realistic expectations of the benefits and hazards involved.

Additionally, G-17 obligations extend to municipal advisory activities, demanding that advisors place the interests of issuers or obligated persons ahead of their own financial or competitive motives. If a dealer acts in multiple capacities—such as underwriting a bond deal while providing advisory services—it needs to disclose clearly the nature of its role and any associated conflicts. This overarching fairness principle underpins numerous MSRB rules, guiding day-to-day practices in the municipal securities markets. Violations can lead to enforcement actions by the SEC or FINRA, reinforcing the rule's pivotal role in protecting both retail and institutional participants.

G-30 (Pricing and Commissions)

MSRB Rule G-30 stipulates guidelines for fair pricing and reasonable commissions or markups in municipal securities transactions. When a dealer sells or buys municipal bonds (or other municipal securities) from customers, the aggregate price—comprising the security's prevailing market value plus any markup or markdown—must be fair and reasonable, considering all relevant factors. Among those factors are the type of security, its credit quality, maturity, liquidity, and the complexity of the transaction. Dealers also weigh prevailing market conditions, the availability of the security, and the expense incurred in executing the trade.

This rule further encompasses agency trades (where the dealer acts solely as an agent) and principal trades (where the dealer owns the bond as principal). In each scenario, the firm's compensation cannot exceed the bounds of fair dealing. Excessive markups—especially in illiquid or infrequently traded bonds—expose dealers to disciplinary action. The MSRB's stance is that customers deserve transparent execution at prices consistent with market norms, protecting them from exploitative spreads. Coupled with rules about best execution and time-of-trade disclosures, G-30 fosters an environment where municipal securities investors can transact with confidence in both pricing and firm practices.

G-45 (Reporting of Information on Municipal Fund Securities)

Rule G-45 obligates underwriters and primary distributors of certain municipal fund securities—commonly 529 plans and ABLE programs—to submit periodic reports on plan information, asset flows, and performance details to the MSRB. By collecting data on contributions, withdrawals, and investment results, the MSRB can observe trends across these education and disability-savings vehicles and potentially pinpoint areas of regulatory concern or emerging risk. Dealers must file the relevant forms electronically, usually on a semi-annual basis, disclosing both aggregated and plan-specific metrics.

This reporting requirement bolsters market transparency, letting regulators and market participants glean insights into how municipal fund securities evolve in terms of asset size, fee structures, or distribution practices. By capturing consistent, standardized data, G-45 also assists in MSRB's investor protection efforts: if certain programs exhibit unexpectedly high fees, minimal take-up rates, or questionable performance claims, the MSRB can investigate more effectively. Consequently, G-45 ensures that oversight extends to municipal fund securities, granting the same rigor of data collection and public accountability that mainstream mutual funds and other registered products typically undergo.

3.3.3 SEC Rules/Regulations

Under the securities laws, the **Securities Exchange Act of 1934** (the "Exchange Act") and the **Investment Company Act of 1940** significantly shape how products are defined, issued, and governed. Specific definitions and regulatory provisions found in these Acts clarify not only which instruments fall under federal oversight but also how fund structures must register, disclose information, and handle shareholders' interests. By establishing uniform requirements, the SEC aims to protect investors from fraudulent practices, ensure fair pricing and liquidity, and maintain confidence in U.S. capital markets.

Exchange Act of 1934 Definitions (3a11-1, 10b-18)
The Exchange Act expanded federal oversight from initial issuance (covered under the Securities Act of 1933) to encompass the **ongoing trading and market activities** of securities. Rule **3a11-1** clarifies the definition of an "equity security," ensuring that any instrument with similar risk-return characteristics to common

stock—such as convertible debt or warrants—receives the same regulatory treatment. By honing the scope of "equity security," the SEC can more consistently apply disclosure and reporting rules, insider-trading prohibitions, and proxy obligations. Meanwhile, **Rule 10b-18** governs how issuers may repurchase their own shares in the open market. This safe-harbor provision stipulates conditions on timing (e.g., not at the market open or near the close), the volume of shares that can be bought, and the bid-ask price constraints designed to avoid manipulative practices. If an issuer complies with 10b-18's guidelines, it benefits from a presumption that the share buybacks are not intended to manipulate the stock price. However, Rule 10b-18 does not grant absolute immunity; if other evidence arises indicating manipulative intent, the SEC can still investigate. In effect, the rule tries to balance an issuer's legitimate desire to return capital to shareholders or improve earnings per share metrics with the marketplace's need for fair and transparent trading.

Investment Company Act of 1940 (Sections 3, 4, 5, 12b-1)

Building on the earlier regulation of offering practices, the Investment Company Act of 1940 focuses on **pooled investment vehicles**—notably open-end mutual funds, closed-end funds, and unit investment trusts—to impose structural, registration, and operational safeguards. **Section 3** enumerates the definitions critical to distinguishing an "investment company" from other entities: if a company holds itself out as investing or trading in securities, or if more than 40% of its assets are in investment securities (excluding certain short-term paper), the Act typically applies. **Section 4** further classifies investment companies—e.g., open-end vs. closed-end—each subject to slightly different protocols for redemptions, pricing, and capital structures. This classification ensures that shareholders in open-end funds can redeem shares at net asset value, while closed-end shareholders buy and sell shares on exchanges at market prices.

Section 5 goes deeper, subdividing management companies into diversified and non-diversified funds, imposing restrictions on how much of a fund's assets can be invested in a single issuer or in controlling stakes. This distinction matters because "diversified" funds promise shareholders that no more than 5% of total assets go into any single issuer, among other concentration limits. Meanwhile, **Section 12b-1** addresses how funds can use their assets to finance distribution costs—a crucial consideration in mutual fund marketing. A "12b-1 fee" can cover expenses like broker compensation, advertising, and sales literature, allowing the fund to expand its shareholder base. However, 12b-1 fees diminish the fund's net returns, so the Act requires clear disclosure of these charges in the prospectus. Funds that enact or increase 12b-1 plans must secure shareholder approval, reflecting the principle that investors deserve a voice in how the fund's assets are spent on distribution versus portfolio management. By establishing these structural guardrails and transparency mandates, the 1940 Act aims to protect investors against excessive fees, self-dealing, or conflicts of interest, thus promoting a robust and trustworthy ecosystem for collective investment products.

Chapter 4 Understanding Trading, Customer Accounts, and Prohibited Activities

4.1 Trading, Settlement, and Corporate Actions

4.1.1 Orders and Strategies

Traders use different types of orders to achieve specific objectives or manage risk in volatile markets. A **market order** seeks immediate execution at the best available price, while a **limit order** specifies the highest acceptable purchase price or lowest acceptable sale price, prioritizing price control over speed. **Stop orders** (often called stop-loss orders) become active market orders once a security trades at or through a predetermined stop price, helping to minimize losses on a long position or protect gains on a short sale. A **good-til-canceled (GTC)** order remains active until the investor cancels it or until it executes, avoiding the need to re-enter the instructions every trading day. Additionally, some accounts allow **discretionary authority**, letting brokers trade on the investor's behalf without prior approval for each transaction, whereas **non-discretionary** accounts require explicit permission for every order. Orders may also be classified as **solicited** (recommended by the broker) or **unsolicited** (requested by the client).

Beyond these order instructions, investors can adopt various strategies reflecting outlook and risk tolerance. A **long** position involves buying shares in anticipation of an upward price move, whereas a **short** position profits if the security declines. Short sales can be **naked**, where the shares are borrowed, or **covered**, where an investor writes a call option against an owned security to generate premium income. Overall sentiment can be **bullish** (expecting prices to rise) or **bearish** (expecting decline). Executions may occur on either a **principal** basis—where the firm trades from its own inventory and charges a markup or markdown—or an **agency** basis, earning a commission for facilitating the trade between a buyer and seller. By matching the right order type and strategy to market conditions, investors and traders can position themselves for potential gains or mitigate downside risk more effectively.

4.1.1.1 Types of Orders (Market, Limit, Stop, GTC)

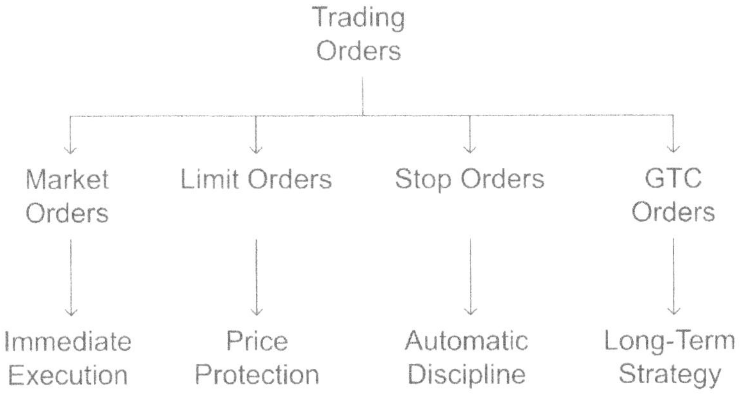

Different order types allow traders to control how and when their trades are executed, letting them balance speed of execution against price certainty. A **market order** seeks the quickest fill at the current best price, often suiting investors who prioritize immediate execution over exact entry points. In a liquid market, this typically results in fills close to the quoted bid-ask price. However, if a stock experiences high volatility or low trading volume, the execution price of a market order might deviate more significantly from the last traded price due to a thin order book or rapid price movements. Still, for actively traded securities, market orders are often used by those confident that short-term fluctuations will not materially affect their investment thesis. Institutional traders and algorithmic systems also rely on market orders to swiftly exit or enter positions when minimal delay is essential.

A **limit order**, by contrast, enforces a specific price ceiling when buying or a price floor when selling. This ensures the investor does not pay more (in the case of a buy) or receive less (in the case of a sell) than the stated limit. Because limit orders only execute if the market reaches the chosen price, they add protection against slippage, though they risk partial or no fill if the price never hits that level. Traders with strong opinions about valuation—believing a stock might temporarily spike or dip, for instance—often use limit orders to capture those favorable prices. If the security trades beyond the limit price rapidly, the order might miss the move, underscoring the trade-off between price certainty and execution speed. Real-time monitoring of fill progress is also key: partial fills can occur if only a portion of the order can be matched at the desired limit.

A **stop order** (sometimes called a stop-loss order) converts into a market order once the security's price trades at or through a designated stop price. Investors long a stock might set a sell stop below the current market to guard against steep losses if the share price falls. Once triggered, the stop becomes a market order, which can lead to executions below the stop price in fast-moving conditions. Conversely, a short seller might use a buy stop to protect profits, setting the stop above the current trading level to automatically repurchase shares if the stock rises. Stops thus provide a measure of "automatic discipline," though they do not guarantee a precise exit price, especially in swiftly changing or thinly traded markets.

A **good-till-canceled (GTC)** order is any limit or stop order that remains active until the investor cancels it or it executes—rather than expiring at the end of a trading day. While some brokerage firms impose their own maximum time frames on GTC orders (e.g., 60 or 90 days), the principle remains that the instructions persist across trading sessions. GTC orders are helpful for those who do not want to re-enter the same limit or stop instructions daily. However, as weeks or months pass, market conditions can shift dramatically, making the original limit or stop price less relevant. Investors typically revisit GTC orders periodically to ensure the order still aligns with their evolving strategy or to adjust the price in response to new developments. Combined intelligently, these order types empower market participants to tailor their trades for varying levels of price protection, speed, and control in dynamic market environments.

4.1.1.2 Discretionary vs. Non-Discretionary, Solicited vs. Unsolicited

A **discretionary account** grants the registered representative (RR) or investment advisor the authority to decide at least one of the "three A's": the asset to be traded, the amount of shares or capital involved, and the action (buy or sell). For instance, if a client signs a limited power of attorney, the RR can purchase shares without first consulting the client about each order, so long as such trades align with the customer's objectives and risk profile. Discretionary authority is often used by busy or less experienced investors who trust their advisor's judgment in spotting opportunities or responding quickly to market swings. However, it introduces heightened compliance obligations: the firm must ensure that each discretionary trade remains suitable for the client, is properly documented, and is approved by a principal. Regulators expect strict internal controls to prevent excessive or inappropriate trading (sometimes called "churning") that could generate commissions without clear client benefit.

In contrast, a **non-discretionary account** requires the RR to obtain the customer's explicit approval for every transaction. The customer typically retains full control over the "three A's" of each trade, with the RR providing recommendations or implementing orders only after securing the client's agreement. Non-discretionary arrangements are common for investors who wish to maintain day-to-day oversight of their portfolios. While this model ensures clients remain deeply involved, it can delay execution during fast-moving markets. If an RR simply chooses time and price but the specific security and quantity are already set by the customer, that limited involvement usually does not count as full discretion. Firms must correctly classify and supervise each account to avoid unauthorized discretionary activity, which can violate industry rules if the customer has not granted formal discretion.

Distinct from these control questions are **solicited vs. unsolicited transactions**. A **solicited** transaction occurs when the RR actively recommends a security or strategy. The firm must document the recommendation's rationale and ensure it meets suitability or Regulation Best Interest standards. By contrast, an **unsolicited** order originates with the customer alone, without the firm's prompting. Although the RR should still verify whether the customer understands the security's risks or complexities, the compliance burden differs. Firms generally label orders as "unsolicited" when the customer initiates them and disclaim direct responsibility for the idea itself—though best practices still require educating clients if their choice appears incompatible with known objectives. In either case, the order ticket must correctly denote whether the trade was solicited or unsolicited so that regulators and supervisors can track patterns, detect possible account abuse, and confirm proper disclosures. By distinguishing discretionary vs. non-discretionary authority and accurately marking trades as solicited or unsolicited, firms maintain clear records of who drives the investment decision, reinforcing investor protection.

4.1.1.3 Long vs. Short, Naked vs. Covered, Bullish vs. Bearish

Investors holding a **long position** in a security own it outright and anticipate that its price will rise. A classic illustration is buying shares of a stock in the hope that the company's positive earnings or market sentiment will push the share price higher. In a long equity position, the maximum risk is limited to the amount invested if the stock price plummets—yet the potential gain theoretically has no ceiling if prices climb substantially. Most retirement and retail accounts engage in straightforward long positions for their growth or income potential, relying on dividends and capital appreciation over time.

A **short position** flips the usual profit motive: the investor sells shares borrowed from a broker with the intention of buying them back ("covering") at a lower price. Short sellers gain if the security's market price drops, but face steep risk if it climbs instead—because losses can compound if the price continues rising. In many jurisdictions, initiating a short sale requires a margin account and the broker must be able to locate shares to borrow. A short sale is thus inherently more complex and risk-intensive than a long position. The difference between the short sale price and the eventual buy-to-cover price determines the net profit or loss, and sudden upward price moves can force short sellers to cover more quickly to limit damage.

Naked vs. Covered strategies often arise in the context of options or short selling. A "naked" position means the investor has not offset the risk with an underlying holding or complementary contract. For instance, a naked call writer sells call options on a stock they do not own; if the stock surges above the strike, they must purchase shares at the higher market price to deliver on assignment, exposing them to potentially unlimited loss. Conversely, a **covered** position—most famously in covered call writing—means the trader owns the underlying security. If they write call options on those shares, they can deliver the shares already in their portfolio if assigned, capping potential losses relative to a naked scenario. Owning the underlying asset also generates potential dividends or interest, though it restricts upside if the stock's price soars well beyond the option's strike.

Bullish vs. Bearish describes broad market outlooks that shape whether investors prefer long or short exposures. A **bullish** perspective implies belief in rising asset prices—hence it aligns with long stock holdings, long call options, or covered call writing as ways to profit from or slightly hedge upside potential. Meanwhile, a **bearish** stance centers on expectations of falling prices, so an investor may short the stock outright, buy put options, or write call options if they anticipate minimal upward movement. Understanding how each position's risk-reward profile connects to bullish or bearish views helps traders structure their strategies precisely. A bull may accept the limited risk of a long position, while a bear might embrace short selling's potential for swift returns—albeit balanced against far more pronounced danger if the market goes against them.

4.1.1.4 Principal vs. Agency Trades (Markup, Commission)

In a **principal** transaction, the broker-dealer (BD) is on the other side of the trade, buying from or selling to the customer directly from the BD's own inventory. Essentially, the BD acts as a dealer, committing capital and assuming the associated risk of holding that position until it is offloaded. To compensate for this risk, the BD may charge a markup (when selling shares from its inventory) or a markdown (when buying shares into its inventory) relative to the prevailing market price. This markup or markdown is factored into the trade's net price, so customers do not see it as a separate line item like a commission. While the markup should be fair and reasonable under industry rules—particularly FINRA Rule 2121 (Fair Prices and Commissions)—it can vary based on factors such as the security's liquidity, the size of the trade, and current market conditions. If a dealer is in a position to provide immediate liquidity for a relatively illiquid security, it might justify a higher markup to reflect the BD's potential difficulty in reselling those shares at a profit. Conversely, highly liquid securities generally incur smaller spreads because the risk of inventorying them is relatively low. Documentation of the markup must be transparent in the trade confirmation's net price, ensuring customers can evaluate their execution quality.

An **agency** transaction, by contrast, positions the BD as a broker or intermediary, matching buyers and sellers without committing its own capital. The firm shops the client's order in the marketplace, earning a clear commission for facilitating the trade rather than a markup on proprietary inventory. Agency commissions appear explicitly on confirmations as separate charges. This model generally suits customers who prefer clear disclosure of execution costs, and it can be advantageous in highly liquid securities where the BD can quickly find counterparties. Since the BD does not carry inventory risk, agency commissions may be lower in theory, but the total transaction cost still depends on the complexity of the trade, order size, and prevailing liquidity. If a large block order demands more sophisticated execution strategies (like negotiating with multiple market participants), the commission might reflect that extra work. Whether acting as a principal or agent, a broker-dealer must abide by best execution obligations, striving to get customers favorable prices given market conditions and client instructions. In practice, customers should verify on confirmations whether the BD acted in a principal or agency capacity, as that detail clarifies the nature of the markup or commission—and underscores the firm's role in the transaction.

4.1.2 Investment Returns

Investment returns reflect the total earnings an investor derives from holding a security over time. Common sources include **interest** (for debt instruments), **dividends** (for equity ownership), and **realized or unrealized capital gains**. Realized gains occur when the security is sold for a higher price than its cost basis, locking in profit, whereas unrealized gains exist on paper until an investor sells. Dividends typically follow a declared schedule and can serve as a steady income source, while interest payments on bonds can vary by coupon rate and credit risk. Some investors reinvest these cash flows to compound growth, while others use the payouts for ongoing income.

Beyond these cash flow components, investors also pay attention to key **yield measurements**. Examples include the **current yield**, which compares annual income to a security's current market price; **yield to maturity (YTM)** and **yield to call (YTC)** for bonds, measuring total return if held to final maturity or an earlier call date; and **total return**, which factors in both price changes and cash distributions over a specific period. Proper **cost basis tracking** ensures accurate reporting of realized gains or losses, especially when shares or lots are purchased at different times and prices. Finally, many investors gauge performance by comparing results to **benchmarks or indices** in similar markets—e.g., the S&P 500 for U.S. large-cap stocks—to judge whether their returns are competitive relative to broader trends.

4.1.2.1 Components (Interest, Dividends, Realized/Unrealized Gains)

Investment returns often arise through multiple channels, each reflecting distinct market dynamics or corporate actions. **Interest** comes into play primarily with fixed-income instruments—bonds, certificates of deposit (CDs), or certain notes—where the issuer agrees to pay a specified coupon rate on principal until maturity. For example, an investor holding a $1,000 face-value bond paying a 5% annual coupon collects $50 per year in interest. The reliability and amount of these payments hinge on the borrower's creditworthiness and the structure of the debt; if interest rates rise sharply after purchase, the market value of the older bond might decline, but coupon payments remain the same unless the issuer defaults. Investors typically report interest income as ordinary income on their tax returns, subject to rates that can differ from the treatment of capital gains or dividends.

Dividends flow mainly from equity investments, such as common or preferred stock. When a corporation's board of directors declares a dividend, existing shareholders receive a proportional distribution of the firm's profits or retained earnings. Some companies consistently pay quarterly dividends, appealing to income-focused investors; others may pay sporadic special dividends or none at all if they prefer to reinvest profits to fuel growth. Dividends can also carry favorable tax rates if designated "qualified," provided certain holding-period rules and other conditions are met. Over time, reinvesting these payouts into additional shares can accelerate growth through compounding. However, if a firm's earnings deteriorate or its capital needs shift, the board may cut or suspend dividends, sometimes causing the stock price to react negatively.

Beyond these direct cash distributions, a security's price fluctuation can generate **capital gains**. These appear in two forms: **unrealized** (paper gains or losses) and **realized** (locked in through an actual sale). **Unrealized gains** reflect the difference between the security's current market price and the investor's original purchase price, but do not produce an immediate tax event. Should the investor decide to sell, any positive difference between sale proceeds and cost basis constitutes a **realized gain**, typically subject to capital gains taxes.

The specific tax treatment—long-term vs. short-term—depends on the holding period. If a position is held for over one year, favorable long-term rates often apply; shorter holds can incur higher rates akin to ordinary income. Conversely, a sale below cost basis solidifies a capital loss that can offset other gains or reduce taxable income, subject to certain IRS limitations. Monitoring both unrealized and realized gains helps investors assess portfolio performance, manage taxation, and gauge the appropriateness of maintaining or liquidating positions in light of evolving market conditions.

4.1.2.2 Dividend Payment Dates (Record, Ex-Dividend, Payable)

When a corporation's board of directors approves a **dividend**, several key dates govern who is entitled to receive it and when. Understanding these dates is vital for investors who wish to capture dividends or avoid unexpected changes in their portfolio's value. The sequence typically includes: the **declaration date**, when the board announces the dividend; the **record date**, which determines which shareholders are on the company's books and thus eligible for the payout; the **ex-dividend date**, set by the relevant exchange or regulatory body, indicating when new buyers no longer qualify for the dividend; and, finally, the **payable date**, when the company actually distributes funds to shareholders.

On the **record date**, the corporation's transfer agent compiles a list of all registered owners. Anyone who appears as a shareholder of record on that date is entitled to receive the declared dividend. However, due to the practicalities of trade settlement, it is not enough to buy the stock on the record date itself to get the dividend; the purchase must settle on or before the record date. Because standard stock transactions usually settle in two business days (i.e., T+2), the **ex-dividend date** is set one business day before the record date for many securities. Starting on the ex-div date, shares trade without the immediate right to that declared dividend, so share prices often adjust downward by approximately the dividend amount at the start of trading on that day. If an investor buys a stock on or after its ex-dividend date, they will not receive the upcoming payout; it goes instead to whoever held the shares prior to the ex-div date. Conversely, if an investor sells shares after the ex-div date, they maintain the right to that declared dividend, even though the transfer of ownership will soon complete.

Finally, the **payable date** (or distribution date) is when the company issues checks or direct deposits to eligible shareholders. Depending on how the investor's account is set up, dividends might appear as cash credited to the brokerage account or might be automatically reinvested in additional shares through a dividend reinvestment plan (DRIP). This final step completes the dividend cycle, delivering actual cash (or new shares) to shareholders who met the record date requirements. By carefully monitoring ex-div, record, and payable dates, investors ensure they understand exactly when they are entitled to dividends and when the market may factor these payouts into a stock's price.

4.1.2.3 Yield Calculations (Current Yield, YTM, YTC, Total Return)

Determining how much an investor truly earns from a security—especially fixed-income instruments—requires a close look at various yield measures, each capturing a different aspect of cash flow and price changes. **Current yield** on a bond, for instance, calculates the annual coupon payment as a percentage of the bond's current market price. If an investor pays $900 for a bond with a $1,000 face value and a 5% ($50) annual coupon, the current yield would be $50 / $900, or approximately 5.56%. This figure helps investors see the income stream relative to what they actually spent, rather than the bond's par value. However, it does not account for potential gains or losses when the bond matures, nor does it incorporate reinvestment of coupon payments or the effect of purchasing the security at a discount or premium to par.

By contrast, **yield to maturity (YTM)** provides a more comprehensive snapshot of a bond's return if held to final maturity. The calculation factors in the coupon rate, the price paid, how many coupon payments remain, and any gain or loss realized at redemption (i.e., the difference between purchase price and par value). YTM also includes an assumed rate at which the investor could theoretically reinvest each coupon. While computing YTM typically involves a financial calculator or iterative methods because of its compounding assumptions, the resulting figure helps compare bonds with different coupons, maturities, and market prices on an apples-to-apples basis. Bonds purchased at a discount generally show a YTM above their stated coupon rate, while bonds bought at a premium reflect a lower YTM.

In some cases, an issuer reserves the right to call—or repay—bonds before maturity, prompting the use of **yield to call (YTC)**. YTC measures the return assuming the bond is called on the first possible call date, with the call price replacing the par value in the formula. This scenario becomes especially relevant when interest rates drop, making it advantageous for issuers to retire old, higher-cost debt and reissue new bonds at lower rates. Investors holding callable bonds must weigh the likelihood of early redemption, as it can shorten the bond's lifespan and reduce the overall yield, especially if they paid a premium for a higher coupon stream. Hence, many quotes for callable bonds include both YTM and YTC, highlighting whichever is lower (commonly known as the yield-to-worst).

Beyond fixed income, equity investors and multi-asset portfolios often refer to **total return**, which encapsulates price appreciation (or depreciation) plus any income distributions, such as dividends or interest, over a given period. Total return thus captures the comprehensive effect of capital gains, reinvestment, and distributions. If an equity pays dividends, the reinvested dividends can compound over time and significantly influence overall performance. Measuring total return is essential for comparing investment managers, funds, or strategies on an even footing, regardless of the specific techniques they use to generate returns. By focusing on both capital changes and periodic cash flows, total return provides a more holistic view of how effectively an investment aligns with the investor's growth or income objectives.

4.1.2.4 Cost Basis Requirements and Tracking

Maintaining accurate cost basis records is crucial for determining taxable gains or losses whenever an investor sells or redeems a security. At its core, a security's cost basis represents the original value of the investment—usually the purchase price plus any associated transaction fees or commissions. Over time, cost basis can be affected by corporate actions (e.g., stock splits, mergers, spin-offs) or other events (such as return-of-capital distributions) that alter an investor's proportionate ownership. For instance, in a 2-for-1 stock split, each share is converted into two shares, and the cost basis is generally halved per share. If the investor neglects to adjust for these splits or other material events, the reported gain or loss upon sale may be inaccurate, leading to possible underpayment or overpayment of taxes. Under federal regulations, broker-dealers must assist in cost basis recordkeeping and report these details to the IRS on Form 1099-B, although it remains the investor's responsibility to verify correctness, especially for older holdings or complicated transactions.

When securities are sold, the investor must decide which shares (i.e., specific lots) are being liquidated if multiple positions with different purchase dates and prices exist. Absent a specified lot ID, most custodians default to FIFO (first in, first out) for determining which shares were sold and what cost basis applies. However, investors can elect other methods—such as LIFO (last in, first out) or specific share identification—provided they document the choice prior to or at the time of the transaction and maintain consistent records. In mutual fund or dividend reinvestment plan (DRIP) accounts, an **average cost** method is often employed for simplicity, particularly if incremental purchases occur monthly. Outside standard purchases, inherited securities typically take on a cost basis equal to the date-of-death market value (often called "step-up" basis), while gifted securities usually retain the donor's historical basis unless their market value has fallen below that basis at the time of the gift. By diligently tracking each purchase, corporate action, and distribution, investors reduce the risk of misreporting capital gains, thus avoiding potential penalties and ensuring fair tax treatment.

4.1.2.5 Benchmarks and Indices

An **index** tracks the performance of a group of securities—stocks, bonds, or other assets—selected according to predetermined criteria such as market capitalization, sector, or geographic region. Well-known equity benchmarks include the S&P 500, Dow Jones Industrial Average, and NASDAQ Composite, each reflecting different segments of the U.S. market. Bond investors may reference the Bloomberg U.S. Aggregate Bond Index or more specific indices covering corporate, municipal, or global debt. By observing the index's daily movement, market participants gauge collective shifts in prices and sentiment, helping them interpret whether gains or losses are localized to certain securities or stem from broader trends. Over time, modifications to an index's composition—like adding fast-growing technology firms to the S&P 500—can reshape its sector balance and risk profile. Index providers set transparent inclusion rules, though some use committees that apply discretion in finalizing or removing constituents.

In a portfolio context, indices serve as **benchmarks** against which investors measure their own performance. If a mutual fund manager states they are targeting U.S. large-cap equities, the S&P 500 might be the yardstick for evaluating their results over monthly, quarterly, or annual periods. Outperforming the benchmark suggests the manager generated "alpha" (excess return), while underperformance indicates a lag behind the broader market. Passive investment vehicles, such as index mutual funds or ETFs, replicate an index by purchasing all (or a representative sample) of its components, effectively delivering the index's return minus fees. As benchmarks, indices also allow risk assessment: a portfolio manager's volatility, drawdowns, or sector allocations can be compared to the index for insights into investment style and potential vulnerabilities. Moreover, global or specialized indices—covering regions like emerging markets or industries like renewable energy—guide investors seeking to diversify beyond mainstream U.S. large-caps. By selecting appropriate benchmarks aligned with a portfolio's mandate, managers and clients maintain clarity on whether returns stem from broad market forces, specific security selection, or style biases.

4.1.3 Trade Settlement

Trade settlement finalizes ownership transfer and payment after a transaction executes. Depending on the security type, standard settlement can be **T+2** (trade date plus two business days) for most stocks and corporate bonds, **T+1** for certain government securities and listed options, or even **same day (T)** for some money market instruments. Adhering to these time frames lets clearing firms match buy and sell details, confirm availability of shares, and ensure funds move to the appropriate parties. If an investor sells a stock on Monday in a market operating T+2, the official ownership and cash exchange typically conclude by Wednesday, barring holidays or other disruptions.

Ownership records can also differ: some securities are still available in **physical certificate** form, though many investors opt for **book-entry** registration, where shares exist electronically and settle through a centralized depository. Book-entry streamlines recordkeeping, lowers administrative costs, and reduces the chance of misplaced certificates. Upon settlement, the buyer's brokerage statement updates to reflect new holdings, and the seller's account receives cash proceeds. Timely settlement is crucial, not only to meet regulatory obligations but also to avoid complications like delayed dividend claims or settlement "fails" that may invite penalties or reputational risk.

4.1.3.1 Settlement Time Frames (T, T+1, T+2)

Settlement time frames represent the interval between a trade's execution date (often called **T**) and the day when the exchange of securities and funds is finalized. In the U.S. equity markets, most common stock and corporate bond trades now settle on **T+2**, meaning two business days after the trade date. If an investor buys shares on Monday, the transaction's settlement—transfer of ownership and payment—ordinarily completes on Wednesday, barring any market holidays. The move from T+3 to T+2 in 2017 accelerated the entire post-trade process, reflecting improved technology and industrywide efforts to mitigate risk by shortening the time unsettled trades remain open. Meanwhile, some securities, notably government bonds and listed options, typically settle on **T+1**, allowing those trades to wrap up within a single business day after execution. At times, certain money market instruments or same-day government debt transactions can settle on **T**, requiring immediate transfer of funds and certificates.

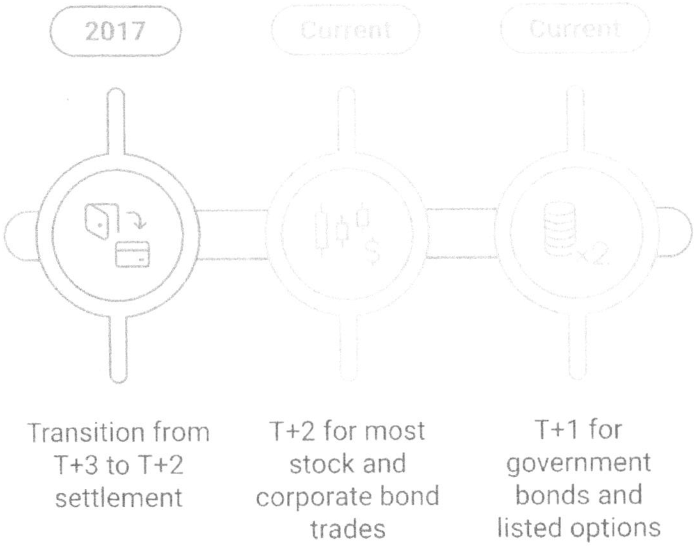

To illustrate why these time frames matter, consider an investor who sells stock on Tuesday for T+2 settlement: they do not officially relinquish share ownership or receive sales proceeds in their brokerage account until Thursday. Dividend entitlements, tax triggers, and corporate action rights hinge on recognized settlement. If another investor tries to claim a dividend record date that falls in between, they must verify that settlement occurs by that date to secure the payout. On an operational level, clearing corporations (e.g., the Depository Trust & Clearing Corporation) handle netting of buy and sell transactions, reconciling which participants owe shares or money to each other. By standardizing to T+1 or T+2, markets minimize the period of counterparty exposure—when something could fail, such as a buyer's inability to provide funds. Any exception trades outside these norms (e.g., a same-day "cash trade") requires special arrangement and often entails extra fees. Overall, adhering to recognized settlement cycles fosters market efficiency, ensures prompt portfolio updates for investors, and reduces systemic risk by not leaving trades in limbo for extended durations.

4.1.3.2 Physical vs. Book Entry

In securities markets, ownership can be documented in two primary ways: **physical certificates** or **book-entry** form. Historically, many investors received paper stock or bond certificates as tangible proof of their holdings. These certificates contained key information—issuer name, registered owner, face value (if applicable), and certificate numbers—and had to be physically delivered whenever the securities were sold or transferred. A notary or medallion signature guarantee would sometimes be required for authenticity. Holding physical certificates, however, introduced several challenges: the risk of misplacing or damaging them, the logistical delays in mailing certificates for settlement, and a potential lag in updating corporate action instructions. To address these issues, financial institutions often offered safe-custody services, but this added another layer of complexity and costs.

Over recent decades, the industry moved toward a **book-entry** system, where no physical certificate changes hands. Instead, ownership records exist electronically on the books of a central depository (e.g., the Depository Trust Company in the U.S.) or through a brokerage's internal ledger. In a book-entry transaction, when an investor buys or sells shares, the depository and the broker adjust their databases to reflect the new owner, eliminating the need to ship paper documents. This approach greatly streamlines trade settlement—trades are confirmed more quickly, and the possibility of certificates being lost in transit disappears. Additionally, corporate actions (like dividend payments, stock splits, or bond redemptions) can be processed automatically, with fewer administrative bottlenecks and a lower chance of errors. Book-entry systems also enhance market liquidity: shares become easier to re-pledge as collateral, and settlement timelines (T+2 or T+1) are more readily met without manual certificate handling.

For investors, book-entry simplifies recordkeeping and reduces costs, as custody fees, manual reissuance charges, or courier expenses for certificates become unnecessary. Some still prefer physical certificates for sentimental or privacy reasons—particularly when collecting memorabilia from historically significant companies. However, the trend remains decisively in favor of electronic ownership, especially given the benefits of real-time transfer, robust security protocols, and the ability to consolidate an investor's entire portfolio on a single brokerage statement. As a result, most modern brokerage firms automatically enroll customers in book-entry unless specifically directed otherwise. By eliminating physical paper trails, the industry enhances both efficiency and transparency, reinforcing confidence in the speed and reliability of the settlement process.

4.1.4 Corporate Actions

Corporate actions are events initiated by a corporation that affect its shareholders or bondholders, with implications for the security's market price and ownership structure. Typical examples include **stock splits** (issuing additional shares to existing holders) and **reverse splits** (consolidating shares to reduce outstanding share count), both of which alter the share price and number of shares proportionally. A company might also conduct **buybacks** or "share repurchases," using its cash reserves to reduce the public float; this can boost earnings per share by lowering the number of outstanding shares. Other noteworthy corporate actions, such as **tender offers** or **mergers**, require shareholders to decide whether to accept new terms or sell their holdings back to the company or another entity at a specified price.

From a logistics standpoint, corporations are responsible for informing shareholders of these actions and providing relevant deadlines. **Cost basis adjustments** often arise from certain corporate actions—such as stock splits or distributions that change the original purchase value—so keeping accurate records is crucial. Meanwhile, **proxy voting** allows shareholders to cast votes on significant matters like electing directors or approving major corporate decisions without attending annual meetings in person. Brokers typically distribute proxy statements on the company's behalf, ensuring that even beneficial owners holding shares in "street name" have the chance to participate in corporate governance decisions.

4.1.4.1 Splits, Reverse Splits, Buybacks, Tender Offers, Exchanges

Companies can modify their share structure and ownership dynamics through a variety of corporate actions, each carrying distinct implications for market price, share counts, and investor decision-making. A **stock split** increases the number of outstanding shares, typically to lower the per-share price and enhance liquidity. In a **2-for-1 split**, each existing share is replaced with two shares, halving the share price while leaving total market capitalization relatively unchanged. This tactic often appeals to firms whose shares have climbed to higher price levels, potentially making the stock more accessible to a broader range of retail investors. Although splits do not alter an investor's proportional stake, they necessitate a recalculation of cost basis per share for capital-gains purposes. Splits are generally viewed as a sign of confidence—management believes the stock's price has outgrown historical norms—yet some companies forgo splitting if they aim to attract only certain investor demographics or maintain a high-priced aura (e.g., Berkshire Hathaway's Class A shares).

By contrast, a **reverse stock split** reduces the number of outstanding shares, effectively consolidating multiple shares into one at a higher price. A **1-for-5 reverse split**, for instance, turns every five existing shares into one share worth roughly five times the previous price. Firms often resort to reverse splits to keep their share price above minimum exchange-listing thresholds or to signal financial stability. However, investors sometimes regard reverse splits skeptically, associating them with companies attempting to "dress up" a declining price. Like regular splits, reverse splits maintain each shareholder's total market value (apart from minor rounding factors), but demand a recalculation of cost basis per share. When such splits take place, broker-dealers and transfer agents handle the administrative changes to shareholders' positions and ownership records.

Beyond splitting shares, corporations may opt for **buybacks** (also called share repurchases) to reduce their public float and potentially bolster earnings per share or support the stock price. Companies can acquire shares on the open market—often guided by safe harbor provisions like SEC Rule 10b-18—or via **tender offers**, inviting shareholders to sell shares back to the company at a set price above current market levels. While buybacks typically occur incrementally, a tender offer has a defined window and maximum share count the company aims to purchase. This approach can be especially beneficial if management perceives the stock as undervalued or if it wants to restructure the firm's capital allocation. However, critics argue that excessive buybacks might divert funds from productive investments or artificially inflate share values.

Sometimes, a corporation or its subsidiary might propose an **exchange offer** that allows security-holders to swap existing securities (e.g., common shares or bonds) for a new issue with different terms—perhaps an alternative coupon, maturity, or share class. Exchange offers frequently arise in restructuring contexts, enabling the issuer to adjust its debt load or equity structure to enhance liquidity or meet regulatory requirements. Shareholders must evaluate whether the new securities better align with their objectives, taking into account risk, payout structure, and potential dilution. Throughout these actions—splits, reverse splits, buybacks, tender offers, or exchanges—investors receive detailed notices describing the rationale, deadlines, and instructions for participation. While none of these events inherently change an investor's percentage stake without consent (except in the case of mandatory actions like splits), they can have significant implications for market perception, share liquidity, and the firm's long-term capital strategy.

4.1.4.2 Impact on Market Price, Cost Basis Adjustments

Corporate actions can prompt immediate or gradual shifts in a security's market price, even if the total economic value for each shareholder remains unchanged. **Stock splits**, for example, typically lower the per-share price while increasing the number of shares proportionally, so investors still own the same overall value. If a company implements a 2-for-1 split and the share price halves from \$100 to \$50, the shareholder who owned 100 shares at \$100 each now holds 200 shares at \$50 each. Although the aggregate investment value (200 × \$50 = \$10,000) remains constant (ignoring any minor market fluctuations), investors often see increased liquidity and sometimes a psychological boost to trading volume. By contrast, **reverse splits** consolidate outstanding shares into fewer shares at a higher price. A 1-for-5 reverse split turning 500 shares at \$2 each into 100 shares at \$10 similarly preserves value while dramatically altering the share count and nominal share price. Reverse splits are commonly used to keep share prices above minimum listing requirements, although market participants may view them skeptically if they perceive the action as masking fundamental challenges. Both standard and reverse splits require broker-dealers to adjust share quantities in shareholders' accounts and recalculate the official open or close prices, usually in coordination with exchange procedures on the effective date.

Simultaneously, these splits necessitate **cost basis adjustments** to maintain accurate tax records. Following a 2-for-1 split, an investor's basis per share effectively halves: if it was $100 per share, it becomes $50—mirroring the new price structure and ensuring the total basis remains identical. Reverse splits accomplish the opposite; the cost basis per share increases so that the total basis remains constant across fewer shares. Other corporate actions can likewise trigger cost basis changes. **Buybacks** reduce the shares outstanding, which might lift the market price, but do not automatically revise existing shareholders' individual cost bases unless there is a partial tender or buyback that redeems some of their shares. In that scenario, the redeemed shares might produce realized gains or losses, which in turn adjust the overall basis in the remaining holdings. **Mergers** and **exchange offers**, where investors swap old shares for new, also carry their own rules—if the transaction is structured as a tax-free reorganization, investors' basis may carry over into the new shares; if it's taxable, a gain or loss could be realized at the time of exchange. Careful documentation throughout these processes helps shareholders and broker-dealers preserve accurate basis figures and avoid surprises when filing taxes or calculating gains and losses upon a subsequent sale.

4.1.4.3 Delivery of Notices and Deadlines

When a corporation undertakes a corporate action—such as a merger, stock split, tender offer, or right issue—it is bound by regulations and market protocols to inform shareholders in a timely, transparent manner. This communication process begins with a formal announcement or disclosure typically filed through regulatory channels (e.g., the SEC's EDGAR system in the United States) and supplemented by direct notices sent to shareholders or their intermediaries. The notice, often called a "corporate action notice" or "offer to purchase" in the case of a tender offer, provides detailed instructions on how investors can participate. It includes key dates (record dates, expiration dates, meeting dates, etc.) and any submission or response requirements. In some cases, the issuer also publishes the announcement via a press release or on its investor relations website for broader visibility. Delays or ambiguities in delivering these notices can jeopardize the entire action's legal standing or deprive shareholders of the chance to exercise their rights.

Because most shares trade in "street name" (beneficial ownership held through broker-dealers or banks), the company seldom contacts investors directly. Instead, it dispatches notices and related materials—like proxy statements or tender forms—to brokerage firms, transfer agents, and other intermediaries. These entities must forward the documentation to individual beneficial owners, ensuring that shareholders, whether large institutions or retail customers, receive the opportunity to review the terms and meet deadlines. The timing is critical: for example, a tender offer might include a short window (such as 20 business days) during which shareholders can accept the offer by instructing their broker. Missing that cutoff could mean forfeiting a premium price or special exchange terms. In addition, certain actions (like mandatory reorganizations) involve strict ex-dates and record dates: if shareholders sell or buy shares after these dates, they may not qualify for the corporate action's benefits.

Clearinghouses, such as the Depository Trust & Clearing Corporation (DTCC), play a major role in standardizing these notices and passing them down the chain. Brokers and custodians, in turn, interpret the event terms—like split ratios or exchange calculations—and present them to end clients, specifying the final day clients can respond (often slightly earlier than the official issuer date) to accommodate internal processing times. For voluntary actions, like tender offers or rights exercises, the broker typically requires the client to file instructions in writing or through an online portal before the broker's own cut-off date, which precedes the issuer's actual expiration date. This buffer prevents last-minute chaos and ensures instructions can be aggregated and transmitted back to the issuer or its agent. In all these interactions, clarity around deadlines and consistent delivery of notices is paramount. Any confusion—such as receiving incomplete instructions or missing the mail date—can lead to unintended consequences for investors, including the inability to participate, unclaimed proceeds, or forced redemption at suboptimal terms. Consequently, regulators impose stringent rules on the content and timing of these notices, requiring plain-language explanations of material factors, the financial impact, and the procedural steps for shareholders to follow.

4.1.4.4 Proxies and Proxy Voting

When a publicly traded corporation schedules a shareholder vote—often at an annual or special meeting—it mails out a **proxy statement** detailing the issues on the ballot and soliciting votes. These ballots can cover topics such as electing the board of directors, approving mergers or other major transactions, and ratifying the company's auditors. By issuing a **proxy**, shareholders appoint someone else (typically the company's management or a designated proxy committee) to vote on their behalf according to the preferences indicated on the proxy card. This arrangement allows investors, especially those spread across different locations, to participate in corporate governance without physically attending the meeting. Under U.S. federal securities laws (particularly Regulation 14A under the Securities Exchange Act of 1934), companies must provide clear, timely disclosures about each proposal, relevant background information, potential conflicts of interest, and the voting procedures to ensure shareholders can make informed decisions.

Beneficial owners who hold shares in "street name" through brokerage firms or banks typically receive proxy materials from their intermediary, which in turn has received them from the corporation or its transfer agent. The broker or bank forwards a voting instruction form that mirrors the official proxy card. Beneficial owners complete this form by the stated deadline, instructing the intermediary how to vote the shares. If no instructions are provided, brokers sometimes have limited authority—governed by FINRA and exchange rules—to vote shares on routine matters (like ratifying the auditor) but not on contested or significant corporate actions (often referred to as "broker non-votes"). Meanwhile, registered owners—those whose names appear directly on the corporate books—receive the official proxy materials directly from the company and cast their votes either by returning the proxy card, voting online, or calling a dedicated telephone line.

The **record date** for a shareholders' meeting—set by the board—determines who is eligible to vote. Only investors on the books as of that record date can cast ballots, even if they sell their shares afterward. Companies then distribute materials, typically including the proxy statement, annual report, and instructions describing how and when to vote (e.g., online, by mail, or telephone). Many proxy statements also provide details regarding **proxy proposals** submitted by shareholders themselves, such as calls for environmental or governance reforms; these proposals must meet certain regulatory thresholds to appear on the ballot. During contested elections or major deals (like mergers), the proxy solicitation process can become highly competitive, with management and activist shareholders issuing separate statements to persuade fellow stockholders.

Accurate tabulation of proxy votes is essential to ensure fair outcomes, and companies often employ independent inspectors of election to validate final tallies. Ultimately, proxy voting is a cornerstone of shareholder democracy, linking corporate control to the dispersed ownership structure prevalent in modern capital markets.

4.2 Customer Accounts and Compliance Considerations

4.2.1 Account Types and Characteristics

Customer accounts can take different forms based on the services, features, and risk profiles they offer. A **cash account** requires the investor to fully fund all purchases, whereas a **margin account** permits borrowing against securities—subject to regulatory and firm-specific maintenance requirements—to buy additional securities. Meanwhile, an **options account** involves additional documentation and suitability measures, since the strategies can be complex and carry higher risk of loss. Whether an account is discretionary or non-discretionary depends on who controls trading decisions: in a discretionary setup, the registered representative can make investment choices without pre-approval on each trade, whereas a non-discretionary one keeps final authority in the client's hands.

Investors and firms also consider how fees are charged. A **fee-based account** combines multiple services under a single fee, potentially benefiting those who trade frequently, while a traditional commission-based model bills per transaction. Special categories include **educational accounts** (e.g., Coverdell ESAs) where contributions and withdrawals serve schooling or related expenses under certain rules. Each account structure aims to balance the investor's goals, risk tolerance, and regulatory constraints, so understanding these distinctions is vital for selecting the account that best fits an individual's or entity's requirements.

4.2.1.1 Cash vs. Margin Accounts

A **cash account** requires that all securities be paid for in full before settlement. Investors deposit funds or transfer in assets, and each purchase transaction must be fully funded by the account holder's available cash. This structure often suits those who prefer a straightforward approach and wish to limit risk, as there is no borrowing involved. Cash accounts are typically the default option for many brokerage relationships, especially for new or conservative investors. Under regulations like the Federal Reserve Board's Regulation T, a cash account must settle in accordance with standard settlement rules—usually T+2 for equity trades—ensuring the investor has sufficient cash on hand to finalize the purchase. If a customer fails to deliver the full payment on time, the broker may issue a **free-riding** violation, freezing the account for 90 days or requiring a deposit. Dividend or interest income, if any, simply accumulates in the account balance, which can then be used for subsequent purchases or withdrawn.

By contrast, a **margin account** allows investors to borrow funds from the broker-dealer to purchase additional securities, using existing holdings as collateral. This leverage magnifies both potential gains and potential losses because it involves trading with borrowed money. A margin agreement, often accompanied by a risk disclosure document, outlines the firm's right to liquidate part or all of the collateralized positions if equity levels drop below maintenance thresholds. Regulatory bodies, including FINRA and the Federal Reserve, impose minimum initial margins (e.g., 50% under Regulation T for equities) and ongoing maintenance margins (which can vary between 25% and 30% or more, depending on firm policy and market volatility). Although margin amplifies buying power and can enable sophisticated strategies—like short selling or hedging—it carries higher risk. Investors must monitor margin calls, ensuring they meet additional deposit requirements if positions decline in value. Failure to satisfy these calls may result in forced liquidation of positions, sometimes at unfavorable prices.

4.2.1.2 Options Accounts

An options account enables customers to trade derivative contracts such as puts and calls on stocks, indexes, or other underlying instruments. Due to the higher risk and complexity associated with options strategies, broker-dealers must follow specific approval processes before permitting a client to open one. This usually begins with gathering detailed financial information—including net worth, liquid assets, investment experience, and the client's tolerance for risk—so the firm can assess suitability. Regulators require that firms provide the **Options Disclosure Document (ODD)**, sometimes called the Characteristics and Risks of Standardized Options, which explains the fundamentals of options trading, potential scenarios for profit and loss, and margin requirements for uncovered positions. The customer must acknowledge receipt of this document and sign an **options agreement**, attesting to their understanding of the risks and consenting to abide by the firm's rules. Firms often categorize approved strategies into different "levels," ranging from basic covered calls (lower risk) to sophisticated combinations or naked positions (higher risk), ensuring the customer's financial profile and experience align with the complexity of trades they plan to execute.

Once the account is approved, ongoing supervision and compliance checks remain essential. Selling options that are not covered by underlying assets (e.g., a naked call) generally requires higher margin and close monitoring, because potential losses could escalate rapidly if the underlying price moves unfavorably. The broker-dealer typically re-evaluates the customer's options authorization periodically, especially if there are material changes to the client's financial situation or trading objectives. Margin calls in options accounts can arise if the value of any uncovered (naked) positions deteriorates and the equity in the account drops below regulatory or house maintenance requirements. Clients should also note that certain strategies, like short straddles or ratio spreads, carry risk profiles that can be quite complex, necessitating a thorough understanding of break-even points, time decay, and implied volatility. Consequently, robust client education, vigilant risk oversight, and proper disclosures are integral to safely operating an options account and meeting regulatory standards.

4.2.1.3 Discretionary *vs. Non-Discretionary*

A **discretionary account** grants a registered representative (RR) or investment adviser the authority to make buy and sell decisions on the client's behalf without needing express permission for each transaction. This arrangement arises after the client signs a formal limited power of attorney or trading authorization, specifying the scope of the professional's authority. In a fully discretionary setup, the RR can determine the security, quantity, and timing of trades, provided the strategy aligns with the client's overall objectives and risk tolerance. Some firms also allow limited or partial discretion, in which the representative may only choose the timing or the price, but not both, or may only decide among certain preapproved securities. Regulations and internal policies demand careful supervision of these accounts, as discretion can open opportunities for unauthorized trading if not monitored. Clients who prefer discretionary accounts typically rely on an adviser's expertise or have limited time to manage daily market developments. Nonetheless, the brokerage firm must periodically review positions and track performance, ensuring the discretionary trades remain suitable and consistent with the investor's stated objectives.

A **non-discretionary account**, by contrast, requires client consent before any trade is executed. The representative or adviser presents recommendations and provides relevant research or analysis, but the client retains final authority over whether to proceed. Often called an "advisory" or "client-directed" relationship, this approach appeals to more hands-on investors who value autonomy or wish to maintain tight control over portfolio changes. Even if the RR believes a particular position should be liquidated or rebalanced, no change can occur until the customer explicitly agrees. Some non-discretionary clients grant "not-held" instructions for a single trade, letting the RR pick execution timing or price without requiring repeated sign-off. However, "not-held" orders do not create ongoing discretionary authority; each trade instruction is transaction-specific. Because non-discretionary customers need to approve every trade, they often receive frequent contact from their representative—especially in turbulent markets—to stay informed about emerging opportunities or risks. This detailed communication fosters a collaborative environment but can also slow execution if multiple approvals are needed quickly.

4.2.1.4 Fee-Based vs. Commission

Choosing how customers pay for brokerage and advisory services can greatly influence trading behavior, account costs, and the advisor-client dynamic. In a **fee-based account**, the investor typically pays an annual or quarterly fee—calculated as a percentage of the total assets under management—covering an array of services such as trade execution, portfolio rebalancing, and ongoing advice. This model appeals to clients who anticipate multiple trades or prefer personalized planning without worrying about individual transaction charges. Advocates of fee-based structures argue that this model aligns the advisor's compensation with the investor's long-term goals: as the portfolio grows, both parties benefit, and as it declines, the advisor's revenue decreases. Fee-based relationships can also mitigate concerns about "churning," since the representative has no direct motivation to generate commissions via frequent trades. However, investors need to confirm that the fee level correlates with the services they actually require. If the portfolio experiences few trades or minimal specialized guidance, the asset-based fee might outweigh transaction-based commissions one would have paid otherwise.

By contrast, a **commission-based account** levies separate charges on each transaction—buys, sells, or other specialized actions like option contracts. In this setup, brokers often rely on markups (principal trades) or commissions (agency trades) for revenue. A commission-based model may be more cost-effective for investors who trade infrequently or adopt a buy-and-hold approach to their portfolios. These clients pay only when they execute a trade, avoiding the blanket expense of an annual percentage fee. Yet, if trading activity escalates significantly, the cumulative commissions can become substantial. Regulators require firms to supervise commission-based accounts for excessive trading or "churning," ensuring that all transaction recommendations remain aligned with the client's best interest rather than commission production. Moreover, in a pure commission model, the adviser's compensation might depend more on transaction volume than ongoing holistic advice, prompting some clients to question whether each recommendation stems from genuine suitability or revenue incentives.

Ultimately, selecting fee-based vs. commission requires comparing the frequency of anticipated trades, desired advice and planning support, and comfort with different cost disclosures. Many brokerage firms now offer "hybrid" arrangements blending fees for certain services—like continuous asset management—alongside standard commissions for specialized transactions, hoping to provide flexibility for diverse client preferences. Regardless of the structure, transparency remains paramount: investors should be able to understand and estimate their total expenses under each model, weigh the pros and cons of paying per trade vs. paying a predictable fee, and confirm that the arrangement suits their investment style and complexity.

4.2.1.5 Educational Accounts

Educational accounts offer tax-advantaged ways to save and invest for a child's future academic expenses. Though **529 Plans** are a well-known option, these are typically categorized as municipal fund securities (discussed elsewhere in this book). Another prominent structure is the **Coverdell Education Savings Account (ESA)**, commonly referred to as an "Educational IRA." A Coverdell ESA allows individuals to make annual, non-deductible contributions (capped at a relatively modest amount per beneficiary) that can grow tax-free if used for qualifying educational costs. Qualified expenses include primary and secondary school expenditures in addition to tuition, fees, books, and supplies at post-secondary institutions. Coverdell ESAs also have income restrictions for contributors: once an individual's modified adjusted gross income (MAGI) exceeds certain thresholds, the allowable contributions phase out. Any unused balance must be disbursed or rolled over to a younger family member by the time the original beneficiary reaches age 30, preventing indefinite tax deferral. This forced distribution rule can result in taxable earnings plus a penalty if the funds are not used for qualified education expenditures.

Beyond Coverdell ESAs, investors sometimes use **Uniform Transfers to Minors Act (UTMA)** or **Uniform Gifts to Minors Act (UGMA)** accounts for educational goals, though these custodial vehicles are not exclusively limited to schooling costs. A custodian manages assets on behalf of the minor until reaching the age of termination (defined by state law), at which point the beneficiary gains full control. While UTMA/UGMA assets can be spent at any time for the child's welfare, not solely on education, many families find them helpful to cover schooling expenses or preliminary college fees. However, UTMA/UGMA balances belong irrevocably to the minor and may have a negative impact on financial aid calculations, since they are treated as the student's assets. When opening any educational account—Coverdell ESA, custodial, or another specialized plan—broker-dealers must verify that clients understand the contribution limits, potential tax consequences, and distribution rules to ensure the vehicle aligns with the family's financial and academic needs.

4.2.2 Customer Account Registrations

Opening a brokerage account begins with selecting a registration style that best suits the investor's goals and legal structure. **Individual accounts** are owned by a single person, who retains full control and accepts all associated tax and trading responsibilities. **Joint accounts**—often labeled as Joint Tenants with Rights of Survivorship (JTWROS) or Tenants in Common (TIC)—involve two or more owners who share assets but differ on how ownership passes if one owner dies. Corporations and other institutions typically register under a corporate or institutional format, requiring documentation proving the entity's legal authority to invest. Additionally, **trust accounts**—either revocable or irrevocable—place management in the hands of a designated trustee, who must oversee investments according to the trust's governing documents and the beneficiaries' best interests.

Various special scenarios also demand unique registration approaches. **Custodial accounts** (UTMA/UGMA) let an adult manage funds for a minor's benefit until the child reaches a specified legal age. **Partnership accounts**, meanwhile, enable a formal partnership to pool resources for trading, with signatories acting on behalf of the group. Retirement accounts, such as **IRAs** or other qualified plans, come with separate rules on contributions and required minimum distributions (RMDs), all designed to encourage long-term saving while imposing tax consequences for early or missed withdrawals. In every instance, the brokerage firm will review the account's legal structure and obtain supporting paperwork—like trust documentation, partnership agreements, or corporate resolutions—to confirm trading authority and ensure compliance with relevant laws.

4.2.2.1 Individual, Joint, Corporate/Institutional

An **individual account** belongs to a single owner who is solely responsible for trading decisions, instructions, and liabilities. In these accounts, the broker-dealer collects identifying information such as name, address, and Social Security number, along with financial background details to assess suitability. Only the owner is authorized to make deposits or withdrawals and direct trades, though they can, if desired, grant power of attorney or trading authorization to another party. Legally, assets in an individual account belong only to that named person, so upon the owner's death, they typically transfer according to the individual's will or designated beneficiaries, rather than to any co-owner (there is no co-owner in this case). Brokers must pay close attention to instructions that vary from the standard arrangement—such as requests to permit an adult child or financial caretaker to trade—ensuring formal documentation is on file.

Joint accounts add complexity by introducing multiple owners. The two most common forms are **Joint Tenants with Rights of Survivorship (JTWROS)** and **Tenants in Common (TIC)**. With JTWROS, if one co-owner dies, the entire account balance automatically transfers to the surviving owner(s), bypassing probate. This arrangement commonly appears in spousal accounts or other close relationships where owners expect the property to stay with the survivors. In contrast, TIC splits ownership according to a specified percentage or proportion for each party; upon one owner's death, their share is distributed according to their estate or named beneficiaries, rather than automatically rolling over to the surviving co-owners. Either way, each owner in a joint account can generally enter trades and withdraw funds on behalf of the entire account, subject to firm policies requiring all owners' signatures on the account documentation. The broker-dealer must also clearly document the method for dividing or transferring assets if a dispute arises or the relationship changes.

When dealing with **corporate/institutional accounts**, the firm must confirm that the entity opening the account has authority to invest and trade. This process often involves obtaining a corporate resolution or similar authorizing document, which specifies who can act on behalf of the company—such as officers or designated employees—and clarifies any limitations on those powers. A board of directors might need to pass a resolution empowering a particular officer to open accounts and execute trades. Institutions, ranging from small nonprofits to large multinational corporations, may impose restrictions on the types of investments that fit their operational or liquidity needs. Broker-dealers thus conduct thorough diligence, reviewing the entity's governing documents and verifying that signatories are duly appointed. Furthermore, institutional accounts often feature advanced trading preferences, specialized settlement instructions, and potentially higher margin capabilities, reflecting the scale and sophistication of these organizations. Once the setup is complete, the broker-dealer remains vigilant about compliance—for instance, ensuring that any changes in authorized personnel or ownership structure are captured in updated account records.

4.2.2.2 Trust Accounts (Revocable, Irrevocable)

A **trust account** is created when the grantor (sometimes called the settlor) transfers assets into a legal entity—called a trust—and appoints a **trustee** to manage and invest those assets for the benefit of designated beneficiaries. From a broker-dealer's perspective, opening such an account requires reviewing the trust documentation (often called the trust agreement or indenture) to verify who has authority to direct trades, whether there are any investment restrictions, and the exact manner in which distributions must occur. This helps ensure that the brokerage firm accepts orders only from the authorized trustee(s) and that it doesn't inadvertently violate the trust's provisions or the grantor's objectives. Generally, the trustee owes a fiduciary duty of loyalty and prudence to beneficiaries, meaning they must manage the assets for the beneficiaries' best interests, not their own.

Revocable (Living) Trusts allow the grantor to alter or terminate the trust at any time during their lifetime. Because the grantor retains a high level of control—often serving as both trustee and beneficiary—assets in a revocable trust remain part of the grantor's estate for tax purposes. Upon the grantor's death or incapacitation, a successor trustee typically steps in to manage or distribute assets according to the instructions contained in the trust document. From a compliance standpoint, a brokerage firm must confirm who can instruct the firm once the initial trustee can no longer serve, especially if the grantor was that trustee. In the interim, because it is revocable, the grantor can remove assets at will, change beneficiaries, and alter the trust terms. This flexibility suits individuals seeking uninterrupted control of their assets while establishing a framework for a seamless transition upon death or disability.

Irrevocable Trusts, by contrast, cannot be changed or dissolved once established, barring very limited exceptions or court intervention. When the grantor places assets into an irrevocable trust, they effectively relinquish ownership—thereby removing those assets from their taxable estate in many cases. However, this also means the grantor loses direct authority over the property. The trustee appointed in an irrevocable trust is bound by the terms of the trust agreement and state laws to manage assets in the best interests of the beneficiaries. With irrevocable trusts, brokerage firms pay close attention to any constraints on investment style or distribution frequency that the trust document spells out. An example might be an irrevocable trust that states dividends must be distributed monthly to a specific beneficiary, while capital gains must be reinvested for another beneficiary's future use. The trustee—often a third-party fiduciary, trust company, or attorney—will carry out these directives. Since the trust is irrevocable, the trust itself will typically be responsible for its own tax liabilities, filing separate returns if required, and reporting gains or losses accordingly.

In both revocable and irrevocable trusts, broker-dealers must confirm the precise trustee powers: whether they can open margin accounts, engage in options strategies, or invest in certain high-risk instruments. Some trust agreements can explicitly forbid speculation or short-selling, while others grant wider latitude. The trustee's fiduciary obligations also mean they must balance the beneficiaries' needs with prudent portfolio management, as any breach of these duties can result in legal or regulatory scrutiny. By thoroughly examining the trust documentation at account inception and periodically updating records if trustees or provisions change, the brokerage firm helps ensure regulatory compliance and protect the interests of the trust's beneficiaries.

4.2.2.3 Custodial Accounts (UTMA/UGMA)

Custodial accounts established under the **Uniform Transfers to Minors Act (UTMA)** or the **Uniform Gifts to Minors Act (UGMA)** allow adults—called custodians—to manage assets on behalf of a minor until that minor reaches the age of termination defined by state law. In either arrangement, the minor is the sole, legal owner of the account's holdings, but lacks the legal capacity to direct trades or withdraw funds. The custodian acts as fiduciary, ensuring that all investments and disbursements serve the best interests of the minor—whether that involves covering educational expenses or, in some states, anything generally deemed beneficial for the child's welfare. Because assets in a custodial account belong irrevocably to the minor, the custodian cannot take them back or list them as personal property. Consequently, these balances may be subject to the "kiddie tax" and can also reduce the child's eligibility for financial aid once they apply to college, as student-owned assets are often weighted more heavily in aid calculations.

A UTMA account typically permits a wider variety of assets (e.g., real estate, tangible property) to be gifted or transferred into custody, whereas UGMA accounts historically allowed only securities and cash. Depending on state law, UTMAs can have a higher age of termination—sometimes 21 or 25, rather than 18—giving custodians additional time to oversee the assets before releasing them outright to the beneficiary. Broker-dealers that open UTMA/UGMA accounts must verify the custodian's authority and confirm that the minor's Social Security number is on record for tax reporting. Since all gains and dividends are taxed in the minor's name, custodians often watch for net unearned income thresholds that trigger higher tax rates under the kiddie tax. Additionally, custodial accounts cannot typically be opened on margin or used to purchase certain riskier instruments, as regulators expect custodians to maintain a conservative profile suited to a minor's best interests. Once the minor reaches the specified age of majority or termination, the custodian's authority ends and the account's control shifts fully to the beneficiary, including the power to withdraw or liquidate all assets without restriction.

4.2.2.4 Partnerships

A partnership account is set up when two or more parties form a partnership entity—often formalized through a **partnership agreement**—and pool their resources for investing or conducting business. The brokerage firm opening the account will typically request a copy of this partnership agreement to confirm who has trading authority, how profits and losses are shared, and any restrictions on permissible transactions. One key feature is that each partner is considered an owner, though the agreement may vest day-to-day decision-making in one partner (a managing partner) or a subset of the partners (an executive committee). For general partnerships, all partners share liability for the entity's obligations, while limited partnerships separate liability among general partners (who bear the most risk and actively manage) and limited partners (passive investors). Because these liability distinctions can affect the partnership's financial exposures, broker-dealers must carefully review the agreement to ensure compliance with relevant rules and to manage risk appropriately.

From a regulatory perspective, each partner's personal financial background, investment objectives, and potential affiliations (e.g., if one partner is affiliated with another broker-dealer) should be accounted for during the new account setup. Typically, the firm will also confirm whether the partnership agreement requires unanimous consent for trades or capital withdrawals, or if certain partners alone may act on behalf of the group. Any subsequent changes—like a new partner joining, a current partner exiting, or shifts in who has trading authority—often necessitate an updated partnership agreement on file. Additionally, broker-dealers must confirm the tax classification of the partnership, since earnings and losses "flow through" to individual partners for tax purposes. This pass-through nature can influence how gains and losses are allocated, as well as the way distributions and capital contributions appear in the firm's records. Ultimately, partnership accounts allow multiple collaborators to combine efforts and invest according to the partnership's collective goals, but the complexities of shared ownership and fiduciary responsibility demand close attention to documentation and ongoing disclosures.

4.2.2.5 Retirement Accounts (IRAs, Qualified Plans) – Contributions and RMDs

Establishing **retirement accounts** requires special attention to both federal tax regulations and each plan's unique rules. Two major categories dominate the retirement landscape: **Individual Retirement Accounts (IRAs)** and **Qualified Plans** sponsored by employers (e.g., 401(k), 403(b), profit-sharing plans). While IRAs are generally personal arrangements between an individual and the financial institution, qualified plans are established by a company for its employees under IRS-approved guidelines. One of the biggest differences lies in who has the fiduciary responsibility over the assets (the plan trustee/employer in a qualified plan vs. the IRA owner in an individual account) and the annual IRS reporting requirements, such as Form 5500 for certain employer plans. Regardless of the account type, tax advantages (e.g., contributions being tax-deductible or growth being tax-deferred) are conditioned on following strict IRS contribution limits, distribution rules, and early withdrawal penalty provisions.

Contributions to traditional IRAs and most qualified plans are typically pre-tax or tax-deductible, meaning the individual (or employer, in the case of a qualified plan) can reduce their taxable income by the contribution amount, subject to annual limits and any phase-outs based on income or coverage under another retirement plan. For instance, the IRS sets an annual dollar limit for IRA contributions (adjusted periodically for inflation), and only individuals under a certain age may qualify for catch-up contributions in addition to the regular limit. Employer-sponsored plans often set their own deferral percentage limits for 401(k) or 403(b) participants, but these too are governed by overall IRS maximums. Roth IRAs, by contrast, involve after-tax contributions (i.e., no immediate tax deduction), yet enjoy tax-free growth and qualified tax-free withdrawals later, if the owner meets certain holding period and age requirements. Similarly, some employer plans now offer a Roth 401(k) component, merging Roth tax treatment with higher 401(k) contribution ceilings.

Required Minimum Distributions (RMDs) become a significant factor once the account owner—or plan participant—reaches a certain age (often 73 under current law for those who turn 72 after 2022, but historically 70½ or 72 in earlier rule sets). With most tax-deferred plans (traditional IRAs, SEP IRAs, SIMPLE IRAs, and 401(k)-type accounts), participants must begin taking annual distributions of at least the RMD amount no later than the required beginning date (RBD). The IRS publishes life expectancy tables, which combined with the prior year-end account balance, determine each year's RMD. Failing to withdraw the RMD promptly triggers a steep excise tax—50% on any shortfall of the required amount, although recent legislative changes have proposed or enacted lowering this penalty in specific scenarios. Roth IRAs, in contrast, do not have an RMD requirement for the original owner during their lifetime, though beneficiaries must observe post-death distribution rules. In employer plans, if the participant is still working past the normal RMD age (and does not own 5% or more of the company), RMDs may be postponed until actual retirement. Brokerage firms opening retirement accounts must guide clients on these nuances—e.g., tracking contributions to ensure they do not exceed annual limits, flagging the plan holder or IRA owner on upcoming RMD deadlines, and ensuring any inherited IRAs or plans comply with designated beneficiary distribution rules. Ultimately, staying compliant with contribution and RMD provisions is essential to preserve the account's tax-advantaged status and avoid IRS penalties.

4.2.3 Anti-Money Laundering (AML)

Anti-Money Laundering (AML) efforts revolve around preventing illicit funds from making their way into the legitimate financial system. At a high level, they require financial firms to identify unusual patterns of transactions, implement safeguards for monitoring customer account activity, and train personnel to recognize potential "red flags." Although the importance of detecting suspicious behavior is self-evident, AML rules underscore the legal obligation to document and escalate such concerns, thereby reducing opportunities for criminals to conceal or "clean" ill-gotten gains. This broad framework is crucial because the financial industry can inadvertently become a conduit for money derived from unlawful acts if proper procedures and oversight are not in place.

In practice, firms maintain compliance by adopting written AML policies, training staff to watch for indicators of questionable transactions, and verifying the identities of clients who open or maintain accounts. In addition, regulatory guidelines require that these programs be regularly tested and updated to address emerging money laundering tactics. Specific reporting obligations and the agencies involved in coordinating AML enforcement are addressed in subsequent sub-sections, but the essential concept is that all securities professionals must remain vigilant and immediately report any transaction that appears atypical or inconsistent with a customer's known business or financial profile.

4.2.3.1 Definition and Stages of Money Laundering (Placement, Layering, Integration)

Money laundering, in its most fundamental sense, is the process of taking funds obtained through illegal activity and masking their origin so they appear legitimate when reintroduced into the financial system. For individuals engaged in illicit enterprises, the goal is to separate the criminal proceeds from their underlying offenses, making it difficult—or ideally impossible—for authorities and financial institutions to trace the money back to its unlawful source. This is a global concern that cuts across borders and involves numerous industries, including the securities sector. While the specific tactics used by criminals can vary widely, the overall process typically follows a three-stage pattern known as placement, layering, and integration.

The **placement** stage is the initial point at which illicit funds enter the financial system. During placement, individuals will often use cash-intensive businesses, structuring (breaking up large sums into smaller amounts), or direct deposits into bank or brokerage accounts to avoid triggering immediate detection. Once successfully placed into a financial institution, the proceeds move to the **layering** stage. Here, launderers create multiple transactions designed to obscure the trail of the funds. They might transfer money across different institutions, convert cash into monetary instruments, or channel funds through complex investments. The more intricate and numerous the transactions, the harder it becomes to determine where the money actually originated. Finally, the **integration** stage reintroduces the laundered funds back into the legitimate economy in a manner that appears normal. At this point, money that began as illegal proceeds may emerge as "clean" capital in the form of real estate, business income, or investment returns.

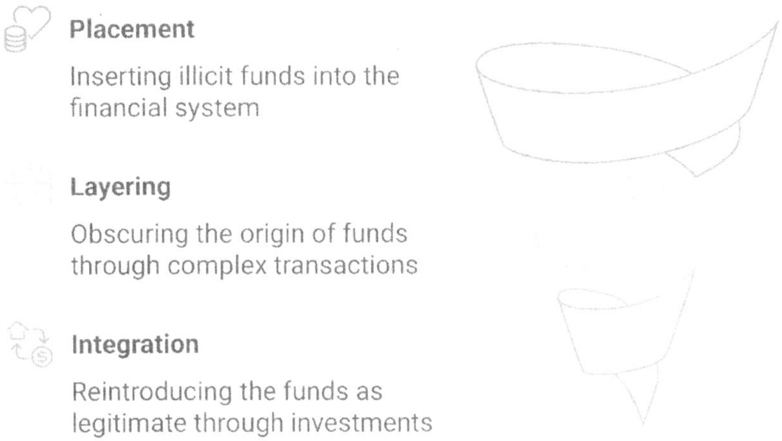

A concise overview of these stages, along with a few representative tactics, is presented below:

Stage	Primary Objective	Common Tactics	Example
Placement	Insert illicit funds into the financial system	Cash deposits, structuring into smaller transactions	Depositing small amounts into multiple bank or brokerage accounts
Layering	Obscure the trail of the illicit origin	Multiple transfers, complex trades, currency exchanges	Wiring funds between foreign and domestic accounts repeatedly
Integration	Reintroduce cleaned funds as legitimate	Using shell companies, purchasing legitimate assets	Investing in real estate or publicly traded securities

Understanding these three phases is crucial because each phase can intersect with legitimate brokerage activities in different ways. A criminal might place funds by depositing illicit capital into a new brokerage account, layer them by converting those assets into various securities and liquidating them through multiple jurisdictions, and finally integrate them by withdrawing the proceeds under the guise of legitimate investment gains. At every point in this chain, financial firms need to recognize anomalies that might signal suspicious activity. For instance, a sudden influx of large deposits from multiple, seemingly unrelated sources could indicate placement, while rapidly shifting funds between unfamiliar counterparties might suggest layering. If each component of a transaction chain is regarded in isolation, it can be difficult to notice illicit patterns. Consequently, a robust understanding of the three stages helps compliance teams tie those pieces together.

Although further sections explore specific reporting obligations and the institutional frameworks designed to detect such misconduct, the stages outlined here remain the core conceptual structure of money laundering. Knowing how placement, layering, and integration function, and how they may appear in a brokerage account setting, equips financial professionals with the insight they need to act swiftly and accurately when suspicious situations arise. By grasping these fundamental stages in depth, firms not only fulfill regulatory expectations but also protect the integrity of the financial markets from criminal exploitation.

4.2.3.2 AML Compliance Programs

A robust Anti-Money Laundering (AML) compliance program is a foundational element in safeguarding brokerage firms and other financial institutions from becoming unwitting conduits for illegal funds. Unlike the general concept of money laundering—discussed previously in terms of placement, layering, and integration—an AML compliance program concentrates on the practical systems, policies, and procedures required to detect and deter such activity. These programs are not simply advisory; they are mandated by various laws and regulations that emphasize the accountability of financial organizations for monitoring customer transactions, identifying irregularities, and reporting suspicious behaviors to the appropriate authorities. While the specific requirements differ across jurisdictions, in the United States these obligations are strongly influenced by the Bank Secrecy Act (BSA) and subsequent legislation that expanded its scope.

Developing and maintaining an AML compliance program typically involves several core components that work together to manage risk. Firms start by implementing firm-wide written policies and procedures tailored to their specific lines of business, ensuring that these guidelines are both clear and enforceable. They designate a qualified AML compliance officer who oversees day-to-day execution of the policies and coordinates with external regulators as needed. Independent testing or audits are then conducted at regular intervals, allowing the firm to verify that its controls are both effective and up-to-date. In parallel, all employees—particularly those involved in handling customer transactions—undergo ongoing AML training that is relevant to their roles. Because these elements must fit together seamlessly, the AML compliance officer plays a critical role in bridging gaps between various departments, ensuring consistent application of the procedures, and promptly responding to any emerging threats or regulatory updates.

On the next page is a concise illustration of the common "pillars" of an AML compliance program:

One of the most important reasons these programs must be carefully tailored to each firm is that risk levels can vary significantly based on customer demographics, geographic exposure, and types of financial products offered. A smaller brokerage that primarily serves local investors might have different vulnerabilities compared to a large multinational firm with clients around the globe. Consequently, AML officers and senior management routinely assess and refine their controls to account for changing business strategies, new products, or updated regulatory guidelines. Effective compliance programs also support timely and accurate reporting of suspicious activity, a topic that the following sections will delve into more deeply. By diligently maintaining these critical elements, firms help protect not just themselves but also the broader integrity of financial markets from criminal exploitation.

4.2.3.3 Suspicious Activity Report (SAR), Currency Transaction Report (CTR)

Suspicious Activity Reports (SARs) and Currency Transaction Reports (CTRs) are two critical tools that financial institutions use to fulfill their anti-money laundering obligations. Unlike broader AML policies, which focus on programmatic frameworks and company-wide controls, SARs and CTRs are tied directly to the detection and documentation of specific transactions. For brokerage firms, these reports signal the presence of activity that could be associated with illegal conduct—ranging from money laundering to terrorist financing—and help build an official record for regulators to identify larger criminal or illicit patterns. Although each report serves a distinct function, both fall under the legal and regulatory umbrella of the Bank Secrecy Act, which compels financial institutions to monitor and disclose certain cash movements and suspicious activities to the appropriate government authorities.

The CTR requirement is triggered when a customer conducts cash transactions of more than $10,000 with a single financial institution in one business day. These can be deposits, withdrawals, currency exchanges, or other cash-related actions that collectively exceed the threshold. The rationale behind this requirement is that large cash transactions are inherently more prone to misuse by criminals seeking to place or layer illicit funds. SARs, on the other hand, come into play when a transaction—or a series of transactions—raises a suspicion of illegal activity or lacks a clear economic or business purpose. Generally, firms file SARs when they detect transactions involving $5,000 or more that exhibit warning signs of money laundering or other criminal enterprises. Suspicion may be triggered by actions such as rapid movement of funds to high-risk jurisdictions, inconsistent customer behavior relative to their stated financial profile, or account patterns that appear artificially structured to evade reporting thresholds.

The table below highlights some core differences and key elements of CTRs and SARs:

Report	Primary Trigger	Threshold	Time Frame for Filing	Purpose
Currency Transaction Report (CTR)	Cash transactions exceeding $10,000 in one business day	$10,000+ in a single day	15 calendar days (in most cases)	Documents large cash deposits, withdrawals, or exchanges to help identify money laundering risks.
Suspicious Activity Report (SAR)	Any transaction that appears to involve illegal activity or lacks a legitimate business rationale	$5,000+ (if suspicious)	30 calendar days from detection (extensions possible in certain scenarios)	Alerts authorities to transactions that may indicate money laundering, fraud, or other criminal activity.

Filing these reports is not just a bureaucratic formality: timely and accurate reporting helps government agencies analyze emerging threats, trace criminal proceeds, and develop targeted enforcement strategies. For firms, failing to file a CTR or SAR when required can result in severe penalties, including substantial fines and potential regulatory sanctions against both the organization and individuals responsible for oversight. Because of these stakes, it is essential that employees remain vigilant, receive adequate training, and understand both the legal thresholds and the context in which SARs and CTRs should be filed. By diligently adhering to these requirements, broker-dealers bolster the broader effort to maintain a transparent, safe, and compliant financial marketplace.

4.2.3.4: FinCEN, OFAC, SDN List

The Financial Crimes Enforcement Network (FinCEN) is a bureau of the U.S. Department of the Treasury tasked with collecting, analyzing, and distributing information related to financial transactions for the purpose of combating money laundering, terrorist financing, and other illicit activities. While FinCEN does not initiate prosecutions or directly enforce criminal statutes, it functions as an intelligence hub. It establishes regulations under the authority of the Bank Secrecy Act (BSA) and leverages the information from Suspicious Activity Reports (SARs) and Currency Transaction Reports (CTRs) to detect and follow the trail of illegal funds. FinCEN also provides guidance to financial institutions on emerging threats and trends, ensuring that broker-dealers remain vigilant against new techniques criminals may employ to conceal illicit proceeds.

On the enforcement side of the Treasury Department's oversight lies the Office of Foreign Assets Control (OFAC). OFAC administers and enforces economic and trade sanctions against targeted foreign countries, entities, and individuals as a matter of U.S. foreign policy and national security. The rationale is to cut off financial support to individuals or organizations deemed a threat, be it because of terrorism, narcotics trafficking, proliferation of weapons of mass destruction, or other destabilizing activities. Any U.S. person or business, including securities firms, is generally prohibited from dealing with sanctioned entities. Compliance departments typically develop protocols to detect and block transactions involving banned parties, often by integrating specialized screening software into the account-opening process or by applying real-time transaction monitoring to ongoing relationships.

Central to OFAC's enforcement regime is the Specially Designated Nationals (SDN) List, which enumerates individuals, companies, and organizations with whom all U.S. persons are forbidden from doing business. If a brokerage firm discovers that a client is listed on the SDN List, or that a prospective customer appears on it, the firm must immediately freeze any assets under its control and refrain from executing further transactions on that party's behalf. It is also required to file the appropriate blocked property and regulatory reports. In many instances, the discovery of an SDN match prompts a thorough internal investigation to confirm that it is not a "false positive," given that certain names can be common. Rapid and accurate identification of true matches is critical, however, because failing to block a transaction for an SDN-designated individual can result in substantial penalties.

On the next page is a quick reference table summarizing the primary responsibilities of FinCEN and OFAC, along with the significance of the SDN List:

Entity	Primary Role	Key Tool	Compliance Implication
FinCEN	Collects and analyzes financial data to fight money laundering and terrorist financing	Regulations under the BSA	Guides broker-dealers in SAR/CTR filing and AML program implementation
OFAC	Enforces U.S. economic and trade sanctions against designated entities and individuals	Sanctions Programs	Requires broker-dealers to block or reject transactions with sanctioned parties
SDN List (OFAC)	Identifies specific individuals and entities subject to asset freezes and transaction bans	Publicly updated listings	Firms must block assets and transactions upon discovering an SDN match

To ensure compliance, broker-dealers and their compliance officers monitor FinCEN advisories for emerging threats, update their AML policies to align with regulatory expectations, and routinely check new and existing clients against the SDN List. This integrated process underscores how FinCEN's intelligence function and OFAC's enforcement protocols intertwine in broader anti-money laundering and counter-terrorism financing efforts. By combining diligent account screening with timely reporting, firms help protect the integrity of the markets and support national security objectives, fulfilling both their legal obligations and their ethical responsibilities as gatekeepers of the financial system.

4.2.4 Books, Records, and Privacy Requirements

The maintenance of accurate books and records is a fundamental responsibility for broker-dealers, as these documents provide a transparent record of all client transactions and firm activities. Regulators expect firms to retain a range of materials—such as transaction confirmations, account statements, and corporate documents—for specific periods of time to ensure that complete information is available for examinations or investigations. In addition, keeping these records in an organized, easily retrievable format helps firms address customer inquiries and resolve any disputes that might arise. Because of the high stakes involved, many broker-dealers use dedicated systems and policies that standardize how documents are created, reviewed, and archived, ensuring consistency throughout the organization.

On the privacy side, firms must also protect their clients' nonpublic personal information from unauthorized access or disclosure. Regulatory guidelines call for safeguarding sensitive data like Social Security numbers, account balances, and other identifying details, and they require clear policies explaining how and why this information is collected. Firms typically provide customers with written notices explaining these practices and offering options for limiting the sharing of such details. By taking both recordkeeping and privacy obligations seriously, broker-dealers demonstrate their commitment to upholding industry standards, preserving customer trust, and maintaining readiness for any regulatory review.

4.2.4.1 Retention Requirements, Confirmations, Account Statements

A cornerstone of regulatory compliance is the obligation for broker-dealers to maintain accurate and accessible records of all activities related to client accounts. These recordkeeping obligations are primarily governed by SEC rules (notably Rules 17a-3 and 17a-4) and FINRA requirements, which stipulate the specific documents that must be created and preserved, along with the length of time those records must be kept. The premise behind these guidelines is straightforward: regulators need a reliable paper (or electronic) trail of transactions to ensure that customer disputes can be resolved, improper conduct can be investigated, and market integrity is preserved. In practice, these demands translate into strict internal protocols for retaining trade blotters, order tickets, communications with clients, and importantly for our purposes, trade confirmations and account statements. By systematically archiving these records, a firm bolsters both its own legal defense and its standing with regulators, since incomplete or disorganized records can result in heavy fines or enforcement actions.

Trade confirmations serve as a critical point of reference for both the customer and the brokerage firm, documenting the key details of each executed trade. These details include the security purchased or sold, the price at which it was executed, applicable fees or commissions, and the settlement date. Although the specifics of how soon confirmations must be provided can vary slightly depending on the transaction type, firms typically send them on or before the first business day following trade execution (commonly referred to as T+1). Under SEC regulations, these confirmations must be kept on file for at least three years, but many broker-dealers opt for longer retention periods to ensure that they can address potential disputes that emerge well after the transaction date. Retaining confirmations also enables auditors to piece together a cohesive history of each client's trading activity and verify that commissions or other fees were properly disclosed.

Customer account statements, on the other hand, present a broader view of a client's overall holdings, typically reported on a monthly or quarterly basis. If an account has activity during the statement cycle—such as trades, deposits, or dividend payments—statements are often issued monthly. If there is little or no account activity, quarterly statements are generally sufficient. These statements outline the securities positions in the account, the cash balance, any margin debit or credit, and a summary of transactions over the period. Compared to confirmations, account statements typically have longer retention requirements under SEC rules, often running six years or more, in part because they capture a cumulative perspective of the client's relationship with the firm. Statements function as a snapshot of the account's status at defined intervals, and their preservation forms an essential part of a broker-dealer's audit trail. They also enable regulators to ensure that firms are delivering transparent, timely information about fees, holdings, and changes in account value—key elements for maintaining trust in the broker-customer relationship.

Below is a concise overview of the usual minimum retention periods for confirmations and account statements:

Document Type	Typical Minimum Retention	Key Regulatory Rationale
Trade Confirmations	3 Years	Proof of transaction terms, enabling audits and dispute resolution
Customer Statements	6 Years	Ongoing record of account balances, transactions, and overall holdings

By diligently adhering to record retention schedules for both confirmations and account statements, broker-dealers fulfill an essential regulatory obligation while also protecting their clients' interests. In the broader context, these documents interact with a firm's other archival responsibilities—including items like account opening forms and correspondence—to form a complete tapestry of activity that regulators can examine. When combined with effective supervisory systems and a consistent privacy policy, robust record retention ensures that a firm's operations remain transparent, organized, and prepared to answer questions or address concerns at any stage of a customer's financial journey.

4.2.4.2 Business Continuity Plans (BCP)

A Business Continuity Plan (BCP) outlines how a broker-dealer will respond to and recover from significant business disruptions, such as natural disasters, cyberattacks, or widespread power outages. While day-to-day compliance requirements ensure that firms protect customer assets and maintain accurate records, a BCP ensures that these obligations continue to be met even under adverse circumstances. In the securities industry, regulators like FINRA mandate that member firms develop and regularly update their BCPs in accordance with Rule 4370, reflecting the high stakes involved: any interruption in brokerage services could delay trades, freeze client assets, and disrupt critical market functions. A thorough BCP, therefore, addresses not only immediate crisis responses but also longer-term steps for restoring normal operations.

Key components of a robust BCP typically include: identification of critical systems and data, assignment of responsibilities to specific personnel, and clear communication protocols for both internal staff and external stakeholders. For instance, the plan will specify how client orders are handled if primary systems go offline, detail the processes for accessing backup facilities or cloud-based servers, and spell out escalation procedures to notify regulators in the event of outages that could affect market integrity. This level of detail is crucial because disruptions can range in scope from a localized power failure to a region-wide natural disaster. By delineating different tiers of response based on the severity of the incident, the BCP ensures that all employees understand exactly what to do in various scenarios and that clients, counterparties, and regulators receive timely updates about the status of the firm's operations.

Just as important as the initial creation of a BCP is the requirement for regular testing and revision. Firms must periodically conduct drills or simulations that gauge whether employees can follow the plan effectively under pressure, and whether the technology solutions still meet current business needs. The results of these tests guide potential refinements to the plan, which may involve incorporating new communication technologies or shifting to more secure, redundant data backup systems. By continually revisiting and improving their BCP, broker-dealers demonstrate both a regulatory commitment and a practical readiness to safeguard client interests and preserve market stability in the face of unforeseen events.

4.2.4.3 Regulation S-P (Privacy Notices, Non-public Personal Information)

Regulation S-P is a pivotal rule enacted by the SEC to protect the privacy of consumers' financial information, placing significant responsibilities on broker-dealers and other financial institutions. At its core, Regulation S-P requires that firms provide clients with clear and conspicuous privacy notices that detail how customer information is collected, used, and safeguarded. The regulation focuses specifically on "non-public personal information" (NPI), which generally includes data that a customer provides in connection with obtaining financial products or services, such as account balances, transaction histories, or even information about the customer's internet usage if it relates to financial services. By mandating transparent disclosure of how and why a firm gathers and shares NPI, Regulation S-P gives customers a clearer view into the security protocols and data handling practices of the institutions with which they do business. Just as importantly, it also establishes a mechanism for clients to opt out of certain types of information sharing with non-affiliated third parties, further reinforcing the principle of informed consumer consent.

An essential aspect of Regulation S-P is the obligation to deliver both an initial and an annual privacy notice to each customer. The initial privacy notice typically accompanies the opening of a new account or the beginning of a client relationship, ensuring that customers understand how their data will be handled from the outset. Subsequent annual notices must reiterate or update these privacy practices, allowing customers to remain aware of any policy changes and re-evaluate whether they wish to limit information sharing. In practice, firms develop privacy policies that not only delineate the categories of NPI they collect but also spell out any circumstances under which that information may be disclosed to affiliates or outside entities—such as service providers or credit reporting agencies—and how customers can opt out of such disclosures if they choose. Compliance with these requirements is more than just procedural: regulators can and do bring enforcement actions against firms that fail to provide adequate notices or that misuse client information in ways that violate the customer's stated preferences.

Beyond notice requirements, Regulation S-P also contains a Safeguards Rule, which compels firms to implement and maintain robust procedures for protecting non-public personal information from unauthorized access. This can involve a combination of technological protections (e.g., encryption or password-protected systems), employee training, and ongoing risk assessments to address potential vulnerabilities. By weaving these safeguards into their daily operations, broker-dealers ensure that customer data remain secure whether stored physically or electronically, underscoring the industry's commitment to privacy and fostering greater confidence among clients. Viewed as part of a broader regulatory framework, Regulation S-P stands out because it mandates not only the adoption of best practices in data security and privacy but also continuous communication with customers regarding those practices. This ongoing dialogue about privacy reflects the SEC's recognition that building and maintaining consumer trust requires both transparency and an active commitment to confidentiality.

4.2.4.4 Customer Protection and Custody of Assets

The cornerstone of safeguarding customer property in the securities industry lies in strict adherence to the SEC's Customer Protection Rule (Rule 15c3-3). Under this rule, broker-dealers must take specific steps to ensure that the cash and securities customers deposit are isolated from the firm's own accounts and are not used to fund its proprietary business. The driving principle is that, even in the event of a firm's insolvency or liquidation, customer assets should remain readily identifiable and retrievable. This is achieved through requirements such as maintaining physical possession or control over fully paid and excess margin securities, setting aside a calculated amount of cash or qualified securities in a special reserve bank account, and regularly reconciling customer balances to confirm that they match exactly what the broker-dealer holds in custody. Taken together, these measures are designed to protect investors from the operational or financial risks faced by the brokerage firm itself.

A critical concept within Rule 15c3-3 is the distinction between "fully paid" securities and those held on margin. Fully paid securities, which customers have purchased outright, must be promptly segregated from firm property and kept in control locations that cannot be accessed to satisfy the firm's obligations. Margin securities, on the other hand, can be partially pledged by the firm to secure loans (in line with Regulation T and other margin rules), but only within the limits established by regulators and with proper disclosures to the customer. In both cases, the broker-dealer is obligated to track each position meticulously and confirm, on an ongoing basis, that its obligations to each client are always backed by a sufficient pool of segregated assets. Failure to segregate client assets or to calculate these segregation requirements properly exposes the broker-dealer to severe regulatory consequences, not to mention reputational harm.

Below is a brief comparison of how customer-owned assets are treated under the Customer Protection Rule:

Type of Asset	Custody Requirement
Fully Paid Securities	Must be segregated and kept in a "control location" where the firm has no liens or claims on them.
Margin Securities	May be partially pledged for the firm's financing needs, subject to strict limits and disclosures.

Another key facet of customer protection is ensuring that each client's free credit balances (i.e., uninvested cash) remain accessible. Broker-dealers must inform customers of these balances and offer them the option to withdraw or otherwise use the funds as they see fit. Additionally, the firm must regularly perform a "reserve formula computation" to determine how much of the firm's own money or qualified securities must be placed into the special reserve bank account, effectively segregating a sum equivalent to all net customer credits. These computed amounts are monitored and adjusted frequently, typically on a weekly or monthly basis, depending on the size and nature of the firm, to maintain strict alignment with the rule's requirements.

Taken as a whole, customer protection and custody procedures serve as a bedrock of investor confidence. They ensure that clients retain clear ownership of the securities and cash held at a brokerage, even if the firm encounters financial or operational difficulties. By preventing customer assets from being siphoned off or comingled, these regulations create a stable foundation on which investors can participate in the securities markets, trusting that their positions are shielded from risks that arise within the broker-dealer's business.

4.2.5 Communications with the Public; Best Interest & Suitability

Communications with the public in the securities industry encompass everything from advertisements and social media posts to formal research reports and direct correspondence. Regulatory guidelines emphasize clarity, fairness, and the prohibition of misleading or exaggerated claims. For example, firms must balance promotional statements with appropriate risk disclosures and avoid any material omissions that could lead investors to form an inaccurate view of a product or service. In most cases, these communications must be reviewed and approved by designated supervisors to ensure adherence to regulatory standards before they reach potential or existing clients.

Another crucial aspect in this area is the requirement to act in the client's best interest when making recommendations, aligning with both the suitability obligation and Regulation Best Interest. Under the suitability standard, a registered representative must have reasonable grounds to believe that a recommended transaction or investment strategy fits the customer's personal objectives, financial status, and risk tolerance. Meanwhile, Regulation Best Interest imposes an additional layer of care, requiring brokers to mitigate conflicts and prioritize the client's welfare above that of the firm. Together, these obligations create a framework in which investors can expect recommendations and communications that not only comply with regulatory rules but also reflect a commitment to transparent, client-focused service.

4.2.5.1 Retail, Correspondence, Institutional Communications

In the securities industry, the term "communications with the public" broadly refers to any written or electronic messages that firms direct to existing or potential clients. However, regulators recognize that not all audiences or message formats pose the same level of risk for misrepresentation or misunderstandings. As a result, FINRA and the SEC categorize these communications into three primary buckets—retail communications, correspondence, and institutional communications—each with distinct review and approval requirements. By segmenting communications in this way, firms can tailor their procedures to the potential impact of each category and ensure that material is accurate, balanced, and fair.

Retail communications are those distributed or made available to more than 25 retail investors within any 30-day period. Because these messages have the broadest reach and may be viewed by a less sophisticated audience, regulators subject retail communications to the most stringent review standards. Depending on the content and format, retail communications often require principal pre-approval to verify that all claims are truthful and not misleading. This category encompasses traditional advertising—such as print ads, television, and radio spots—as well as newer channels like social media posts and mass emails. Detailed disclosures, particularly regarding risks and costs, become especially critical here to avoid projecting a misleading or overly optimistic depiction of a product or service.

Correspondence, on the other hand, includes written or electronic communications sent to 25 or fewer retail customers within a 30-day period. Because of the smaller scope, correspondence typically has a more limited regulatory burden when it comes to pre-approval, although firms must still maintain robust supervision and recordkeeping systems. Examples include personalized emails, letters responding to individual client inquiries, or communications directed at a small group of prospective investors. Firms often adopt supervisory policies that allow these communications to be sampled and reviewed on a post-distribution basis, ensuring that potential issues—such as exaggerated claims or missing disclosures—are detected promptly without hindering day-to-day client interactions.

Institutional communications are directed exclusively to institutional investors such as banks, registered investment companies, insurance companies, or any person with at least $50 million in total assets. Given that these recipients are presumed to have greater financial expertise, regulators generally permit a more flexible approach to institutional communications. Principal pre-approval may not be mandatory if the content is unlikely to be forwarded to retail clients. Nonetheless, the firm must still employ effective internal controls to confirm that institutional messages remain accurate and do not inadvertently reach or mislead a retail audience. In other words, the classification of a communication can change if institutional content is redistributed in ways that make it visible to retail investors, thus triggering stricter standards and potential review requirements.

On the next page is a concise comparison of these categories:

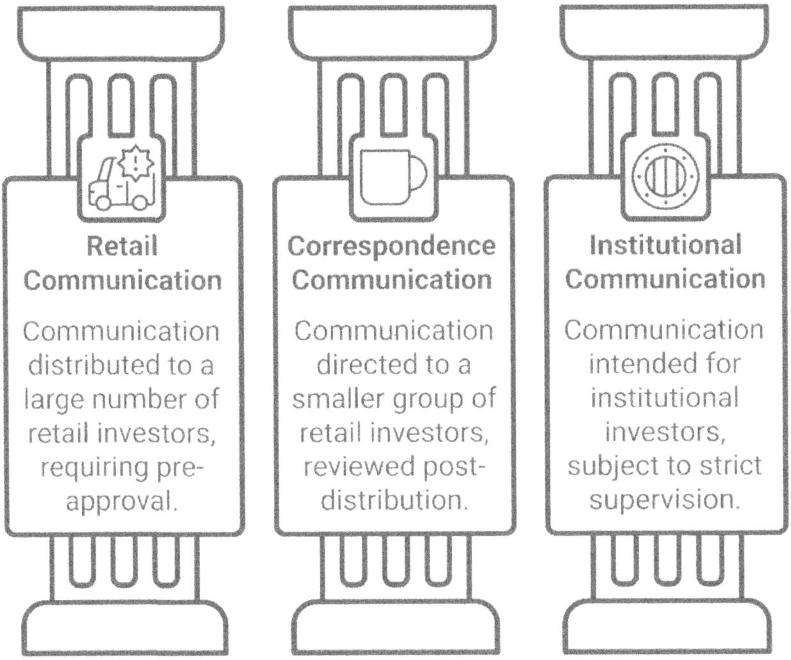

An important point is that each firm's supervisory procedures should clearly delineate how to classify different types of communications, what level of review is needed, and how records are retained for regulatory inspection. Firms must also keep up with ever-evolving communication technologies—like chat apps, video conferencing platforms, and emerging social media channels—to ensure they remain compliant if these methods are used for business purposes. By doing so, broker-dealers are better equipped to maintain consistent messaging and present information responsibly, thereby enhancing investor protection and reducing the risk of regulatory violations.

4.2.5.2 Telemarketing Rules and Do-Not-Call Lists

Telemarketing in the securities industry is governed by a mix of federal regulations, including the Telephone Consumer Protection Act (TCPA) and FINRA rules, all aimed at preventing unwanted solicitations and protecting consumer privacy. Broker-dealers that engage in telephone solicitations must therefore comply with specific requirements regarding the permissible times for contacting potential clients, the manner in which the call is conducted, and the maintenance of both internal and external do-not-call (DNC) lists. In general, calls cannot be made before 8 a.m. or after 9 p.m. in the potential client's time zone, and the representative placing the call must immediately provide certain identifying information—such as name, firm affiliation, and a telephone number or address where the caller can be reached—so that the call recipient knows who is contacting them and why. These disclosures are meant to enhance transparency and enable consumers to report or opt out of future calls if they wish.

Central to telemarketing compliance is the concept of the do-not-call list. At the national level, the Federal Trade Commission (FTC) maintains a registry that allows individuals to opt out of telemarketing calls from all businesses, including broker-dealers and other financial firms. Broker-dealers must regularly consult this National Do Not Call Registry, scrubbing their call lists to remove any phone numbers that appear there, except in certain limited scenarios such as an existing business relationship. In addition, each firm must maintain its own internal do-not-call list, which records specific requests from recipients who, even if not on the national registry, directly indicate they no longer wish to be contacted by that firm. Once a customer makes such a request, the firm must honor it indefinitely. Firms also have to document and preserve records of these internal requests, updating their calling procedures so that representatives do not inadvertently contact someone who has opted out.

Time-of-day restrictions and do-not-call lists are not the only elements of telemarketing regulations; firms must also ensure that the content of the call is not misleading or high-pressure in a way that conflicts with other regulatory mandates. This means representatives should refrain from making any exaggerated claims or failing to disclose material facts that might mislead potential customers. Broker-dealers typically implement rigorous supervisory systems, including call monitoring or recording, to verify that these standards are being met. Through these combined measures—adherence to time-of-day restrictions, clear identification and disclosures, and accurate tracking of both national and internal DNC lists—firms demonstrate their commitment to responsible outreach practices and uphold consumer protections in telemarketing activities.

Below is a simplified comparison of the two main do-not-call lists:

List	Scope	Update Frequency	Key Exceptions
National Do Not Call Registry (FTC)	Covers telemarketing calls across all industries; consumers register their numbers to opt out nationwide	Firms must synchronize at least every 31 days	Existing business relationships; prior written consent
Firm-Specific (Internal) DNC	Maintained individually by each broker-dealer; reflects direct requests from call recipients	Must be updated promptly upon each opt-out request	None (once a customer requests "no calls," it must be honored)

4.2.5.3 Suitability (FINRA Rule 2111) vs. Regulation Best Interest (SEC 15l-1)

FINRA Rule 2111 imposes a "suitability" obligation on broker-dealers, requiring them to base recommendations on a reasonable understanding of a customer's investment profile. In practice, this means a registered representative must consider the customer's financial situation, investment objectives, and risk tolerance—among other factors—before suggesting a security or strategy. Suitability under Rule 2111 is generally broken down into three essential components: (1) **Reasonable-Basis Suitability**, demanding that the broker understand the potential risks and rewards of a recommended product; (2) **Customer-Specific Suitability**, requiring the product to align with the individual client's unique profile; and (3) **Quantitative Suitability**, focusing on whether the frequency and volume of trading (or the recommended strategy) might constitute excessive or abusive activity in light of the client's circumstances. Taken together, these obligations aim to ensure that every recommendation is grounded in thoughtful analysis and an understanding of the individual investor's best interests.

Regulation Best Interest (Reg BI), codified as SEC Rule 15l-1, builds upon the suitability standard by imposing an even higher threshold of care for broker-dealers when making recommendations to "retail customers." Specifically, it obligates firms and their associated persons to "act in the best interest" of the customer at the time a recommendation is made, rather than merely ensuring that the recommendation is suitable. Reg BI sets forth four main obligations: **Disclosure**, **Care**, **Conflict of Interest**, and **Compliance**. The Disclosure Obligation compels broker-dealers to disclose key information about their relationship with the client, including fees, services, and any potential conflicts. The Care Obligation closely resembles FINRA's suitability rules but explicitly states that the firm cannot place its own interests—or those of its personnel—ahead of the retail customer's interests. The Conflict of Interest Obligation requires firms to establish policies reasonably designed to identify, mitigate, or eliminate conflicts that could compromise the quality of a recommendation. Finally, the Compliance Obligation calls on firms to create and maintain effective procedures that ensure compliance with all aspects of Reg BI. By stipulating that broker-dealers proactively address conflicts and consistently place the client's benefit first, Regulation Best Interest expands the principles underlying traditional suitability into a more robust framework.

One significant distinction, therefore, is the shift from a "could this recommendation fit the client's needs?" test under suitability to a more explicit "does this action serve the client's best interest?" standard under Reg BI. In other words, while Rule 2111 primarily aims to prevent unsuitable recommendations, Regulation Best Interest addresses the broader concern of conflicts and incentives that might bias a broker-dealer's advice. Although many of the day-to-day processes for gathering client financial information, understanding investment goals, and approving recommendations remain similar, broker-dealers now have a heightened obligation to demonstrate that their recommendations do not benefit the firm or the representative more than the customer. Compliance departments typically respond by refining their supervisory procedures, enhancing disclosure documents, and regularly training registered representatives on how to apply Reg BI's principles throughout the sales process.

Ultimately, Reg BI does not eliminate or supplant FINRA's suitability rules but rather coexists as a complementary, higher-level regulatory standard specifically targeting retail investor protection. Broker-dealers must navigate both frameworks, ensuring all recommendations satisfy the well-established suitability criteria while also meeting the broader expectations of acting in the "best interest" of the client. This dual compliance environment underscores a broader shift in regulatory philosophy: the industry's focus on "knowing your customer" remains essential, but it is now accompanied by a rigorous expectation that firms place the customer's welfare at the forefront of every recommendation.

4.2.5.4 Know-Your-Customer Requirements

Know-Your-Customer (KYC) requirements obligate broker-dealers and their registered representatives to collect and evaluate key information about a prospective or existing client before making any recommendations or facilitating transactions that might not be appropriate for that individual. Although these obligations overlap conceptually with the suitability and best-interest standards, KYC is more fundamentally about understanding who the customer is—their financial profile, investment experience, and overall objectives. By taking the time to learn these details, a broker-dealer can tailor its recommendations and services more effectively, minimize the risk of introducing products that may lead to significant losses or illiquidity, and help promote trust in the broker-customer relationship. Regulators expect that KYC processes will be embedded into new account paperwork, personal interviews, and ongoing updates as the client's situation evolves over time.

Firms typically capture a range of data that goes beyond simple demographic details. For instance, they may request the customer's occupation, net worth, liquid assets, and any outstanding obligations, along with investment objectives and tolerance for risk. These details combine to form a comprehensive client profile that influences which investment strategies may be presented. A young professional just starting out, for example, might prioritize growth-oriented investments, while a retiree might need regular income and a lower risk threshold. The thoroughness of the KYC process is central to consistently meeting other regulatory obligations, such as maintaining accurate customer records and ensuring that any recommendations align with the client's financial outlook. In that sense, KYC is not a one-time event; it is an ongoing process that necessitates regular communication with customers about their goals, changes to their personal finances, and shifts in market conditions that might affect their portfolios.

Below is an overview of common KYC data points that firms gather and review:

Data Category	Examples
Personal Identification	Legal name, date of birth, Social Security number (or taxpayer ID), address
Financial Information	Annual income, net worth, liquid assets, existing debts or obligations
Investment Experience	Previous exposure to stocks, bonds, derivatives, or other securities
Risk Tolerance & Objectives	Level of comfort with volatility, time horizon, primary goals (e.g., growth, income)

KYC requirements also help broker-dealers fulfill various compliance tasks, such as monitoring for suspicious transactions or activity that deviates significantly from a client's known profile. While Anti-Money Laundering (AML) frameworks focus on detecting illicit funds, KYC provides the foundational knowledge to spot anomalies in account behavior. By integrating KYC into their day-to-day practice, firms can not only offer more personalized service but also reduce the likelihood of regulatory infractions and potential harm to investors who might otherwise be introduced to unsuitable or overly complex products. Ultimately, the KYC rule exemplifies the securities industry's commitment to transparency, investor protection, and the alignment of advisory services with each customer's unique needs.

4.3 Prohibited Activities

4.3.1 Market Manipulation

Market manipulation generally refers to any activity designed to deceive or mislead investors by artificially affecting the price or trading volume of a security. Such conduct can encompass spreading false rumors to spark unwarranted buying or selling, orchestrating a "pump and dump" scheme where a stock is inflated in price through misleading promotion before major shareholders sell off their positions, or engaging in front running by trading ahead of large customer orders. The unifying thread across these tactics is the intent to distort natural market forces for personal gain, thereby compromising fair price discovery and undermining investor confidence.

Regulators view market manipulation as a grave violation because it corrupts the integrity of financial markets and harms unsuspecting participants who base their trading decisions on misleading signals. For instance, "marking the close" involves placing trades or bids late in the trading day with the primary aim of influencing a security's closing price, potentially affecting margin calculations or the perceived success of a particular security. Collectively, these manipulative practices destabilize the markets and diminish public trust, which is why they are actively policed and subject to significant penalties when detected.

4.3.1.1 Definition and Types (Market Rumors, Pump & Dump, Front Running, Marking the Close/Open, etc.)

Market manipulation, in its broadest sense, involves any deliberate attempt to interfere with the natural forces of supply and demand in the securities markets for personal or collective gain. The primary objective of such schemes is to create an artificial price or trading volume that misrepresents the true value or liquidity of a security. At its core, this distortion undermines the principle of fair and efficient markets and can erode investor confidence. Because of the deceptive tactics employed, regulators and self-regulatory organizations treat market manipulation as a serious violation, capable of triggering significant penalties and reputational damage for the perpetrators and their affiliated firms.

Within this overarching definition, several well-known manipulative strategies fall under the umbrella of prohibited conduct. One example is **market rumors**, where individuals or groups spread false or exaggerated information—often via social media, electronic message boards, or word of mouth—to influence buying or selling behavior. If successful, the rumors trigger a surge or drop in price that speculators exploit by trading before the market corrects itself. Another classic form is the **pump & dump**, where manipulators first acquire a large position in a security—often a thinly traded or low-priced stock—and then generate hype by disseminating misleadingly positive news or price predictions (the "pump"). Once the price rises due to the artificial enthusiasm, the manipulators liquidate their holdings at the inflated price (the "dump"), leaving unsuspecting buyers with large losses when the price collapses. A related tactic, **front running**, occurs when a broker-dealer or a registered representative places personal trades ahead of large customer orders, anticipating that the forthcoming bulk trade will shift the market price favorably. By trading in advance, front runners seek to profit from a subsequent price move that their client's substantial order is likely to produce. Meanwhile, **marking the close** or **marking the open** involves placing orders at or near the market's closing or opening moments with the primary aim of influencing the official closing or opening price. These trades may be small in volume but strategically timed and priced to give the impression of a last-minute surge or dip, potentially affecting margin calculations, settlement prices, or investor sentiment for the next trading session.

Below is a concise illustration of common market manipulation types:

Manipulative Practice	Primary Mechanism	Typical Outcome
Market Rumors	Spreading false or exaggerated claims about a company's prospects	Artificial buying or selling momentum caused by misinformation
Pump & Dump	Promoting a stock to inflate its price, then selling at the peak	Unsuspecting investors left with overpriced shares as manipulators exit
Front Running	Trading in advance of a known large customer order	Illegal profits made by taking advantage of expected price movements
Marking the Close/Open	Executing trades right before the market closes/opens	Distorted closing or opening prices, affecting market perception

These methods, although distinct in their approaches, share a common goal of manipulating the perception or behavior of other market participants. Because they compromise the fairness of the trading environment, regulators enforce strict rules and impose heavy sanctions when such activities come to light. By understanding the nuances of each tactic, industry professionals and investors alike can better identify unusual market patterns and help uphold the integrity of the securities markets.

4.3.2 Insider Trading

Insider trading typically occurs when an individual buys or sells a security based on material non-public information (MNPI) in breach of a duty of trust or confidence. This can involve corporate officers, directors, or any person who misappropriates confidential knowledge about a company's financial condition, mergers and acquisitions, or upcoming product announcements. The essence of the violation is that the trader exploits an unfair informational advantage to profit (or avoid losses) at the expense of other market participants who lack access to the same data.

Regulatory authorities enforce insider trading rules because such behavior undermines the fairness and transparency that markets depend on. Violations may lead to severe penalties, including fines several times the amount of illicit gains and potential prison sentences. Those who tip material non-public information to others, along with those who knowingly trade on such tips, can be liable under insider trading laws. By aggressively policing these offenses, regulators aim to preserve investor confidence and foster an environment where all market participants are on an equal informational footing.

4.3.2.1 Material Non-public Information

Material non-public information (MNPI) lies at the very heart of insider trading rules. "Material" in this context means that the information could significantly affect an investor's decision to buy or sell a security if it were made public. Such information might include an upcoming merger, a major earnings announcement, a regulatory approval or denial for a key product, or financial troubles that have not yet been disclosed. Whether a fact is material often hinges on whether a reasonable investor would view it as altering the "total mix" of data available for assessing a company's performance or future prospects. This determination can be nuanced, depending on the nature and timing of the disclosure and the security involved. What appears immaterial in one context may be highly impactful in another, particularly if it points to a fundamental shift in a company's valuation.

The non-public aspect of MNPI focuses on whether the information is broadly available to the investing public. Even if a fact is undoubtedly material, it does not trigger insider trading restrictions unless it remains confidential. Once the information is disseminated widely—through official press releases, SEC filings, or credible media coverage—it is considered public, and trading on it typically is no longer restricted. However, a common misconception is that discussing partial or "soft" information—such as a vague hint of a forthcoming corporate event—absolves one from insider trading rules. In reality, any meaningful detail not previously disclosed to the marketplace can qualify as non-public if it provides a significant edge to those privy to it. Because the integrity of the markets depends on all participants operating with comparable data, regulators aggressively pursue individuals who exploit even fragments of unreleased information for personal or third-party gain.

Below is a brief illustration of scenarios that often involve MNPI:

Scenario	Why It May Be Material
Pending Merger or Acquisition	Can dramatically alter a company's valuation
Not-Yet-Released Earnings Figures	Directly impacts share price if results differ from market expectations
Regulatory Approvals or Rejections	May significantly influence a company's operations or product viability
Major Contract Wins or Losses	Can affect both immediate revenue and long-term growth prospects

When an insider—be it a corporate executive, employee, or someone with a duty of trust—possesses MNPI, they must refrain from trading on that information or sharing it with others who might do so. Violations typically occur when individuals pass along insider details to friends or family, or when they engage in trades themselves before a public announcement. While upcoming sections will discuss the penalties and liabilities for such conduct, it is the concept of MNPI that forms the legal and ethical boundary. If the information is both material and has not been made public, it falls under the strict purview of insider trading regulations. Understanding precisely what MNPI is and recognizing it in various forms is thus essential to complying with securities laws and maintaining fair, transparent markets.

4.3.2.2 Involved Parties and Liability

Insider trading liability typically extends beyond just the corporate officers or directors who possess confidential details; it can ensnare any individual who knowingly trades on material nonpublic information (MNPI) or shares such information with others who then capitalize on it. While traditional "insiders" (such as a company's executives or board members) often come to mind first, liability can also attach to professionals who gain inside knowledge through a relationship of trust—like lawyers, investment bankers, accountants, or even close family members. In the classic "tipper-tippee" scenario, the tipper (the insider or misappropriator who shares the information) breaches a fiduciary or other duty of confidentiality, and the tippee (the person who receives and trades on that information) becomes equally liable if aware that the tipper violated that duty. Courts have consistently held that a tippee must know or should have known that the information was confidential and that the tipper stood to benefit in some tangible or intangible way from the disclosure. This broad net means that people far removed from the original insider can be pursued if they continue to disseminate or trade on the information.

Beyond tippers and tippees, the concept of misappropriation also imposes liability on those who steal or misuse information in violation of a duty owed to the source of that information. For example, a consultant or an outside attorney given privileged corporate data could face insider trading charges if they trade on that data without authorization. In some cases, even "temporary insiders" may fall under these rules if they develop a special relationship of trust and confidence by virtue of their access to sensitive details. Liability can also extend to "control persons," such as supervisors or firm principals, if they knowingly or recklessly fail to prevent violations by individuals under their watch. In all instances, the core principle remains the same: exploiting MNPI for personal gain—whether by trading oneself or by enabling others to trade—

undermines market fairness and transparency, and thus is vigorously prosecuted by regulators.

Below is a concise overview of the primary parties and how liability may arise:

Party Involved	Liability Trigger
Insider	Trades or tips MNPI in breach of a duty of trust/confidence
Tipper	Discloses MNPI to a tippee for personal benefit or with knowledge it will likely be misused
Tippee	Trades on MNPI received from a tipper, knowing (or having reason to know) the tipper violated a duty
Misappropriator	Obtains MNPI by deceit or violation of a duty owed to the source of the information
Control Person	Fails to prevent or detect insider trading violations when responsible for supervising the violator

4.3.2.3 Penalties (Fines, Incarceration)

Penalties for insider trading can be severe, reflecting the significant harm done to market integrity and the confidence of ordinary investors. On the civil side, individuals found liable by the SEC may face financial sanctions that extend well beyond any profits realized or losses avoided. For instance, the SEC can seek disgorgement of illicit gains plus a monetary penalty that often equals up to three times the amount of those gains or losses. If the inside information was passed along to others, "tippees" can also be pursued for similar penalties when they trade on the tip. Moreover, civil injunctions might prohibit further participation in the securities industry, effectively barring violators from working as registered representatives, officers, or directors of public companies. Because insider trading undermines the basic principle of fairness in the markets, courts and regulators typically impose these penalties as a strong deterrent to future misconduct.

Criminal penalties can be even more daunting. Under the federal securities laws, individuals convicted of insider trading may face substantial fines, which in certain cases can reach millions of dollars, as well as prison sentences that may extend up to 20 years. These criminal charges are pursued by the Department of Justice when there is evidence of willful intent to trade or tip based on material non-public information. The severity of a sentence often depends on factors such as the scale of the wrongdoing, the duration over which the misconduct occurred, and whether the individual cooperated with investigators once the activity came to light. This dual exposure—civil enforcement actions by the SEC and potential criminal prosecution by the Department of Justice—creates a high-stakes environment in which individuals engaged in insider trading risk not only losing ill-gotten gains but also their personal freedom and professional reputations.

4.3.3 Other Prohibited Activities

Beyond market manipulation and insider trading, several additional activities violate regulatory standards and can result in significant penalties for both individuals and firms. In many cases, these violations undermine the fundamental trust that must exist between financial professionals and their customers. For example, brokers may not improperly use customer securities or funds by borrowing from clients without approval or misrepresenting how assets are being held. Regulators also disallow practices like sharing in accounts without proper authorization, exploiting seniors who may be vulnerable due to cognitive or financial circumstances, and withholding or falsifying documents that could help illuminate the true nature of a transaction. Any effort to mislead regulators—through manipulative devices, incomplete recordkeeping, or deliberately distorted disclosures—runs contrary to the goal of maintaining open and transparent markets.

In addition, specific rules such as FINRA Rule 5130 limit who can participate in initial public offerings to ensure fair distribution and prevent conflicts of interest. Activities involving unregistered persons—those lacking the proper credentials to solicit or advise on securities—are similarly monitored, as regulators expect all market participants to meet basic competency requirements. Taken as a whole, these prohibitions aim to prevent dishonest behavior that could harm customers or erode market integrity. By enforcing clear boundaries around how securities transactions must be handled, the industry preserves confidence that brokerage firms and their representatives are prioritizing client interests and adhering to established ethical and legal standards.

4.3.3.1 IPO Purchase Restrictions (FINRA Rule 5130)

FINRA Rule 5130 is designed to uphold the integrity of the IPO (initial public offering) process by preventing "restricted persons" from unfairly profiting at the expense of the investing public. In essence, the rule seeks to ensure that shares of a new public offering are not allocated to individuals and entities who, by virtue of their industry affiliations or influence, might gain a special advantage. This includes certain broker-dealer personnel, finders, fiduciaries, and portfolio managers who are in a position to direct business to underwriters.

The fundamental principle is that IPOs should be offered in a manner that fosters broad participation and limits potential conflicts of interest.

Under Rule 5130, firms distributing an IPO must obtain written representations from purchasers affirming they are not restricted persons. The categories of restricted persons span more than just registered representatives and firm principals; immediate family members of those individuals can be deemed restricted if their investments are directed by or have notable ties to the industry insider. In practical terms, this means the underwriter and broker-dealers involved in the IPO must carefully verify eligibility before allocating new-issue shares, often by requiring certifications or questionnaires from prospective investors. Violations not only compromise the fairness of the distribution process but can also trigger regulatory sanctions for both the individual and the firm. By disallowing insiders from gaining a head start on potentially lucrative IPO shares, Rule 5130 promotes a level playing field and reinforces the notion that retail and institutional investors alike should have a fair shot at participating in public offerings.

Below is an overview of common categories of restricted persons under Rule 5130:

Restricted Category	Why Restricted
Broker-Dealer Personnel	Could exploit industry connections for preferential IPO share allocations
Immediate Family of Broker-Dealer Personnel	May receive beneficial treatment due to personal ties with industry insiders

Finders and Fiduciaries	Positioned to influence investment banking decisions or IPO allocations
Portfolio Managers	Might direct future underwriting business to favor certain firms in exchange for IPO shares

While each category has specific parameters, the overarching goal is the same: ensure that new issues are fairly distributed, curb conflicts of interest, and maintain public confidence in the equity markets. By requiring rigorous pre-allocation certifications and ongoing diligence, firms can demonstrate their commitment to impartiality, reducing the likelihood of scrutiny by FINRA or the SEC. Ultimately, FINRA Rule 5130 underscores the significance regulators place on transparent and equitable procedures surrounding the distribution of IPO shares, preserving the broader health and fairness of the underwriting process.

4.3.3.2 Manipulative/Deceptive or Fraudulent Devices

From a regulatory standpoint, the phrase "manipulative, deceptive, or fraudulent devices" encompasses a broad spectrum of illegal behaviors that breach the trust investors place in the securities markets. Unlike insider trading, which hinges on misuse of confidential data, these tactics generally rely on deliberate falsehoods or misleading actions to deceive others. Whether it involves spreading fabricated claims about a company's performance, forging client documents, or masking actual trading intent through concealed arrangements, each instance aims to trick market participants or customers into making choices they would not otherwise make. The ultimate harm extends beyond direct monetary losses—these deceptive acts corrode confidence in the fairness and transparency of the market itself.

Regulators rely on anti-fraud provisions, such as SEC Rule 10b-5, to define and penalize the use of manipulative or deceptive devices. Under this rule, it is unlawful for any person to employ a scheme, device, or artifice to defraud; to make untrue statements of material fact or omit material information; or to engage in any act that operates as a fraud upon another in connection with the purchase or sale of securities. As a practical matter, this prohibition applies to a range of behaviors that create a false impression of market interest or distort information flowing to investors. These practices might include misrepresenting key details about a security's risk profile, doctoring internal records, or entering into contrived arrangements to suggest higher trading volume than truly exists. Regardless of the exact mechanism, the common thread is that perpetrators deceive others—regulators, customers, or the broader investing public—to secure financial gain or competitive advantage. Below is a brief overview of several manipulative or fraudulent tactics:

Tactic	Description
False Statements	Disseminating misleading or outright fabricated claims about a company's prospects or financials
Wash Trades/Matched Orders	Arranging trades with oneself or a co-conspirator to create the illusion of market demand
Document Falsification	Forging customer signatures, altering records, or concealing information needed to evaluate transactions
Omissions of Material Fact	Withholding critical data that would change an investor's decision had it been disclosed

These devices often do not require insider access to confidential data; rather, they exploit trust and the open flow of information that underpins an efficient market. Because of this, regulators aggressively pursue both individuals and firms engaged in such schemes, leveraging substantial civil and criminal penalties to deter future misconduct. By clearly defining manipulative, deceptive, or fraudulent acts, the industry underscores its commitment to maintaining a level playing field and protecting investors from the unscrupulous practices that would otherwise undermine the securities markets.

4.3.3.3 Improper Use of Customer Securities/Funds

Maintaining the integrity of customer assets is paramount in the securities industry. Any unauthorized or unethical use of client securities and funds can expose firms and individual representatives to severe regulatory and legal consequences. Regulators view such infractions as a fundamental breach of fiduciary duty and a direct threat to investor confidence. When representatives handle customer accounts, they must exercise the highest standards of care to ensure that all transactions and account activities align with the client's best interests, the firm's written supervisory procedures, and applicable regulations.

One of the most serious concerns in this area is the temptation for registered personnel to use customer property—be it cash or securities—for their own personal advantage or for purposes not explicitly authorized by the customer. Even if a representative's intentions are benign, such actions are strictly prohibited and can constitute conversion or misuse of customer funds. Whether it involves placing trades without client knowledge, "borrowing" shares under the guise of a temporary arrangement, or misdirecting customer funds to cover firm expenses, any unauthorized appropriation of client assets undermines the confidence and trust that investors place in their brokerage firms.

Borrowing from/Loaning to Customers

Borrowing money from or loaning money to customers is highly restricted in most brokerage firm environments because of the potential for conflicts of interest and the appearance of impropriety. Representatives might justify these arrangements as short-term loans or "bridges" to help a valued client or to solve a personal financial need. However, regulators generally discourage such financial entanglements because the representative's objectivity could be compromised, leading to advice or trade recommendations that serve the personal financial arrangement rather than the customer's true investment goals. In many cases, firm policies prohibit these relationships outright unless the customer is an immediate family member or a lending institution in the regular course of business.

Even in situations where the firm's policies permit limited forms of borrowing or lending (such as arrangements between family members), strict guidelines typically apply. Firms often require written disclosures, supervisory approval, and documentation demonstrating that the transaction is in no way tied to the brokerage account's balances or securities. Representatives who bypass these procedures risk disciplinary action, including termination or regulatory sanctions. The rationale behind this strict stance is that borrowing arrangements can easily morph into quid pro quo scenarios, in which the representative feels compelled to recommend products or strategies beneficial to the customer providing the loan—or conversely, detrimental to the long-term needs of that customer. By strictly regulating or forbidding these arrangements, the industry aims to preserve an unclouded fiduciary relationship.

Sharing in Accounts

Another area of potential misuse involves representatives sharing in the profits or losses of a client's account. In most circumstances, industry rules and firm policies prevent a registered person from directly or indirectly participating in an account's gains or losses unless they have a bona fide joint account relationship with the customer (such as a spouse) or meet specific exceptions laid out by regulatory agencies. The rationale is straightforward: when a representative has a financial stake in the account's outcome, it can create a conflict of interest and might influence the representative's recommendations, trading patterns, or willingness to accept certain risks.

Even if the rules allow some form of joint participation—for instance, in accounts involving certain family relationships—broker-dealers typically require prior written approvals and verifications of proportional contributions to the account. These checks are designed to confirm that any sharing is equitable and does not disguise an impermissible compensation structure or an undisclosed arrangement. Without these safeguards, an unscrupulous representative could take advantage of client relationships or circumvent standard commission practices, potentially overtrading to chase short-term gains or otherwise jeopardizing the client's assets. Consequently, the combined effect of regulatory guidelines and firm policies around sharing in accounts is meant to eliminate hidden incentives, maintain transparent compensation structures, and keep the representative's primary focus on the customer's best interests.

4.3.3.4 Exploitation of Seniors

Exploitation of seniors involves any attempt to manipulate or misuse the assets of older adults for personal gain. Although such misconduct can occur with clients of any age, seniors are often targeted because they may have substantial accumulated wealth yet may also be more vulnerable to deceptive practices. The vulnerability can stem from diminished cognitive capacity, lack of familiarity with complex financial products, or social isolation that leaves older investors more dependent on their financial professionals for advice. Because regulators and the industry at large recognize these heightened risks, broker-dealers and their representatives are obligated to take extra precautions to detect and prevent potential abuse. This may include closer scrutiny of unusual withdrawal requests, sudden changes to account beneficiaries, or frequent transfers of funds that appear inconsistent with a senior client's established financial objectives.

Many firms institute specialized training programs to help their personnel identify red flags, such as abrupt shifts in a senior client's decision-making, uncharacteristic requests for large cash distributions, or the sudden involvement of a previously unknown third party who claims authority over the account. In addition, some regulators encourage or require broker-dealers to obtain the name of a trusted contact person who can be approached if concerns arise about the client's capacity or the legitimacy of account instructions. While the precise legal requirements vary from one jurisdiction to another, a general best practice is that representatives maintain careful documentation of any suspicious communications or directives, escalate issues to the firm's compliance department, and halt transactions if there is a credible belief that exploitation is occurring. The overarching aim is to protect older clients from financial harm by ensuring that firms act swiftly and responsibly whenever signs of possible abuse emerge.

Below is a concise overview of some common indicators that may suggest potential senior exploitation:

Potential Red Flag	Description	Example Scenario
Unusual or Sudden Fund Withdrawals	Large, unexpected withdrawals contrary to prior account patterns	A client requests repeated large-sum wire transfers to unfamiliar recipients
Abrupt Changes in Account Authorizations	Rapid addition or replacement of a power of attorney or beneficiary	A new "friend" claims to hold power of attorney without clear documentation
Significant Shift in Investment Strategy	Investing in high-risk products despite a history of conservative choices	A senior begins speculation in volatile penny stocks after no prior interest

When these red flags appear, a firm's internal procedures—often detailed in its written supervisory policies—guide staff on how to respond. This might entail contacting a designated supervisor, placing a temporary hold on transactions, or reaching out to the trusted contact person if doing so aligns with applicable regulations. While no single precaution can eliminate all instances of senior exploitation, a vigilant approach backed by clear policies helps mitigate the risk and underscores the industry's commitment to safeguarding one of its most vulnerable client segments.

4.3.3.5 Activities of Unregistered Persons

Broker-dealer personnel who are not properly registered face strict limitations on the scope of their activities. Registration is the mechanism by which financial professionals demonstrate their qualifications and agree to abide by regulatory standards. If an individual lacks the appropriate license—such as the Series 7 or Series 6 for representatives, among others—they cannot legally engage in tasks that involve effecting securities transactions or providing investment recommendations. This includes not only the execution of trades but also solicitations to potential clients, discussions of specific investment products in a way that promotes sales, or handling detailed inquiries about a security's suitability for an investor. Even administrative tasks, if they stray into the territory of suggesting particular trades, can cross the line from clerical support into registered activities. As a result, unregistered individuals who step outside their limited function risk severe penalties for both themselves and the firm that allows such conduct to occur unchecked.

Firms typically maintain written supervisory procedures that delineate exactly what unregistered persons may and may not do. For instance, unregistered staff might be permitted to greet walk-in clients or forward calls to a properly licensed representative, but they must refrain from discussing product features or providing investing advice. Regulators also scrutinize compensation structures to ensure that unregistered persons are not indirectly rewarded for bringing in new customers or recommending trades. If an unregistered assistant or intern, for example, is compensated based on a percentage of commissions generated from clients with whom they interacted, that arrangement may be viewed as tantamount to paying them for conducting registered activities. Below is a simplified illustration of permitted vs. prohibited functions for unregistered personnel:

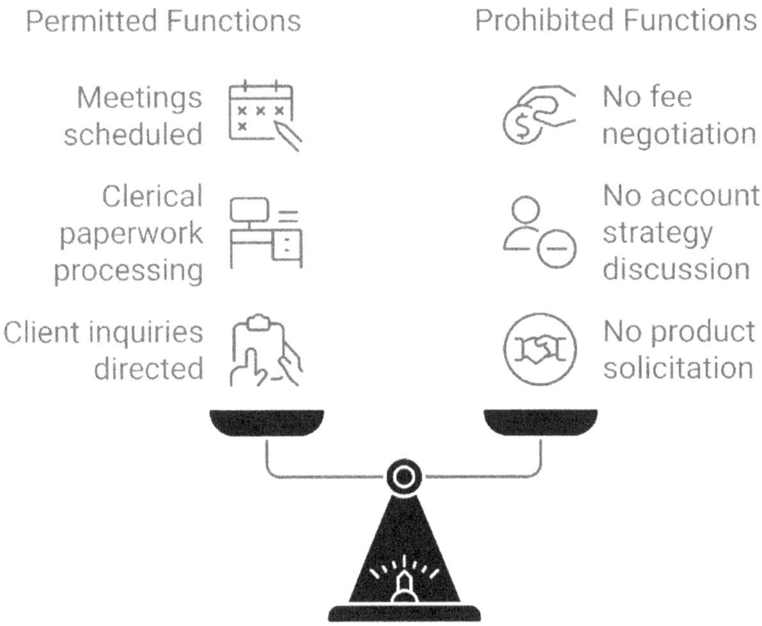

Firms bear responsibility for monitoring and training all staff to ensure that lines do not blur between allowable administrative work and functions reserved exclusively for registered persons. This includes educating unregistered individuals about the legal ramifications of engaging in sales-related tasks or offering guidance that goes beyond factual, scripted information. Failure to enforce these boundaries can prompt disciplinary actions from regulatory bodies, which may range from censures and fines to suspension or revocation of the firm's license. Ultimately, these rules exist to protect investors by guaranteeing that anyone who offers securities advice or facilitates trades has undergone the necessary vetting, examination, and ongoing education to carry out those responsibilities ethically and competently.

4.3.3.6 Falsifying or Withholding Documents

Falsifying or withholding documents strikes at the core of fair dealing and transparency within the securities industry. Regulators hold broker-dealers, registered representatives, and associated personnel to strict standards for accurate recordkeeping precisely because these documents serve as the primary evidence of transactions, customer instructions, and firm operations. When records are intentionally doctored—through altered signatures, fabricated account entries, or misrepresented terms—this deceptive conduct can mask fraud, mislead clients, or frustrate regulatory examinations. Similarly, withholding documents, such as failing to provide complete trade blotters or required disclosures, deprives auditors and investigators of critical information needed to verify that all transactions align with the rules. These practices not only jeopardize the rights and interests of investors but also erode the integrity of the market as a whole.

One common scenario involves an attempt to conceal losses or risky trading strategies by modifying statements or confirmations before showing them to a supervisor or client. In other cases, a representative might withhold documents that highlight unauthorized or excessive trading, hoping to avoid detection by compliance officers. Regardless of the motive, regulators classify document falsification and withholding as willful violations, typically subjecting offenders to rigorous penalties—including hefty fines, suspension, or permanent bar from the industry—because the damage extends beyond any single transaction. The records a firm maintains are essential for ensuring that each client's assets are properly accounted for and that regulators have a complete, unadulterated view of a firm's business practices.

Below is a summary of possible forms of document falsification or withholding, along with the implications for clients and the firm:

Activity	Example	Implication
Altering Customer Signatures	Forging or transferring a signature from one document to another	Undermines a client's consent and invalidates the authenticity of instructions
Backdating Contracts or Agreements	Changing dates on disclosures or purchase agreements to circumvent a regulatory requirement	Creates a misleading timeline, obscuring whether the transaction was compliant
Withholding Account Statements or Confirmations	Failing to deliver statements that document unauthorized trades	Prevents clients from detecting irregularities or disputing questionable activity
Misrepresenting Operational Data	Editing trade blotters to hide unapproved or high-risk trades	Conceals misconduct from compliance oversight and regulatory examinations

In practice, a robust supervisory system and a culture of compliance are critical to deterring document manipulation. Firms often deploy checks—like mandatory electronic recordkeeping, dual sign-off procedures, and periodic audits—to catch discrepancies before they lead to deeper systemic abuses. When combined with thorough training programs, these measures remind personnel that the potential short-term gain from falsifying or withholding documents pales in comparison to the severe legal and ethical consequences that typically follow such violations.

4.3.3.7 Prohibited Book/Record Maintenance Activities

Accurate and consistent recordkeeping is fundamental to the health of the financial markets, as it ensures that regulators, auditors, and customers can reliably assess a firm's activities. Prohibited book and record maintenance practices generally involve concealing or misrepresenting information in the official ledgers that document trades, client data, and other critical details of day-to-day operations. While common sense dictates that books and records should reflect the actual business conducted, some firms or individuals attempt to maintain "off-the-books" accounts or create parallel systems to hide unauthorized trades or fees. These hidden ledgers, partial records, or intentionally mislabeled entries prevent full transparency and can mask illicit practices, such as unapproved customer transactions, improper fee arrangements, or risk exposures that far exceed a firm's stated policies. Importantly, such misconduct can occur at any point in the transaction lifecycle—whether in the trade capture phase, the clearing and settlement stage, or even during routine internal reconciliations—and thus must be guarded against through rigorous supervisory procedures.

To reinforce the importance of maintaining correct and comprehensive records, regulators impose specific rules around how long documents must be retained, what form they should take, and when they must be made available for inspection. Firms that fail to meet these requirements risk civil or criminal penalties, given that incomplete or inaccurate books can thwart regulatory oversight and undermine investor protection. For instance, a broker-dealer that systematically omits certain categories of trades from its central trade blotters, or that stores crucial records in inaccessible or unapproved locations, directly hampers the ability of compliance officers and examiners to identify unauthorized patterns. Likewise, any attempt to alter or destroy records prematurely—especially if done to avoid scrutiny—will draw serious enforcement actions. Below is a summary of common violations:

Prohibited Practice	Description	Impact
Maintaining "Shadow Books"	Keeping secret sets of ledgers separate from official records	Obscures actual financial positions and transactions from regulators and internal oversight
Incomplete Documentation	Omitting required details from transaction logs or blotters	Prevents accurate reconstruction of trades and hampers the compliance process
Unauthorized Off-Site Storage	Storing records in unapproved locations that are not readily accessible for audits	Delays or obstructs regulatory examinations, impeding timely verification
Premature Destruction of Records	Destroying documents before the regulatory retention period ends	Eliminates audit trails necessary for dispute resolution and fraud detection

Enforcing proper recordkeeping protocols requires continuous training and vigilant oversight. Firms often rely on automated systems that log all trade activity, reconcile positions daily, and flag anomalies for management review. Additionally, internal audits help verify that logs match actual business activity. By following these best practices and avoiding any attempt to conceal, distort, or selectively omit data, firms uphold the industry's reputation for transparent operations and maintain a defensible position in the event of regulatory inquiries or customer disputes.

4.4 Key Rules and Regulations for Trading & Prohibited Acts

4.4.1: FINRA Rules

FINRA (Financial Industry Regulatory Authority) rules form a comprehensive framework that governs virtually every aspect of broker-dealer conduct, from ethical obligations to specific operational details like margin requirements, recordkeeping, and communications with the public. At their core, these rules seek to protect investors and maintain fair, orderly markets. Among the foundational standards is **FINRA Rule 2010**, which establishes that members and associated persons must observe "high standards of commercial honor" in the conduct of their business. Though succinct in language, Rule 2010 underpins many subsequent enforcement actions because it sets a broad baseline for ethical conduct. Closely related is **FINRA Rule 2020**, which addresses manipulative and fraudulent devices. By prohibiting practices that mislead or deceive investors, it reinforces the principle that market participants should not secure an advantage through false representations or distortions of information.

Several rules focus on investor protection through proper diligence and transparency. **FINRA Rule 2090** is often referred to as the "Know Your Customer" rule, mandating that firms understand the essential facts about each client before making any recommendations, while **FINRA Rule 2111** sets forth suitability requirements, obligating representatives to recommend only those products or strategies aligned with a customer's objectives, risk tolerance, and financial situation. In scenarios where safeguarding vulnerable clients is paramount, **FINRA Rule 2165** allows broker-dealers to place a temporary hold on disbursements if there is reasonable suspicion of financial exploitation—particularly important for senior investors. Meanwhile, **FINRA Rule 2150** prohibits unauthorized use of customer funds or securities, serving as a reminder that registered persons must never borrow from a client without specific firm authorization or share in a customer's account beyond limited, regulated exceptions.

Communications and disclosures also receive significant attention. **FINRA Rule 2210** details how broker-dealers must craft and review retail communications, correspondence, and institutional communications to ensure they are fair, balanced, and not misleading. For account-level transparency, **FINRA Rule 2231** outlines the frequency and content requirements for sending customer account statements, while **FINRA Rule 2232** focuses on trade confirmations, requiring explicit disclosures of transaction-related costs and fees. Additionally, **FINRA Rule 2264** addresses margin disclosures from the perspective of warning customers about the potential risks of borrowing to invest. In concert with these, **FINRA Rule 4210** provides the core guidelines for margin trading itself, detailing how much collateral is necessary and how shortfalls must be handled if asset values change.

On the firm operations front, **FINRA Rule 3150** covers electronic data storage and retrieval, ensuring that critical records are maintained in an accessible and tamper-resistant manner. **FINRA Rule 4511** extends recordkeeping obligations, stipulating that firms must preserve certain documents for specified periods, while **FINRA Rule 4512** requires accurate and up-to-date customer account information, including essential facts needed for suitability and AML compliance. Firms also shoulder significant responsibilities under **FINRA Rule 3310**, which mandates the establishment of a robust Anti-Money Laundering (AML) program—an aspect deeply intertwined with the Patriot Act requirements covered elsewhere in this book.

In the trading and underwriting arena, **FINRA Rule 5130** restricts how IPO shares can be allocated to industry insiders, seeking to prevent conflicts of interest and favoritism during initial public offerings. **FINRA Rule 5270** prohibits front running—where a broker-dealer or associated person trades ahead of customer orders—while **FINRA Rule 5310** codifies best execution standards, ensuring that firms handle customer orders in a way that maximizes the likelihood of favorable pricing and minimal transaction costs. Finally, overarching ethical mandates—like those found in Rule 2010—apply as a catch-all to any improper conduct not specifically enumerated in other rules. Taken together, these regulations underscore FINRA's overarching mission: to foster a transparent, fair, and responsible marketplace where investors can participate with confidence.

Rule	Key Focus/Requirement	Purpose/Impact
2010	High standards of commercial honor	Broad ethical guideline prohibiting dishonest or unethical practices
2020	Manipulative, deceptive practices	Bars use of fraudulent devices to mislead or harm investors
2090	Know Your Customer	Ensures firms gather essential facts about clients before recommending products
2111	Suitability of recommendations	Requires that any recommendation aligns with a customer's investment profile and objectives
2150	Improper use of customers' securities or funds	Prohibits borrowing from or lending to customers without proper authorization, and sharing in accounts without approval
2165	Financial exploitation of seniors	Allows firms to place a temporary hold on suspicious disbursements affecting senior or vulnerable adult customers
2210	Communications with the public	Governs how broker-dealers create and disseminate retail, institutional communications, and correspondence
2231	Customer account statements	Specifies how often customers should receive statements and what information must be disclosed
2232	Customer confirmations	Requires clear disclosures of execution prices, commissions, and other pertinent transaction details
2264	Margin disclosures	Informs customers of margin risks, obligations, and potential financial exposures

3150	Electronic storage of data	Mandates secure, retrievable systems to store and protect firm records
3310	AML compliance programs	Requires member firms to develop, implement, and test effective anti-money laundering policies
4210	Margin requirements	Establishes collateral requirements and procedures for handling margin deficiencies
4511	General recordkeeping requirements	Sets minimum periods for preserving firm records (e.g., account documents, trade blotters)
4512	Customer account information	Requires accurate customer data (name, address, financial profile) for suitability and AML checks
5130	IPO allocations to industry insiders	Limits how underwriters distribute shares to avoid conflicts of interest
5270	Front running restrictions	Prohibits trading ahead of customer orders to capitalize on pending block transactions
5310	Best execution	Obligates firms to execute trades in a manner most favorable to the customer, considering price, speed, and cost

This table consolidates many of the key FINRA rules relevant to trading, account management, and ethical standards, helping illustrate how each regulation fits into FINRA's broader mission of investor protection and market integrity.

4.4.2: MSRB Rules

The Municipal Securities Rulemaking Board (MSRB) is the principal regulator responsible for creating and enforcing rules that govern the municipal securities market. Unlike FINRA, which primarily oversees the corporate securities space, the MSRB's authority covers broker-dealers and banks underwriting and trading in municipal bonds, as well as municipal advisors providing advice to state and local governments. MSRB rules address everything from recordkeeping and investor disclosures to ethical obligations and advertising standards, forming a comprehensive regulatory scheme aimed at protecting both retail and institutional investors. Because municipal securities can be complex—often involving tax considerations, varying maturities, and potentially large funding projects—MSRB rules help ensure that investors receive timely, accurate information and that market intermediaries uphold consistent professional standards.

These rules, often cited by their alphanumeric designations, are enforced in concert with the SEC and FINRA. Firms must adopt robust supervisory policies and compliance frameworks to meet MSRB requirements. From obligations to maintain detailed books and records (G-8, G-9) to specific guidelines on fair pricing and transaction reporting (G-13, G-14, G-15, G-18), MSRB rules demand careful attention to detail. Additional provisions like G-21 (advertising standards) and G-25 (improper use of assets) underscore the Board's focus on fair dealing and customer protection. The result is a set of standards that parallels, but remains distinct from, those established for corporate securities, reflecting the unique features and risks of municipal debt instruments. Below is an in-depth look at major MSRB rules and their significance.

Rule	Key Focus/Requirement	Purpose/Impact
G-8	**Books and Records**	Requires municipal securities dealers to maintain detailed records of transactions, customer account details, and related documents. Ensures audit-ready transparency for regulatory inspections.
G-9	**Preservation of Records**	Specifies how long certain records must be kept (e.g., correspondence, trade blotters) and in what format. Noncompliance can impede regulatory review and lead to potential penalties.
G-13	**Quotations**	Governs how quotes (bids or offers) for municipal securities must be disseminated. Seeks to prevent misleading or inaccurate quotes, supporting fair price discovery.
G-14	**Transaction Reporting**	Mandates real-time reporting of trades in municipal securities. Facilitates transparency by providing timely data on market prices and execution volumes through the MSRB's reporting systems.
G-15	**Confirmation, Clearance, Settlement**	Details how dealers must confirm transactions (including disclosures on price, yield, and commissions). Addresses uniform settlement practices, helping avoid confusion or disputes between parties.
G-18	**Best Execution**	Requires municipal securities dealers to use reasonable diligence in finding the best market and most favorable price for customer transactions, in line with the security's characteristics and market conditions.

G-21	**Advertising**	Imposes standards to ensure advertisements are fair, balanced, and not misleading (similar to FINRA Rule 2210). Includes guidelines on performance comparisons and the use of hypothetical or projected data.
G-25	**Improper Use of Assets**	Prohibits dealers from making unauthorized use of customer funds or securities. Reinforces a fiduciary mindset and protects clients from misappropriation or undisclosed risk exposures.
G-39	**Telemarketing**	Mirrors federal and other SRO rules on telephone solicitations, including time-of-day restrictions and do-not-call lists. Seeks to protect investors from unwanted or harassing calls.
G-41	**Anti-Money Laundering Compliance**	Requires municipal dealers to implement AML programs that detect and report suspicious activities, in harmony with the Bank Secrecy Act and USA PATRIOT Act requirements.
G-47	**Time-of-Trade Disclosures**	Obligates dealers to disclose all material information at or before the time of trade, ensuring that retail and institutional investors alike can make informed decisions about the securities they purchase or sell.

Books and Records (G-8, G-9)

MSRB Rules G-8 and G-9 form the foundational layer of administrative compliance by dictating what records municipal securities dealers must create, how these records are organized, and for how long they must be retained. G-8 requires detailed recording of every transaction and account activity, mirroring SEC and FINRA recordkeeping rules. This includes maintaining trade tickets, confirmations, customer information, and any correspondence related to municipal bond transactions. G-9 then builds upon G-8 by specifying the minimum retention periods for each record type, often spanning several years. By mandating clear and consistent documentation, the MSRB facilitates regulatory oversight and ensures that dealers are always prepared for audits or customer inquiries.

Quotation and Transaction Reporting (G-13, G-14)

Accurate quotations and real-time trade reporting are critical in the municipal bond market, where liquidity can vary significantly among different issues. Rule G-13 addresses how dealers should quote prices, requiring that quotes be bona fide and not designed to mislead market participants. In turn, Rule G-14's transaction reporting obligations feed data into the MSRB's trade reporting system, making trade prices and volumes visible to the public. This transparency helps investors and regulators gauge market health, identify pricing anomalies, and establish fair values for municipal securities.

Confirmations, Settlement, and Best Execution (G-15, G-18)

Rule G-15 focuses on the content and timing of transaction confirmations. Dealers must inform customers about the price, yield to maturity (if applicable), commissions, and settlement terms—vital details in a market where interest rate changes and other factors can affect a bond's value. Under Rule G-18, dealers assume an obligation akin to "best execution," requiring them to find the most favorable terms for their customers. The rule considers the character of the market for the security, the size and type of transaction, and other relevant factors. These combined rules aim to prevent confusion, ensure timely and accurate settlement, and promote fairness in the pricing process.

Advertising and Improper Use of Assets (G-21, G-25)

Through Rule G-21, the MSRB imposes restrictions on how municipal securities dealers advertise their products and services. Advertisements must not exaggerate or omit material facts, and any performance claims require balanced context. Similarly, Rule G-25 prohibits the misuse of customer assets, underscoring a fundamental ethical principle: that client funds and securities exist for their benefit, not for covering firm shortfalls or personal pursuits. By bolstering transparency in promotion and preventing the misappropriation of customer property, these rules strengthen investor confidence in the municipal marketplace.

Telemarketing and AML Compliance (G-39, G-41)

Rule G-39 aligns with federal telemarketing regulations, instructing municipal dealers on permissible calling hours, mandatory disclosures, and the handling of do-not-call lists. This emphasis on customer privacy and autonomy extends beyond day-to-day communications into broader compliance. Under Rule G-41, dealers must implement anti-money laundering (AML) programs, mirroring the obligations found in other corners of the securities industry. AML measures aim to detect and report red flags—such as suspicious patterns of fund movement or the placement of illicit proceeds—thereby protecting the integrity of the municipal bond market.

Time-of-Trade Disclosures (G-47)

Finally, Rule G-47 mandates comprehensive time-of-trade disclosures, ensuring that customers are fully informed about the characteristics and risks of a municipal bond before they purchase or sell it. These disclosures may include call features, the tax status of interest, credit ratings, and any material events affecting the issuer. The rule compels dealers to provide such details promptly and proactively, recognizing that municipal securities can carry unique local-government risks—such as infrastructure funding challenges or shifting economic conditions—that might not be obvious at first glance.

Taken together, these MSRB rules collectively uphold the principles of transparency, fairness, and investor protection. Whether guiding how dealers store records, quote prices, settle trades, or interact with customers, each provision reflects the MSRB's effort to maintain orderly markets where the interests of issuers, investors, and the general public are respected. By promoting consistent standards of conduct across all facets of municipal securities activity, the MSRB builds greater confidence in a market that funds critical public projects—from schools to roads to public utilities—nationwide.

4.4.3: SEC Rules and Regulations

The Securities and Exchange Commission (SEC) stands as the principal federal regulatory authority overseeing U.S. financial markets, including exchanges, broker-dealers, and publicly traded companies. Through a broad array of rules and regulations, the SEC strives to maintain fair, orderly, and efficient markets while protecting investors from fraudulent or abusive practices. This section explores several key SEC regulations and legislative acts—ranging from anti-manipulation measures to investor privacy mandates—that collectively shape the landscape in which broker-dealers operate. The intent is to highlight how each rule enforces transparency, promotes accountability, and addresses specific challenges posed by evolving market structures and financial products.

Regulation M

Regulation M is designed to prevent market manipulation in connection with securities offerings, particularly when an issuer or its underwriters might be tempted to inflate or stabilize a stock's price around the time of distribution. By restricting certain bidding and purchasing behaviors, Reg M aims to protect the integrity of the pricing process during public offerings. Key provisions include **Rule 101**, which limits how distribution participants can bid for or purchase covered securities in the restricted period leading up to a new offering, and **Rule 102**, which applies similar prohibitions to issuers and selling security holders. Additionally, **Rule 103** provides a framework for passive market making on Nasdaq, allowing firms engaged in an offering to continue making markets in a stock under tightly controlled conditions.

In practical terms, these restrictions help ensure that the offering price reflects genuine supply-and-demand dynamics rather than the artificial effects of underwriter interventions or issuer buybacks. Broker-dealers participating in a distribution must pay careful attention to the applicable restricted period (ranging from one to five business days before the pricing date), as violations can lead to significant penalties. This constant vigilance fosters a level playing field, protecting existing and prospective shareholders alike from manipulative or deceptive pricing schemes.

Regulation S-P

Regulation S-P enshrines investor privacy protection by governing how broker-dealers, investment companies, and registered investment advisers handle nonpublic personal information (NPI). Under this regulation, firms must issue initial and annual privacy notices to customers, detailing what information they collect, how it is used, and the circumstances (if any) under which it is shared with nonaffiliated third parties. These notices also inform consumers about their right to opt out of certain forms of information sharing, empowering them to maintain tighter control over personal data.

Compliance with Regulation S-P goes beyond mere disclosure. Institutions must implement robust procedures—both technological and procedural—to safeguard NPI against unauthorized access or misuse. This includes physical security measures, encrypted electronic recordkeeping, and ongoing employee training. Breaches or weak protocols can expose firms to legal repercussions and damage their reputations, as regulators view client confidentiality as a cornerstone of investor protection. By clearly defining how personal data is managed, Regulation S-P reinforces trust in the financial system and reassures clients that sensitive details about their accounts will remain secure.

Exchange Act of 1934 (Sections 10, 11(d), 14, 15, 20A, 21A)

The Securities Exchange Act of 1934 established the SEC and laid the groundwork for regulating securities markets and participants on an ongoing basis. Within the act, several sections stand out for their direct impact on broker-dealers:

1. **Section 10**: This section underpins many of the SEC's anti-fraud provisions, including the famous **Rule 10b-5**. Section 10 broadly prohibits manipulative or deceptive devices in connection with the purchase or sale of any security, authorizing the SEC to enact specific rules that give teeth to this principle.

2. **Section 11(d)**: Addresses restrictions on broker-dealers who extend credit on new issues. The provision typically prohibits a dealer who is participating in a distribution from financing the customer's purchase of that distributed security. It seeks to reduce conflicts of interest and manipulation risks in newly offered securities.

3. **Section 14**: Governs proxy solicitations, mandating disclosure requirements when shareholders are asked to vote on corporate matters. Although it may not directly touch every broker-dealer transaction, broker-dealers serving in advisory or fiduciary capacities must be aware of its implications when relaying materials and recommendations to clients.

4. **Section 15**: Establishes the requirement for broker-dealers to register with the SEC, thereby subjecting them to ongoing regulations and oversight. It also includes rules for associated persons' registration, capital requirements, and supervisory obligations, effectively shaping the entire broker-dealer regulatory ecosystem.

5. **Section 20A**: Codifies liability for insider trading, clarifying how tippees, tippers, and other participants in insider trading schemes can be held responsible. It often interacts with more specific rules such as Rule 10b-5 to ensure that all parties who knowingly benefit from illicit trades face potential legal consequences.

6. **Section 21A**: Grants the SEC authority to impose civil penalties for insider trading violations. This includes substantial monetary fines, often far exceeding the amount

of any illicit gains, reflecting the seriousness with which the SEC treats insider abuse.

Collectively, these sections pave the way for the modern approach to market regulation: robust disclosures, fair dealing, firm registration standards, and severe penalties for fraudulent or manipulative behaviors.

Insider Trading Acts (ITSFEA 1988)

The Insider Trading and Securities Fraud Enforcement Act of 1988 (ITSFEA) strengthened the SEC's hand in pursuing insider trading violations by increasing the monetary penalties for those found guilty and establishing provisions for rewarding whistleblowers. It also highlighted the liability that supervisors can face if they fail to take appropriate steps to deter employees from illegally trading on material nonpublic information. While insider trading was already illegal under the Exchange Act and earlier case law, ITSFEA formalized the structure for imposing severe financial sanctions—up to three times the profit gained or loss avoided—and clarified that individuals and firms must implement adequate compliance procedures to detect and prevent insider trading.

A key upshot of ITSFEA is the clear impetus it provides for broker-dealers to maintain proactive supervisory systems, such as restricted lists and watch lists, to track which securities employees have access to nonpublic data. Many firms have also adopted mandatory "blackout periods" for trading certain stocks to avoid even the appearance of impropriety. By embedding these safeguards, broker-dealers minimize the risk of firmwide liability should an associated person engage in illicit activity.

Anti-Fraud and Disclosure Rules: 10b-5, 10b5-1, 10b5-2, 10b-10, 15c1-2, 15l-1 (Reg BI)

- **Rule 10b-5**: This cornerstone anti-fraud rule prohibits any act or omission resulting in fraud or deceit in connection with the purchase or sale of a security. Its broad wording captures a wide range of deceptive practices, from making false statements to insider trading schemes. Courts have repeatedly used Rule 10b-5 as the framework for adjudicating securities fraud.

- **Rule 10b5-1**: Provides an affirmative defense for insiders who trade in their own company's stock according to pre-arranged, binding trading plans established before possessing inside information. If strictly followed, these plans can protect insiders from liability claims that they traded while in possession of material nonpublic information.

- **Rule 10b5-2**: Clarifies what constitutes a "duty of trust or confidence" for purposes of insider trading cases, especially in "misappropriation" scenarios. For instance, if someone learns sensitive information from a family member under an understanding of confidentiality, Rule 10b5-2 can establish that a duty was breached if that person trades on the information.

- **Rule 10b-10**: Governs the content and timing of broker-dealer confirmations to customers, ensuring that investors receive prompt, detailed transaction information. The rule mandates that confirmations disclose transaction prices, commissions, and whether the broker-dealer acted as an agent or principal, among other details.

- **Rule 15c1-2**: Prohibits broker-dealers from engaging in fraudulent, deceptive, or manipulative acts in connection with the offer, sale, or purchase of any security. It expands on the Exchange Act's general anti-fraud provisions, emphasizing fair dealing and transparency in interactions with prospective customers.

- **Rule 15l-1 (Regulation Best Interest, or Reg BI)**: Imposes a higher standard of conduct on broker-dealers when they recommend securities transactions or investment strategies to retail customers. Reg BI goes beyond suitability by requiring firms to act in the best interest of the customer at the time of the recommendation, addressing conflicts of interest, and enhancing disclosures. It represents a shift toward a more fiduciary-like duty, though not identical to the standard for Registered Investment Advisers under the Investment Advisers Act of 1940.

Federal Reserve Board Regulation T

Although not an SEC rule, Regulation T (often abbreviated "Reg T") is integral to broker-dealer operations since it governs the extension of credit by broker-dealers for securities transactions. Administered by the Federal Reserve Board, Reg T sets the initial margin requirements—commonly 50%—that an investor must deposit when purchasing securities on margin. It also addresses conditions under which broker-dealers can lend securities to customers for short sales and how margin accounts must be maintained.

The interplay between Reg T and the SEC's own margin and net capital rules ensures that broker-dealers remain adequately capitalized and that the risk of default from margin transactions is contained. Reg T typically applies to new purchases of exchange-listed securities, but additional margin requirements can be layered on through self-regulatory organization (SRO) rules, such as FINRA

Rule 4210. By limiting leverage, Reg T helps prevent excessive speculation and systemic instability that might arise if investors borrowed too freely in pursuit of short-term gains.

USA PATRIOT Act (Sections 314, 326, 352)

Enacted in the wake of the September 11, 2001 attacks, the USA PATRIOT Act expanded the scope and obligations of financial institutions—including broker-dealers—to help combat money laundering and terrorist financing. Three sections are particularly pertinent:

1. **Section 314**: Enables information sharing among financial institutions, law enforcement, and regulatory authorities to detect and prevent money laundering or terrorist activities. Broker-dealers may, for instance, receive 314(a) requests from FinCEN directing them to check customer records for matches with known or suspected criminals or terrorists.

2. **Section 326**: Introduces the Customer Identification Program (CIP) requirement, mandating that firms verify customer identities at account opening, maintain records of the methods used, and screen customers against government watchlists (e.g., the OFAC SDN list). CIP guidelines ensure that firms do not inadvertently facilitate the financing of illegal operations.

3. **Section 352**: Requires financial institutions to establish AML programs complete with written policies, designated compliance officers, ongoing employee training, and independent testing. This statutory mandate dovetails with other SEC and FINRA AML requirements (e.g., FINRA Rule

3310), reinforcing the need for robust internal controls that detect suspicious account activities or transactions.

Ultimately, the PATRIOT Act extends broker-dealers' responsibilities beyond traditional investor protection, tasking them with an active role in national security efforts. Failure to comply can lead to severe enforcement actions, reflecting the Act's centrality in preventing illicit flows of capital and maintaining market integrity.

These SEC rules and regulations—together with Regulation T and the AML provisions of the USA PATRIOT Act—define the essential obligations broker-dealers must meet to uphold transparency, honesty, and accountability in the securities markets. Whether preventing manipulative practices during offerings under Regulation M, enforcing robust privacy safeguards through Regulation S-P, or elevating the standard of conduct via Regulation Best Interest, the collective aim is to foster an environment where all investors can confidently participate, free from the threat of fraud, abuse, or undue systemic risk. By adhering to these detailed frameworks, broker-dealers affirm the trust placed in them and help maintain the credibility upon which modern capital markets depend.

Chapter 5 Overview of the Regulatory Framework

5.1 SRO Regulatory Requirements for Associated Persons

5.1.1 Registration and Continuing Education

Registration for associated persons is the first critical step in demonstrating their qualifications to work in the securities industry. Individuals must typically pass relevant exams to confirm their competency in specific product areas, such as general securities or investment banking. After successful completion, they formally register with their firm and the appropriate self-regulatory organization (SRO). Throughout this process, background checks help ensure that candidates meet certain standards of trustworthiness, and in many cases, additional state-level "Blue Sky" registration requirements also apply.

Continuing education (CE) requirements help maintain high professional standards even after someone is registered. Most registered representatives participate in two principal types of CE: the Firm Element and the Regulatory Element. The Firm Element addresses job-specific training needs, varying based on the products and services offered by the firm, while the Regulatory Element provides periodic updates on industry rules and best practices. By requiring individuals to remain current on evolving regulations, continuing education programs protect the integrity of the financial system and reinforce each participant's commitment to responsible conduct.

5.1.1.1 SRO Qualification and Registration Requirements

Self-Regulatory Organizations (SROs), such as FINRA and the MSRB, play a critical role in setting and enforcing the standards by which financial professionals must abide. One of their primary functions is to establish qualification examinations and registration processes that ensure associated persons have the requisite knowledge and skills to serve customers properly. Individuals who wish to engage in securities activities, whether on a retail or institutional desk, typically must complete the SIE (Securities Industry Essentials) exam plus an appropriate "top-off" exam, such as the Series 7 or Series 6. This two-tier approach, introduced several years ago, helps SROs filter out unqualified candidates early while allowing prospective registrants to specialize further based on the types of products or services they intend to offer. At the firm level, broker-dealers submit applications on behalf of new hires through the Central Registration Depository (CRD) system, linking each individual's exam credentials to a specific firm affiliation. In parallel, each firm must adopt internal supervisory procedures to oversee registrants, verifying not only their exam credentials but also their adherence to day-to-day compliance requirements.

The scope of registration does not stop at the fundamental level of "general securities representative." SROs maintain an extensive list of specialized categories designed for associated persons who handle particular product lines, supervisory roles, or even compliance oversight. For instance, there are dedicated qualification exams for operations professionals, research analysts, municipal advisors, and investment banking specialists. Each category outlines the range of permissible activities for the registrant; for example, a Series 79 registration (limited to investment banking) authorizes a professional to advise on or facilitate M&A transactions and equity offerings but does not allow broad retail securities sales. Some SROs also require certain individuals to register as principals—such as branch managers or department heads—if they supervise or oversee other representatives. In these cases, passing an additional principal-level examination, like the Series 24 (General Securities Principal) or Series 26 (Investment Company/Variable Contracts Products Principal), becomes mandatory. By structuring the qualification and registration framework in this granular way, SROs effectively tailor the regulatory oversight to the specific responsibilities of each person, thereby reducing the risk that someone without the appropriate training could inadvertently (or intentionally) act outside their professional scope.

Below is an illustrative overview of some common registration categories and the associated examinations:

Registration Category	Typical Exam(s)	Scope of Activities
General Securities Representative	SIE + Series 7	Broad authority to trade and sell most types of securities
Investment Company/Variable Contracts	SIE + Series 6	Sales of mutual funds, variable annuities, and similar packaged products
Investment Banking Representative	SIE + Series 79	M&A advisory services, equity/debt offerings, and other corporate finance
Municipal Securities Representative	SIE + Series 52	Municipal bond underwriting, sales, and advisory work

Research Analyst	SIE + Series 86/87	Preparation and publication of research reports on securities or industries
Operations Professional	SIE + Series 99	Back-office functions, client onboarding, account administration

Maintaining these registrations is not a one-time event. SROs expect all registered persons to keep their knowledge current through mandatory continuing education, both on regulatory changes and on the firm's evolving product offerings and procedures. The registration framework, therefore, operates as a dynamic life cycle: it begins with the individual's initial application and exam passage, extends to more specialized registrations as their career progresses, and continues through ongoing training meant to reinforce ethical conduct and up-to-date expertise. By vigorously enforcing these qualifications, SROs aim to protect the investing public, promote efficient markets, and sustain confidence in the professionals who serve as intermediaries in the securities industry.

5.1.1.2 Registered vs. Non-Registered Person (Permitted Activities)

Within broker-dealers and other financial services firms, activities involving the offer or sale of securities generally must be conducted by registered personnel. Registration indicates that the individual has passed relevant qualification exams and is authorized to discuss, recommend, or execute trades for securities transactions. Conversely, non-registered persons—often referred to as "unregistered staff" or "non-licensed individuals"—are limited to performing administrative or clerical tasks that do not require specialized product knowledge or direct engagement in securities solicitation. This fundamental distinction is enforced by self-regulatory organizations (SROs), which require broker-dealers to maintain clear written policies preventing non-registered employees from stepping into roles meant for registered representatives.

Because the line between permissible administrative functions and impermissible sales activity can blur, SROs routinely emphasize internal training and supervision. Non-registered persons may greet clients who walk into a branch office, forward inbound calls to a registered representative, or provide clerical assistance in processing already-approved transactions. However, they may not discuss product features or suitability, solicit orders, or recommend purchases or sales of securities. Even seemingly incidental conversations—if they stray into discussing investment strategies or how a particular product might fit a client's needs—can trigger regulatory scrutiny. From the SRO perspective, these rules protect investors by ensuring that only qualified, properly supervised individuals provide advice and sell products in the securities marketplace.

Below is a comparison of permitted vs. prohibited activities for non-registered individuals:

Non-Registered Person	Permitted Activities	Prohibited Activities
Office Assistant/Clerical Staff	• Greeting customers, directing calls • Handling basic account forms at the customer's request • Scheduling appointments	• Offering or discussing investment recommendations • Soliciting trades or transactions • Explaining product features or risks

Intern/Administrative Intern	• Collecting general information for administrative records • Organizing seminar materials (pre-approved by compliance)	• Attending client meetings if recommending securities • Negotiating commissions or fees • Discussing suitability in detail
Non-Licensed Customer Service Rep	• Providing account balances or transaction status • Handling routine service inquiries (e.g., address changes)	• Providing market opinions or insights • Advising on portfolio allocations • Recommending new investment products

In many situations, non-registered staff collaborate closely with a supervising principal or registered representative to facilitate day-to-day operations. For instance, they might gather certain customer documents and pass them along to a licensed individual who completes the actual recommendation process. If compensation structures for non-registered employees are tied to performance metrics such as sales volumes or commissions generated, however, regulators may view this as encouraging unregistered sales behavior. To mitigate risks, broker-dealers often rely on compensation frameworks that avoid direct ties to sales production for unregistered individuals, such as salaries or bonuses based on overall firm profitability.

By keeping these boundaries clear, firms help maintain compliance and protect both their employees and customers. Proper oversight, combined with ongoing training about what non-registered staff can and cannot do, reduces the possibility of inadvertent regulatory violations. In the event that an unregistered person crosses into prohibited activities—such as recommending a stock or bond—both the individual and the supervising firm risk penalties or sanctions, emphasizing the seriousness with which regulators treat registration requirements.

5.1.1.3 Statutory Disqualification, Background Checks, Fingerprinting

Statutory disqualification refers to specific criteria under federal securities laws that automatically prevent an individual from becoming or remaining associated with a broker-dealer unless they obtain special permission from the regulatory authorities (such as the SEC or FINRA). Although commonly described as a "ban," statutory disqualification does not always lead to a permanent bar. Instead, it places the burden on the disqualified person and the employing firm to demonstrate why, despite the disqualifying event, that individual should be allowed to continue operating in the securities industry. Qualifying events for statutory disqualification often include convictions for securities-related crimes or felonies, injunctions involving investment-related misconduct, expulsions or suspensions from other self-regulatory organizations, or willful violations of federal or state securities laws. Because these scenarios imply a breach of trust or a risk to investor protection, regulators are typically stringent in determining whether an exception is warranted.

When a firm seeks to associate with a statutorily disqualified individual, it must file a detailed application known as a **Membership Continuance Application (MC-400)** with FINRA or the SEC. This filing lays out the circumstances of the disqualification, the individual's role, and the firm's supervisory plan to ensure there is no further misconduct. Regulators weigh factors such as the severity of the violation, the applicant's track record post-disqualification, and the effectiveness of the proposed oversight measures. In many instances, even if permission is granted, the disqualified person may be subject to heightened supervision, periodic compliance reviews, or restrictions on their activities, reflecting the regulators' commitment to shielding investors from undue risk.

Background Checks and the Role of Form U4

Broker-dealers must conduct thorough background checks before employing registered representatives or principals. This requirement is typically fulfilled via Form U4—an extensive disclosure form that collects personal, employment, and disciplinary information. Prospective representatives must enumerate their employment history, state if they have experienced any legal or financial issues (like personal bankruptcies or liens), and disclose customer complaints or prior regulatory actions. By capturing such data, Form U4 enables firms and regulators to assess whether the individual might pose a risk to investors or fail to meet the industry's "good moral character" standard. Should the person have a history suggesting potential misconduct, it does not necessarily trigger automatic statutory disqualification; however, it may prompt heightened scrutiny or additional questions about the applicant's fitness for registration.

Firms are also expected to verify the accuracy of the information provided on Form U4 to the extent possible. This may involve contacting previous employers, examining court records, or reviewing credit reports. If the individual has been named in arbitration awards, has outstanding judgments, or has faced regulatory fines, the firm must weigh whether these red flags indicate a risk that could endanger investors or the firm's reputation. Failure to conduct appropriate background checks can expose broker-dealers to regulatory sanctions and legal liability should the individual later engage in fraudulent or unethical activities.

Fingerprinting Requirements

Fingerprinting requirements serve as an additional layer of due diligence to help identify individuals with criminal records. Under Section 17(f)(2) of the Securities Exchange Act of 1934 and related FINRA and SEC rules, almost every person employed in a broker-dealer's office who is involved in the sale of securities (or who has regular access to the handling of cash or securities) must submit a set of fingerprints to the U.S. Attorney General for identification and processing. The aim is to detect any undisclosed criminal convictions that could bear on an individual's character and suitability for employment in a sensitive financial position.

In practice, broker-dealers integrate fingerprint collection into the onboarding process. Often, employees are fingerprinted as part of their initial application or on their first day at the firm. The results, processed by the FBI, are reported back to the employing broker-dealer, which then decides if any newly discovered convictions or outstanding warrants disqualify the individual from working in a registered capacity. In tandem with Form U4 disclosures, fingerprinting ensures that candidates cannot conceal a criminal background by omission or by providing misleading information. Firms that neglect or delay fingerprinting obligations risk not only regulatory censures but also expose themselves to potentially serious reputational harm if unvetted individuals commit illicit activities while under their employ.

Ensuring Robust Compliance

Taken together, statutory disqualification, background checks, and fingerprinting underscore how rigorously the securities industry polices its own membership. Regulators demand this thorough vetting to maintain high standards of integrity and professionalism, protecting investors and the broader financial system from bad actors. For broker-dealers, implementing policies that adhere to these requirements is part of everyday compliance: Human Resources and Compliance Departments must collaborate to verify applicants' histories, promptly flag any discrepancies, and determine if formal filings—such as MC-400 applications—are necessary. The continuous monitoring of individuals, through timely updates to Form U4, periodic re-fingerprinting in certain jurisdictions, and prompt disclosure of any new legal or financial entanglements, further strengthens the gatekeeping framework. This vigilance reduces the incidence of misconduct and builds trust among clients, counterparties, and regulatory bodies alike.

5.1.1.4 State Registration (Blue-Sky Laws)

State securities laws, often referred to as "Blue-Sky Laws," supplement federal regulations by imposing their own registration and compliance requirements on broker-dealers, agents, and investment advisers operating within a particular state. The term originates from early 20th-century statutes designed to protect investors from speculative schemes "as airy as the blue sky." Modern versions of these laws typically follow the framework of the Uniform Securities Act (USA), though each state's administrator retains the authority to adapt or expand upon that model. The result is a patchwork of requirements that can vary in subtle yet significant ways from one jurisdiction to the next. Consequently, firms with multi-state footprints must stay abreast of each location's filing procedures, fee structures, and deadlines for renewing registrations.

From an associated person's perspective, meeting Blue-Sky registration requirements involves more than simply holding a federal license such as the Series 7. In many cases, states mandate passing a state-law exam—commonly the Series 63 (Uniform

Securities Agent State Law Exam) or, for investment adviser representatives, the Series 65 or 66. These tests cover core elements of the USA, rules on fraudulent and prohibited practices, and the authority of the state administrator to investigate potential violations. Once licensed, individuals must keep their records current, updating the state administrator with any changes in employment, disciplinary events, or material alterations to personal information. Failing to register properly before engaging in securities business can result in serious consequences, including fines, forced rescission of completed trades, or even barring an agent from future licensure in that state.

In addition to individual agent requirements, broker-dealers themselves must register in each state where they transact business—whether because they maintain a physical office, have resident clients, or actively solicit new accounts. Some states offer limited or de minimis exemptions for firms that operate infrequently within their borders, but these carve-outs generally apply only if certain strict conditions are met (for example, having a minimal number of non-institutional clients). Similarly, states may grant special exemptions for isolated private placements or non-public offerings. However, these exemptions can be narrow, and a slight misstep or expansion of activity may trigger full registration obligations. Given the variations across jurisdictions, most broker-dealers designate internal or external compliance experts to track and manage each state's filing cycles, renewal fees, and disclosure updates, ensuring full alignment with local Blue-Sky statutes.

Although each state's Blue-Sky Laws function somewhat independently, they share a common purpose: to protect investors by ensuring that any securities professional who operates within the state is adequately qualified and transparent about their business practices. By demanding that individuals demonstrate not only general industry competence but also familiarity with local consumer protection rules, states reinforce a multi-layered regulatory system. In tandem with federal oversight, these rules create a robust framework that benefits both investors—who can expect consistent safeguards across state lines—and the securities industry as a whole, which enjoys a more credible and trustworthy marketplace.

5.1.1.5 Continuing Education (Firm Element, Regulatory Element)

Continuing education (CE) ensures that registered representatives stay current with evolving industry practices, regulatory developments, and firm-specific policies. While initial qualification exams (e.g., Series 7, Series 6) confirm baseline competence, the CE framework serves to reinforce and update that knowledge throughout a professional's career. SROs, particularly FINRA, oversee these programs, mandating that registered individuals fulfill certain requirements on an ongoing basis. Firms also have a duty to design training that addresses any unique risks or new products that have emerged in their lines of business. In this way, CE is a collaborative effort: regulators set the general parameters, and broker-dealers tailor supplemental content to the precise needs of their representatives and clientele.

From a structural standpoint, CE generally comprises two distinct elements: the Regulatory Element and the Firm Element. The **Regulatory Element**, administered electronically by FINRA, focuses on broad rule updates, ethical standards, and industry priorities. Registered individuals must complete these modules according to a prescribed schedule (historically every three years, though recent regulatory changes have shifted toward an annual model for many). Failure to complete the Regulatory Element within the required time frame can lead to the individual's registration becoming inactive, effectively barring them from conducting securities business. On the other hand, the **Firm Element** is planned and executed internally by each broker-dealer. Its content varies based on a documented needs analysis, which takes into account the firm's product offerings, customer profiles, internal control environment, and any regulatory concerns highlighted in past examinations. Topics might include updates on complex financial instruments, refresher courses on anti-money laundering protocols, or briefings on the proper handling of senior client accounts. By incorporating both the broader Regulatory Element and the firm-tailored Firm Element, the CE program endeavors to maintain a consistently high level of competence and ethical awareness throughout the industry.

Regulatory Element

The Regulatory Element has a uniform curriculum developed by FINRA, in consultation with the SEC and other industry bodies. Delivered via an online portal, these modules immerse registered persons in scenarios that test their judgment on ethical dilemmas, rule interpretations, and best practices. Real-world case studies often illustrate how rule violations occur and what preventive measures can be taken. The content is updated regularly to address emerging issues—such as changes in margin requirements, new SEC rules on disclosure, or revisions to best-interest obligations. If individuals do not complete the Regulatory Element by the deadline, their registration goes into a "CE inactive" status, meaning they cannot perform any activities that require registration until the requirement is fulfilled. This ensures that outdated or incomplete knowledge does not compromise investor protection. Firms must monitor each representative's CE status and cannot allow them to engage in registered functions if they have lapsed.

Firm Element

Where the Regulatory Element deals with industry-wide standards, the Firm Element is highly customized. Each year, firms conduct a "needs analysis" to pinpoint areas where their employees require additional training. This process could be triggered by new products in the firm's lineup, heightened regulatory scrutiny in certain business lines, or patterns of customer complaints that suggest gaps in representative knowledge. Once the needs are identified, firms develop or procure relevant training modules—sometimes in collaboration with third-party providers—and schedule them for completion by those who handle the targeted products or services. Topics can range from ethical sales practices in options trading to updated procedures for verifying client identities as part of anti-money laundering compliance. Firms also track participation and test outcomes to ensure employees absorb the material. If repeated deficiencies appear—for instance, if many employees struggle with the same concept—management may elect to expand the training scope or add refresher sessions throughout the year.

The emphasis on individualized training under the Firm Element recognizes that no two broker-dealers operate in precisely the same environment. A firm specializing in municipal bonds might focus on MSRB rule updates and best execution obligations unique to that market, whereas a retail-focused brokerage might concentrate on product disclosures for mutual funds and annuities. Yet in all cases, the core objective remains the same: to maintain a knowledgeable and ethical workforce equipped to navigate the day-to-day regulatory and operational challenges in their respective roles.

Integrating Both Elements for Ongoing Compliance

The dual structure of CE—Regulatory Element plus Firm Element—helps ensure that critical knowledge gaps never widen to the point of harming customers or undermining market integrity. By systematically reinforcing industry rules, ethical norms, and firm-specific procedures, continuing education serves as a frontline defense against misconduct and operational error. Successful completion of both elements is not merely a checkbox exercise; it is an ongoing commitment that enhances the professionalism and accountability of the entire securities industry. In practice, many firms weave CE into their broader compliance calendars, aligning them with staff performance reviews, new product launches, or regulatory deadlines, thereby creating a culture where continued learning and ethical conduct are the norm rather than the exception.

5.2 Employee Conduct and Reportable Events

5.2.1 Employee Conduct

Employees in the securities industry must uphold high ethical standards and comply with all relevant rules regarding disclosure and customer interaction. A key aspect of meeting these standards involves accurately completing the necessary registration forms, such as Form U4 and Form U5, which capture details about an individual's employment, disciplinary record, and other professional qualifications. Any omissions or misleading statements on these forms can lead to significant consequences for both the employee and the firm, including regulatory sanctions or termination of employment. Once registered, employees are also subject to ongoing requirements that mandate timely updates to their records when personal or professional circumstances change.

In addition to registration obligations, employees must handle customer complaints seriously and be vigilant for possible signs of misconduct or red flags. If a client lodges a complaint, it must be documented and escalated according to the firm's internal procedures and applicable regulatory guidelines. Failing to address legitimate customer concerns in a transparent and timely manner can result in reputational damage and legal repercussions. By consistently monitoring for irregularities in customer accounts, such as unexplained changes in investment strategies or unusual patterns of transactions, employees can help maintain the firm's commitment to ethical business practices and overall market integrity.

5.2.1.1 Form U4 and U5 (Purpose, Updates)

Form U4 (Uniform Application for Securities Industry Registration or Transfer) and Form U5 (Uniform Termination Notice for Securities Industry Registration) are pivotal documents in the lifecycle of a registered representative. They not only establish the individual's registration with regulators and self-regulatory organizations (SROs), but they also capture critical personal and professional data that can be reviewed by potential employers, clients, and regulators alike. Both forms are filed electronically in FINRA's Central Registration Depository (CRD) system, ensuring that the individual's disclosures remain in a centralized database accessible to all relevant authorities.

The **Form U4** serves as the entry point when someone begins or changes a registered role. It covers a wide array of information, including employment history, residential addresses, and any prior disciplinary actions. Of particular importance are the "disclosure questions," which ask about criminal charges, regulatory sanctions, customer complaints, and financial matters such as bankruptcies or liens. If the answer to a question is "Yes," the registrant must provide explanatory details, including supporting documents or settlement agreements. This level of transparency allows prospective employers and regulators to assess whether an individual poses risks to investors or the firm's reputation. Once the Form U4 is filed, it must be promptly updated whenever a material change in the representative's status or history occurs (for example, a newly filed lawsuit or a recently settled customer complaint). Failure to amend the form in a timely manner can lead to serious regulatory consequences—ranging from fines to potential disqualification—because accurate U4 data is considered foundational to investor protection and market integrity.

Where Form U4 captures the start or continuation of a registration, the **Form U5** documents its end. When a registered individual leaves a firm for any reason—voluntary resignation, termination, or layoff—Form U5 must be filed within 30 days of the separation. This form details the circumstances of the departure and indicates whether it was ordinary (e.g., the individual left for a new role) or due to a rule violation or internal investigation. If the latter is the case, the firm must provide a succinct explanation on the U5, allowing future employers and regulators to see if the individual was "permitted to resign" or dismissed for misconduct. The U5 is also subject to ongoing updates; if a firm obtains new information that could alter the reason for termination, an amended filing is required to keep the CRD record accurate. This follow-up responsibility helps prevent a scenario in which an ex-employee's record remains misleadingly clean if further details of misconduct emerge after they have left.

Maintaining the accuracy of both forms is critical. A single incomplete or misleading statement on the U4 could later result in regulatory actions under FINRA Rules 2010 or 2020, or disqualification under the Exchange Act if the omission involves certain criminal or disciplinary histories. The U5 likewise carries weight: if a termination is coded incorrectly or reported late, the departing representative and the firm may each face repercussions. For professionals, the challenge is twofold: ensuring their own records remain up to date, and monitoring any changes to their status that a prior firm might file in the CRD system. Because these documents serve as the industry's primary mechanism for tracking an individual's regulatory and employment track record, the U4/U5 process stands as a cornerstone of transparency, enabling informed hiring decisions and promoting a culture of accountability in the securities industry.

5.2.1.2 Consequences for Misleading/Omitted Information

When a securities professional provides incomplete or inaccurate information—intentionally or otherwise—it undermines the foundational trust that investors, regulators, and firms rely upon for fair and transparent markets. In the registration context, this often arises when individuals submit or update Form U4 with missing or incorrect disclosures on topics such as criminal history, prior regulatory sanctions, or financial problems. But other situations can be equally problematic: for instance, someone downplaying the severity of a customer complaint, omitting an outside business activity, or misrepresenting their professional qualifications. Regardless of the specifics, a failure to disclose is taken seriously by regulators and may trigger enforcement action under core rules like FINRA Rule 2010 ("Standards of Commercial Honor") or the Exchange Act's anti-fraud provisions.

Once an inaccuracy is discovered—perhaps via a FINRA cycle exam, a background check, or a customer dispute—the potential ramifications can extend far beyond a simple administrative correction. The individual and their supervising firm may face fines, suspensions, or even industry bars in extreme cases. If the misstatement involves criminal conduct or other serious misconduct (e.g., a felony that was never disclosed), the employee could be deemed statutorily disqualified, requiring a separate application process for them to continue working in the industry. Moreover, the firm itself might be found culpable for inadequate supervision, leading to additional disciplinary measures. These outcomes not only damage professional reputations but also can severely limit future career prospects, since all such violations remain accessible in regulatory databases. Beyond formal punishment, firms often lose confidence in representatives who have demonstrated dishonesty, resulting in termination or refusal to hire for future roles.

Below is a brief overview of some common examples of misleading or omitted information and their typical implications:

Misleading/Omission Scenario	Potential Impact
Failing to disclose a prior bankruptcy on Form U4	Possible fine or suspension; jeopardy for future registration renewals
Omitting criminal charges or convictions	Statutory disqualification; potential industry bar or heightened supervisory requirements
Downplaying or failing to report a major customer complaint	Regulatory fines for the representative and firm; extended audits or scrutiny on complaint-handling processes
Concealing outside business activities	Violations of firm policies and FINRA rules; risk of conflicts of interest and subsequent disciplinary actions

From the regulator's perspective, ensuring that investors can access accurate data on a securities professional's background is integral to preventing fraud and abuse. For that reason, even "minor" omissions—like forgetting to update contact information or failing to mention a small consumer complaint—can escalate if they signal an overall pattern of disregard for compliance obligations. The industry's emphasis on full disclosure reflects a zero-tolerance approach toward false or misleading information, underscoring the notion that honesty and transparency form the bedrock of ethical conduct. By recognizing these high stakes and diligently confirming that all required details are accurate and up to date, registered representatives help maintain their standing in the industry and protect the interests of the investing public.

5.2.1.3 Customer Complaints and Red Flags

Customer complaints are a critical indicator of whether a firm's internal controls and supervisory systems are functioning properly. A "complaint" can be defined broadly as an expression of dissatisfaction related to the broker-dealer's or registered representative's services, and it often comes in a documented form—such as a written letter or an email—though some regulators also allow for complaints lodged via recorded phone calls. Firms have a regulatory obligation to investigate every complaint promptly and impartially, documenting the outcome and any corrective actions taken. This process not only helps resolve the immediate problem but also provides valuable feedback that can uncover systemic issues like overly aggressive sales practices, poor communications about fees, or inadequate disclosures. Because unresolved complaints can escalate into regulatory inquiries or legal disputes, compliance departments typically maintain comprehensive logs to track complaint trends and identify potentially problematic patterns that might require further scrutiny.

Identifying and responding to red flags is equally vital. Red flags may arise when a client's account shows sudden spikes in trading activity or changes in investment objectives that do not align with the customer's financial profile. Other signs include repeated customer inquiries about unexplained fees, requests for large cash withdrawals without reasonable justification, or allegations that a representative is conducting unauthorized trades. Brokers should approach these signs with heightened vigilance, as they can indicate deeper misconduct or misunderstandings that, left unchecked, could lead to formal complaints or enforcement actions. Early detection can allow the firm to intervene, either by engaging the customer in clarifying conversations or by escalating the matter to supervisors who can determine if the activity constitutes negligence, intentional wrongdoing, or a simple communication gap.

Below is a concise illustration of common red flags that might precede or accompany formal complaints:

Potential Red Flag	Possible Concern
Unusually rapid turnover in account ("churning")	Excessive trading primarily to generate commissions
Frequent margin calls without clear explanation	Overuse of leverage beyond customer's risk tolerance
Abrupt or unsanctioned changes to account profiles	Possible unauthorized trading or incorrect suitability assessment
Customer confusion about fees or commissions	Inadequate disclosures or misrepresentation of product costs
Consistent pattern of small, undisclosed withdrawals	Suspected misappropriation or exploitation

When a complaint does materialize—either triggered by these red flags or emerging unexpectedly—firm policies usually direct representatives to notify supervisors or compliance personnel immediately. A formal investigation then commences, which may involve reviewing account statements, transaction logs, and any relevant communications between the customer and the representative. If wrongdoing is detected, the firm may take disciplinary measures against the employee involved and, in more serious cases, file a report with regulators. Throughout the process, accurate recordkeeping becomes essential, both for demonstrating responsiveness to the complaint and for defending the firm if the matter advances to arbitration or litigation. By systematically addressing complaints and red flags, firms foster a culture of accountability and enhance their overall capacity to protect customer interests.

5.2.2 Reportable Events

Certain employee actions, known as "reportable events," must be disclosed to the broker-dealer and, in many cases, also reported to regulators. These actions can range from engaging in outside business activities or private securities transactions to receiving certain gifts or gratuities, making specific political contributions, or experiencing a significant personal financial event like a bankruptcy. By requiring disclosure, firms can better supervise how these situations intersect with employees' professional roles, ensuring that conflicts of interest or compliance risks are identified and mitigated early.

The objective of reporting these events is to maintain transparency and avoid any appearance of impropriety that could harm a firm's reputation or regulatory standing. Employees who neglect to report outside activities or other potentially compromising events may inadvertently violate industry rules and firm policies, triggering supervisory or disciplinary measures. Ultimately, a proactive and open approach to disclosure supports the broader goal of fostering ethical conduct and maintaining confidence in the financial industry.

5.2.2.1 Outside Business Activities

Outside business activities (OBAs) refer to any business pursuits a registered representative undertakes outside the scope of their primary employment with a broker-dealer. This could encompass positions such as managing a small family business, providing financial consulting services for a fee, or even running a separate e-commerce venture. Regulators like FINRA (under Rule 3270) require registered persons to provide prior written notice to their firm when engaging in these activities. The firm's obligation, in turn, is to evaluate potential conflicts of interest and decide whether to approve, restrict, or prohibit the activity. Failure to disclose an outside business activity can compromise the firm's ability to supervise potential risks—such as overlapping customer bases or incompatible fiduciary duties—and may result in disciplinary actions against both the individual and the broker-dealer.

At the core of these rules is the recognition that outside engagements may create situations in which a representative's responsibilities to the firm or its clients could conflict with the representative's other interests. For example, a representative who holds a senior role at an unrelated financial services startup might be tempted to promote that startup's products to the broker-dealer's clients, thereby blurring professional boundaries. In other instances, undisclosed OBAs can mask personal financial pressures—like large debts or investment obligations—that increase the risk of improprieties such as churning or misappropriating client funds. By requiring advanced notice and ongoing review of any outside activity, firms can pre-empt such issues, install additional supervisory controls where necessary, and maintain a higher level of transparency across all facets of a representative's professional life.

Below is an example illustrating key aspects of OBAs:

Scenario	Potential Risks & Considerations
A registered representative starts a real estate brokerage on weekends	• Customers of the broker-dealer might seek property transactions, raising the question of dual compensation. • The firm must confirm that the rep will not recommend real estate deals to current securities clients, potentially risking conflict of interest.

In practical terms, firms often require representatives to fill out an OBA disclosure form, specifying the nature of the outside pursuit, anticipated time commitments, compensation structures, and any client overlap. Compliance or supervisory personnel then assess whether the activity might erode the representative's objectivity or compromise sensitive client information. Sometimes, the firm may approve the activity under certain conditions—like restricting solicitation of the broker-dealer's customers. In other cases, the risk profile may be deemed too high, resulting in a denial of the request. Once authorized, OBAs are often subject to periodic reviews, particularly if a representative's role in the external venture evolves over time. This ongoing vigilance helps ensure that the previously approved arrangement remains valid and does not morph into a more intrusive or conflicted scenario.

While these disclosure and approval processes can be time-consuming, they serve an essential function in safeguarding investors and preserving the integrity of the securities industry. By maintaining clear lines of communication and setting firm expectations for representatives' extracurricular endeavors, broker-dealers can minimize the likelihood of conflicts, protect their reputation, and comply with the regulatory requirement to supervise all aspects of registered personnel's business conduct.

5.2.2.2 Private Securities Transactions

Private securities transactions are often referred to as "selling away" when they are conducted outside the regular scope of a representative's employment with a broker-dealer. Under FINRA rules (notably, FINRA Rule 3280), registered representatives must provide prior written notice to their firm before participating in any private securities transaction, regardless of whether they anticipate direct or indirect compensation. This requirement applies to a range of securities offerings that take place away from the employing firm's supervision, including private placements, limited partnership interests, or even certain crowd-funded investments. The core purpose of these regulations is to ensure that broker-dealers maintain clear oversight over any securities-related activity involving their representatives, mitigating conflicts of interest and protecting customers from risks that the firm has neither sanctioned nor supervised.

When representatives fail to disclose their intent to engage in these transactions—particularly if they are soliciting or recommending private deals to potential investors—they expose both themselves and the firm to liability. First, the representative may violate federal and state securities laws if the offering is improperly structured or lacks proper disclosures. Second, the employing firm could face regulatory scrutiny for failing to supervise its associated persons effectively, even if it was unaware of the activity. FINRA and other regulators take such misconduct seriously, as off-the-books securities dealings can mask fraudulent schemes, create unrecognized conflicts, and deprive investors of the safeguards afforded by a fully supervised transaction. If a representative breaches these rules, disciplinary outcomes can range from monetary fines to industry suspensions or, in egregious cases, a permanent bar from the industry.

Below is an illustration of key considerations in the private securities transaction landscape:

Element	Relevance to Private Securities Transactions
Written Notice to Firm	Must disclose the nature, compensation arrangement, and participant information in advance.
Firm Approval or Denial	The broker-dealer assesses the risk; if approved, the firm may impose supervision protocols.
Compensation	Rules apply whether the rep is directly or indirectly compensated; volunteer involvement can also trigger disclosure.
Ongoing Oversight	If the firm approves, it must monitor the transaction's progress and compliance.

In practice, if a representative wishes to, for example, invest in or promote a friend's startup that issues equity, they must submit detailed documentation describing the offering's structure, their role in soliciting or advising potential investors, and any expectation of compensation. The firm's compliance department will evaluate the offering for compliance with securities regulations and determine whether the representative's participation is permissible. This might entail ensuring that the startup's offering memorandum is consistent with Regulation D (if it's a private placement), verifying that the representative isn't extending promises outside of what is disclosed, or reviewing any marketing materials to confirm their accuracy and alignment with regulatory guidelines. If approved, the firm remains responsible for supervising the representative's activities in connection with that offering, which can require periodic reporting, additional training, or specialized oversight of customer communications.

Ultimately, effective controls around private securities transactions are crucial in preventing "selling away" from morphing into a vehicle for fraudulent or misleading sales. By enforcing these rules, FINRA and the employing firm seek to maintain transparency, protect customers from unvetted opportunities, and uphold the integrity of the registered representative's relationship with the firm. Representatives who observe these procedures—in conjunction with disclosing any outside business activities—help safeguard themselves against regulatory violations while reinforcing a culture of compliance and investor protection within the industry.

5.2.2.3 Political Contributions (MSRB Rule G-37)

MSRB Rule G-37 addresses concerns about "pay-to-play," a practice where firms or individuals might make political contributions to public officials or candidates in the hope of securing municipal underwriting or advisory business. The rule imposes strict prohibitions on municipal securities dealers, municipal advisors, and certain associated individuals. In broad terms, if a firm or a covered individual makes a political contribution to an official involved in awarding municipal securities business, the firm can be banned from engaging in negotiated municipal underwriting business with that issuer for a specified period—commonly two years. This extends to both direct contributions and indirect contributions funneled through political action committees or "conduits." The rule's purpose is to preserve fairness in public financing transactions, ensuring that awards are based on merit rather than political favoritism.

At the heart of G-37 is the requirement that firms track and publicly disclose all relevant political contributions. Each quarter, municipal dealers and advisors must file a Form G-37 with the MSRB, listing contributions made by the firm and its Municipal Finance Professionals (MFPs) to officials of municipal issuers with which the firm does or seeks to do business. Failure to report or an attempt to conceal contributions can lead to enforcement actions, heavy fines, or even suspension from the industry. The rule also differentiates between different types of contributors and the maximum allowed personal contributions, often referred to as a "de minimis" exemption for contributions made by an MFP to candidates in their home voting district. For instance, an MFP may legally contribute a small amount (e.g., up to $250) to a candidate for whom they are eligible to vote without triggering the automatic ban. However, surpassing that threshold—even unknowingly—could prompt a two-year ban that prohibits the firm from negotiating municipal securities business with the affected issuer.

Below is a simplified illustration of Rule G-37's primary components:

Key Element	Description
Covered Persons	Municipal Finance Professionals (MFPs), including advisors, principals, underwriters, and certain supervisors
Prohibited Contributions	Contributions that exceed de minimis levels or are intended to influence an official to award business
Two-Year Ban	If a prohibited contribution is made, the firm is banned from negotiated underwriting/advisory work for two years
Disclosure (Form G-37)	Firms must file quarterly reports of political contributions to issuer officials and bond ballot campaigns

From a supervisory standpoint, broker-dealers implement internal policies requiring pre-clearance of all political contributions by employees who qualify as MFPs. This helps the firm avoid inadvertently breaching the threshold and triggering the ban. Compliance departments also monitor external political action committees to ensure the firm is not indirectly contributing beyond what is legally permissible. The significance of these controls cannot be overstated: a single unauthorized contribution could cause the firm to lose large underwriting assignments, seriously impacting both revenue and reputation. Ultimately, Rule G-37's emphasis on disclosure and prohibition serves to deter the use of contributions as a lever for securing municipal securities business, upholding transparency and investor confidence in the municipal bond market.

5.2.2.4 Gifts, Gratuities, Non-Cash Compensation Limits

Gifts, gratuities, and other forms of non-cash compensation are subject to strict rules in the securities industry to safeguard impartiality and uphold investor protection. Regulators, including FINRA (notably under Rule 3220) and the MSRB, set limits on the value and nature of gifts that can be given or received by registered representatives without creating conflicts of interest. The classic example is the $100 per-person, per-year limit imposed by many such rules, but there are nuances and exceptions. For instance, ordinary and customary business entertainment—such as a modest dinner or tickets to a local sporting event—may be permissible if attended by the host and if it directly relates to fostering a professional relationship. However, lavish outings, extravagant vacations, or purely personal gifts that exceed the threshold likely cross the line and could expose both the giver and recipient to regulatory scrutiny.

The purpose of these limits is to prevent scenarios where a broker-dealer's representative might feel pressured to recommend products or services as a "favor" in exchange for an expensive gift. Conversely, gifts from customers, product sponsors, or other third parties could undermine the representative's objectivity when making recommendations. Firms must often keep detailed logs of gifts and non-cash perks and require employees to submit requests for pre-approval if the value appears to exceed set thresholds. Some broker-dealers also maintain internal guidelines that are even more stringent than the regulatory minimum, for example restricting event sponsorships or capping meal expenditures to amounts below the regulatory safe harbor. By setting clear policies and reviewing them frequently, firms reduce the risk that these benefits become a lever for undue influence, while preserving the business relationship building that comes from normal hospitality.

Below is an illustrative example of how firms categorize permissible vs. impermissible gifts or non-cash compensation:

Category	Typical Examples	Compliance Approach
Nominal Gifts	A pen or T-shirt under $100, small holiday token	Usually allowed without prior approval unless frequent or repetitive
Customary Business Entertainment	Meals, sporting events, cultural outings (host attends)	Permitted if "ordinary and usual," directly related to a business relationship
Excessive or Lavish Items	Luxury hotel stays, overseas trips unrelated to business	Generally disallowed or subject to strict pre-approval & documentation
Cash Equivalents	Prepaid gift cards, gift certificates, or other "near-cash" items	Often treated like cash; usually disallowed if over $100 total value

Firms must also pay attention to non-cash compensation from product sponsors, such as mutual fund or annuity providers, which could be structured as contests, awards, or sales incentives. Regulatory guidance typically mandates that such programs be based on total sales across a broad product line, rather than tied to a specific investment or security. This ensures that representatives are not "steered" toward pushing one particular product purely for the sake of winning a pricey reward. Ultimately, compliance in this arena balances relationship management and healthy networking with the imperative to avoid inappropriate influence. By maintaining transparent gift logs, enforcing adherence to stated thresholds, and training staff on the rationale behind these policies, broker-dealers foster an environment in which objective advice remains paramount.

5.2.2.5 Disclosures of Felonies, Financial Misdemeanors, Liens, Bankruptcies

Revealing criminal or financial background details is a fundamental component of maintaining transparency and integrity in the securities industry. Registered representatives and applicants must disclose felonies, certain misdemeanors (especially those relating to financial crimes), and significant financial events like bankruptcies or unsatisfied liens. These disclosures typically occur through Form U4 updates, which capture pivotal information used by regulators and employing firms to evaluate an individual's suitability for continued registration. A felony or a financial-related misdemeanor can raise concerns about trustworthiness and potential vulnerabilities, such as the temptation to commit fraud to address personal financial pressures. Likewise, bankruptcies and liens can prompt heightened supervision and may factor into a firm's hiring or retention decisions, as they may imply recurring financial troubles that could put customer interests at risk.

Although the presence of a felony conviction or certain misdemeanors can result in statutory disqualification under federal securities laws, not every offense automatically precludes one from working in the industry. Regulators assess the nature, severity, recency, and context of these convictions, while the individual or employing firm can, in some situations, pursue a waiver or an MC-400 application to seek permission for continued employment. With bankruptcies and liens, the critical concern is whether these events indicate a pattern of poor financial management that could undermine one's fiduciary obligations. While such disclosures do not automatically disqualify a registered representative, they can trigger extra scrutiny from compliance departments or result in conditions such as mandatory direct deposit for commissions or a requirement to notify supervisors before conducting personal transactions. By enforcing strict reporting requirements—and verifying that all relevant facts are fully disclosed—regulators and firms promote an environment in which customer protection remains paramount, and potential conflicts stemming from an individual's financial challenges are responsibly managed.

Below is a brief illustration of different disclosures and their general implications:

Disclosure Type	Regulatory/Employment Impact
Felony Conviction	Can lead to statutory disqualification; requires detailed review, possible MC-400 application for continued employment
Financial-Related Misdemeanor	May result in restricted duties or heightened supervision; can also contribute to statutory disqualification if the offense is severe enough

Bankruptcy (Personal or Business)	Raises concerns about financial stability; typically requires additional oversight and/or disclosures to customers if relevant
Outstanding Liens or Judgments	Implies ongoing financial risk; may lead to probationary measures, enhanced reporting, or conditions imposed by the employing firm

In practice, firms must verify these disclosures and keep them updated throughout a representative's tenure. Any new felony charges, financial misdemeanor indictments, or significant changes in credit status (like a new lien or a second bankruptcy filing) must be reported promptly on Form U4. Delays or omissions in reporting can lead to severe disciplinary actions, including fines and possible registration revocations. By insisting on full candor in this realm, regulators help shield investors from representatives who might misuse their positions if under personal financial stress, and they bolster overall trust in the securities industry's standards of professionalism.

5.3 Key Rules and Regulations

5.3.1 FINRA By-Laws (Articles I, III, IV, V, VI, XII, XV)

The FINRA By-Laws form the foundational governance framework through which FINRA carries out its mission of overseeing broker-dealers, protecting investors, and ensuring market integrity. While FINRA Rules often address specific operational and conduct standards, the By-Laws establish the organization's core structure, its decision-making processes, and the rights and responsibilities of its members. Taken together, they define how FINRA is organized, how it levies fees and dues, how its leadership is constituted, and how disciplinary matters are administered. This section explores seven key Articles within the By-Laws (I, III, IV, V, VI, XII, and XV), illustrating how each guides FINRA's role as an industry self-regulator.

Many of these Articles lay out essential elements such as membership obligations, governance procedures, and disciplinary authority. Articles I and III clarify foundational concepts of membership and scope, while Articles IV and V describe the inner workings of FINRA's Board of Governors and its officers. Articles VI, XII, and XV address financial matters, disciplinary processes, and amendments, respectively. By understanding the nuances in each Article, industry participants—ranging from broker-dealers to individual associated persons—gain insight into the processes that shape their interactions with FINRA and, by extension, their regulatory obligations.

Article I: Definitions and General Provisions

Article I provides the definitional backbone for the entire set of By-Laws. It clarifies key terms and phrases, such as "Board," "Firm," "Member," and "Associated Person," ensuring that the rest of the By-Laws can be interpreted consistently. By establishing precise definitions, FINRA eliminates ambiguity about who or what falls under its regulatory oversight. For instance, the Article might specify that a "Member" is a broker-dealer admitted to FINRA's membership and subject to all applicable rules, while an "Associated Person" includes registered representatives, principals, and certain key employees.

Although definitional in nature, Article I has concrete regulatory implications. For example, clarifying what constitutes a "Member" or "Associated Person" ensures that FINRA can accurately assert jurisdiction, whether it is carrying out an examination or initiating a disciplinary action. This Article may also detail how the term "Exchange Act" or "Rules" is to be understood within the context of the By-Laws, avoiding confusion between FINRA's own rules and those promulgated by the SEC or other authorities. Without Article I's carefully worded definitions, enforcement and compliance efforts could be hamstrung by interpretive disputes, weakening the overall regulatory structure.

Article III: Membership

Article III deals with the prerequisites, processes, and ongoing obligations for broker-dealers seeking FINRA membership. Typically, a prospective firm must demonstrate financial and operational competence and agree to abide by FINRA rules. Applicants undergo a detailed review in which FINRA assesses the firm's capital adequacy, supervisory systems, and the background of its principals to ensure the prospective member can conduct business without posing undue risk to investors or the public.

Beyond the initial admission requirements, Article III may outline the conditions under which membership can be suspended or terminated. For instance, if a firm fails to meet net capital requirements, or if it becomes subject to certain disciplinary sanctions, FINRA can impose restrictions or revoke membership outright. This Article often works in tandem with other By-Law sections—particularly those covering disciplinary authority—to ensure that membership remains a privilege contingent upon ongoing compliance. By defining the grounds for admission and exit, Article III underscores FINRA's gatekeeping function, which helps maintain high standards of conduct among broker-dealers.

Article IV: Board of Governors

Article IV addresses the composition, roles, and responsibilities of FINRA's governing body, the Board of Governors. It typically spells out how Governors are elected or appointed, the length of their terms, and the balance of industry versus public representatives. The mix of public members and industry insiders is crucial to maintaining both subject-matter expertise and an independent perspective—two elements that help reinforce investor trust in the self-regulatory system.

Paragraph 2

This Article often includes stipulations on quorum requirements, voting procedures, and committees formed under the Board's oversight (e.g., an Executive Committee or an Audit Committee). The Board's powers might include approving rule proposals for submission to the SEC, overseeing FINRA's budget, and guiding strategic initiatives. In essence, Article IV ensures that governance remains transparent and accountable; it also allows the Board to delegate specific tasks to committees or FINRA management, while reserving key policy decisions and rulemaking authority for itself.

Article V: Officers and Agents

Article V typically shifts focus to the individuals charged with executing the Board's directives, including FINRA's Chief Executive Officer, President, Secretary, Treasurer, and any other designated officers. It spells out how these officers are elected or appointed, their terms of service, and the general scope of their responsibilities. For instance, the CEO may oversee day-to-day operations and represent FINRA in external matters, while the Treasurer might handle the organization's finances and ensure compliance with budgeting protocols set forth by the Board.

Beyond describing each officer's function, Article V may also address succession planning, the removal or replacement of officers, and indemnification provisions that shield them from personal liability when acting in good faith on FINRA's behalf. These details help ensure continuity in leadership and clarify the chain of command for implementing the By-Laws and the Board's policy decisions. By codifying officers' roles and responsibilities, Article V contributes to a well-defined organizational structure where accountability flows from top to bottom.

Article VI: Dues, Assessments, and Fees

Article VI tackles the financial underpinnings of FINRA's regulatory operations. As a self-regulatory organization, FINRA derives much of its funding from membership assessments, user fees, and other dues paid by member firms. This Article typically spells out how these assessments are calculated—for instance, based on firm size, trading volume, or other metrics—and how often they must be paid. Failure to remit dues can lead to sanctions or suspension, ensuring that members contribute their fair share to the cost of regulation.

In many cases, Article VI also covers the process for adjusting fee structures in response to changes in market conditions or FINRA's regulatory needs. For example, if the industry sees a surge in trading volume, FINRA might adjust specific fees to ensure it can handle increased surveillance demands. Conversely, if economic downturns reduce the total number of registered representatives or active firms, FINRA might revise its fees to maintain enough revenue to fulfill its mission without imposing undue burdens on the remaining members. Overall, Article VI ensures that the organization's financial base remains stable and transparent.

Article XII: Disciplinary Proceedings

Article XII outlines FINRA's authority and procedures for investigating and adjudicating disciplinary matters against members and their associated persons. It may detail how formal complaints are initiated—sometimes by FINRA staff or after the discovery of potential violations during routine exams—and how a firm or individual can respond. The By-Laws might specify the role of hearing panels and the appeals process, including potential escalation to the National Adjudicatory Council (NAC) or even the SEC if further review is warranted.

In addition to laying out the mechanics of the disciplinary process, Article XII often enumerates the possible sanctions that FINRA can impose, ranging from censures and monetary fines to suspensions or permanent bars. It may also address the settlement process, enabling respondents and FINRA to resolve cases without a full hearing if they can reach a mutually acceptable agreement. By making disciplinary procedures transparent and accessible, this Article reinforces investor confidence that violations will be pursued fairly and consistently.

Article XV: Amendments to By-Laws

Article XV governs how changes to FINRA's By-Laws themselves can be introduced, debated, and ultimately approved. It usually requires that any proposed amendment go through multiple layers of review—starting with the Board of Governors and potentially involving public commentary or direct input from member firms. If the proposal is approved internally, it may still require the SEC's final sanction before becoming effective, reflecting FINRA's status as an SRO under SEC oversight.

This Article might also delineate the conditions under which urgent or emergency amendments can be made—for example, if a sudden market development necessitates a swift regulatory response. Such provisions aim to balance the need for thorough deliberation with the realities of a rapidly evolving financial landscape. By detailing the formalities for altering its governing documents, Article XV provides a structured pathway for modernization, ensuring that FINRA's core regulatory architecture remains adaptable yet grounded in due process.

Summary Table of FINRA By-Laws (Select Articles)

Article	Subject	Core Focus	Key Implications
I	Definitions	Establishes clear terminology for all By-Laws	Clarifies who is considered a Member, Associated Person, etc.; removes interpretive ambiguity
III	Membership	Admission requirements, membership obligations, suspension/termination	Gatekeeping function; ensures broker-dealers meet standards for financial and operational competence
IV	Board of Governors	Composition, responsibilities, committee delegations	Provides for balanced representation (industry vs. public); sets policy, approves rule proposals

V	Officers and Agents	Roles of CEO, President, Secretary, Treasurer, etc.	Defines chain of command, outlines succession and removal procedures, establishes accountability
VI	Dues, Assessments, and Fees	Funding mechanism for FINRA operations through member fees, user charges	Ensures stable revenue stream; adjustable fee structures to address market changes or budgetary needs
XII	Disciplinary Proceedings	Formal complaint process, hearing panels, sanction powers	Establishes due process for alleged rule violations; potential for fines, suspensions, bars
XV	Amendments to By-Laws	Procedure for proposing, reviewing, and finalizing amendments	Balances thorough review with responsiveness to industry changes; requires SEC oversight for adoption

Taken as a whole, these Articles reveal how FINRA manages its internal governance and external oversight responsibilities. Article I's definitional clarity ensures that FINRA's regulatory purview is applied consistently, while Articles III and IV formalize the membership and leadership structures essential to self-regulation. Articles V and VI delve into operational facets, ensuring that qualified officers run day-to-day affairs and that members financially support the organization's regulatory mission. Finally, Articles XII and XV provide the enforcement and evolutionary frameworks—defining how FINRA disciplines its members and how the By-Laws can be reconfigured over time. By examining each Article in depth, participants in the securities industry gain a richer understanding of FINRA's foundational pillars and the procedural safeguards that guide its mission of protecting investors and maintaining market integrity.

5.3.2 FINRA Rules (Registration, CE, Reporting, etc.)

FINRA's regulatory framework consists of a broad set of rules that govern how broker-dealers and their associated persons conduct business. These rules address everything from the initial registration of individuals (including qualification exams) to continuing education requirements and the reporting of relevant disciplinary or customer-related events. Firms must implement comprehensive supervisory systems to ensure compliance with these standards, while individuals bear personal responsibility for understanding and adhering to the obligations that apply to their specific roles. The FINRA rules discussed in this section—spanning the 1000 Series and particular rule numbers such as 1122, 1240, 2060, 2263, 2267, 3110(e), 3220, 3270, 3280, 4513, 4530, and 8312—represent some of the key pillars of FINRA's oversight. When examined in aggregate, these rules help maintain high ethical standards, protect investors, and preserve market integrity.

A unifying theme across these requirements is the emphasis on transparency and accountability. Whether by enforcing rigorous registration criteria (1000 Series), mandating the prompt reporting of changes to an individual's background (Rule 1122), or obligating firms to keep meticulous records of complaints and compensatory arrangements (Rules 4513 and 3220), FINRA's rules aim to create an environment in which potential risks are identified early and handled proactively. At the same time, they allow for a measure of flexibility: many rules provide space for firm-level policies that may be more restrictive than the regulatory minimum, thus enabling broker-dealers to adopt best practices suited to their unique business models. This blend of structured directives and adaptable guidelines underpins the self-regulatory principle: the industry polices itself within a well-defined framework, all while remaining subject to the SEC's overarching authority.

1000 Series: Member and Associated Person Registration

The 1000 Series lays out the requirements for broker-dealer membership in FINRA, as well as the registration of associated persons. It covers the process by which individuals must pass qualification examinations (e.g., the SIE plus a specialized top-off exam) to demonstrate their competency in handling securities transactions. Additionally, these rules address re-testing, permissive registrations, and the responsibilities of principals who supervise registered representatives. Firms must ensure that each individual's category of registration aligns with their functional role—be it a General Securities Representative, an Investment Banking Representative, or an Operations Professional.

A key feature of the 1000 Series is the stipulation that individuals and firms must keep their registration information current, reflecting any material changes such as name, address, or employment status. This requirement works in tandem with Form U4 filings and updates (explored in detail elsewhere in the text) to provide a transparent view of the industry's active participants. If a firm or representative fails to maintain registration or engages in prohibited activities without the proper licensing, FINRA may impose a range of sanctions. This underscores how the 1000 Series forms the baseline for ensuring that every person operating under FINRA's umbrella has the requisite knowledge, ethical orientation, and accountability measures.

Rule 1122: Filing of Misleading Information as to Membership or Registration

Rule 1122 prohibits any member or associated person from filing false or misleading information regarding membership or registration status. For instance, if an individual omits past disciplinary actions on a Form U4, or if a firm misrepresents its net capital to secure membership, the rule serves as a direct enforcement mechanism. In practical terms, this means that both initial filings and subsequent amendments must be scrupulously accurate. Oversight of these disclosures typically falls to a firm's compliance department, which must verify the veracity of background information, test results, and financial metrics submitted to FINRA.

Violations of Rule 1122 can carry severe repercussions. Fines are the most common sanction, but FINRA may also suspend or bar individuals from association with any member firm, particularly if the misconduct indicates a broader pattern of deceit. At the firm level, knowingly submitting false information can result in heightened regulatory scrutiny and even jeopardize membership standing. Rule 1122 thereby reinforces the industry's emphasis on honesty and full disclosure, dovetailing with the moral imperative that shapes many other FINRA regulations.

Rule 1240: Continuing Education Requirements

Continuing education (CE) is central to ensuring that registered persons stay informed about evolving products, services, and regulations. Rule 1240 outlines the two main components: the Regulatory Element and the Firm Element. The Regulatory Element, administered by FINRA, focuses on broader industry updates and ethical case studies, typically requiring completion on a cycle (traditionally every three years, though recent changes have shifted many registrations to an annual framework). The Firm Element is customized by the broker-dealer, based on a yearly needs analysis identifying skill gaps or areas of regulatory focus.

Noncompliance with Rule 1240 can lead to a "CE inactive" status, meaning a registered representative cannot legally perform functions requiring registration until the requirement is fulfilled. Firms must therefore track each representative's CE schedule and remind them to complete modules promptly. In practice, compliance departments integrate these deadlines into broader training calendars, ensuring that employees continually refresh their knowledge of securities rules, emerging risk factors, and firm-specific procedures.

Rule 2060: Use of Information Obtained in Fiduciary Capacity

Rule 2060 prevents member firms from exploiting confidential information acquired in a fiduciary or special relationship for the purpose of soliciting or obtaining business. An example might be a trustee who learns about a large forthcoming share sale by a beneficiary or an escrow agent privy to sensitive data about a merger deal. If a firm or representative uses this privileged insight to market products or engage in targeted solicitations, they breach Rule 2060. Violations can also overlap with insider trading regulations if the information is deemed material and nonpublic.

The rationale for Rule 2060 is clear: the securities industry depends on fiduciaries respecting client confidences. Breaching that trust for personal or corporate gain undermines not only the interests of the client but also the integrity of the marketplace. Firms typically address this rule within their written supervisory procedures, calling for strict protocols around the handling and dissemination of confidential information. Representatives are trained to compartmentalize data gleaned from fiduciary relationships and to seek supervisory guidance before using any sensitive details outside the narrow scope in which they were entrusted.

Rule 2263: Arbitration Disclosure to Associated Persons

Under Rule 2263, firms must provide a specific disclosure statement to associated persons about the arbitration process as it pertains to employment controversies. This disclosure ensures that employees understand they may be required to arbitrate disputes—including statutory discrimination claims—through the FINRA arbitration forum rather than taking them to court. The rule aims to keep employees fully informed of the arbitration clause within their Form U4 or employment agreements.

While many employees sign these clauses as a condition of their registration, controversies occasionally arise when an employee later claims they were unaware of the binding nature of arbitration. Rule 2263 eliminates that argument by mandating a clearly worded notice. Firms document the representative's receipt of this disclosure, creating a transparent and documented agreement on dispute resolution methods.

Rule 2267: Investor Education and Protection

Investor education stands at the heart of FINRA's mission, and Rule 2267 exemplifies that commitment. The rule obligates member firms to provide customers with the FINRA BrokerCheck hotline number and website address, along with the firm's own contact details. By doing so, it directs investors to FINRA's BrokerCheck database, where they can review a broker or firm's disciplinary history, registration status, and employment background.

This mandatory communication typically appears on account statements or in client correspondence, ensuring that the information is regularly in front of customers. The transparency provided by BrokerCheck helps investors make informed decisions about the professionals handling their money. A firm's failure to include these details can result in regulatory actions, as it denies clients a critical resource for verifying the trustworthiness and track record of their brokers.

Rule 3110(e): Supervisory Systems (Background Investigations)

Rule 3110(e) compels member firms to ascertain the good character, business repute, qualifications, and experience of prospective associated persons, via thorough background checks. This process often includes verifying the accuracy of Form U4 disclosures, fingerprinting, credit checks, and direct outreach to previous employers. The aim is to detect red flags—such as undisclosed criminal charges or repeated customer complaints—that could pose a risk if the individual were allowed to handle client assets or sensitive information.

If a firm neglects to perform adequate due diligence, it risks fines and other penalties, particularly if the newly hired individual commits violations. Beyond regulatory concerns, insufficient vetting can damage a firm's reputation and invite litigation from harmed customers. Consequently, most broker-dealers treat 3110(e) as a key plank of their supervisory regime, conducting not just initial but also periodic re-checks to ensure ongoing compliance.

Rule 3220: Influencing or Rewarding Employees of Others (Gifts)

Rule 3220 sets a $100 annual limit on gifts given by a member or associated person to employees of another business. While business entertainment events (where the host is present) may be exempt from certain aspects of the limit if considered "ordinary and usual," purely personal or extravagant gifts are restricted. The rule's objective is to prevent improper inducements that might sway the judgment of employees at another firm, leading them to recommend certain products or services for personal gain.

Firms often maintain gift-tracking systems to log the date, recipient, and estimated value of items given. They also issue guidelines distinguishing nominal tokens from lavish perks. A violation of Rule 3220 not only risks sanctions but can raise serious ethical concerns and erode confidence among institutional partners or retail investors who expect unbiased recommendations. In tandem with other non-cash compensation rules, it forms an important barrier to pay-to-play arrangements across the industry.

Rule 3270: Outside Business Activities

Outside Business Activities (OBAs) refer to any revenue-generating pursuits a registered individual engages in outside their affiliation with the broker-dealer. Rule 3270 mandates that representatives provide written notice to the firm prior to starting or modifying any such activity. Firms then evaluate the potential for conflicts of interest, customer confusion, or regulatory infractions. If the firm deems the OBA too risky or time-consuming, it may reject the request or impose conditions (e.g., limiting client overlap).

In practice, OBAs can range from part-time real estate sales to positions on the boards of private companies. Representatives who fail to disclose these pursuits can face disciplinary action for "selling away" or for undisclosed financial relationships. This rule thus protects customers, ensuring they are not misled about a representative's outside loyalties or possible preferential ties to external businesses.

Rule 3280: Private Securities Transactions

Rule 3280 addresses "private securities transactions," a subset of OBAs that specifically involve the buying, selling, or recommending of securities outside the regular scope of the representative's employing firm. The rule requires prior written notice, detailing the specifics of the transaction, compensation (if any), and the role of the representative. If the firm approves, it must supervise the activity, effectively adopting it as part of the firm's overall business. If disapproved, the representative must refrain from participating.

A classic concern is "selling away," where a representative promotes unvetted securities to their clients, potentially circumventing the firm's supervisory structures. Violations of Rule 3280 can result in severe penalties, reflecting FINRA's priority to ensure that all securities transactions fall under the firm's compliance umbrella. Investors rely on that oversight for consistent due diligence and risk disclosures, and "private" deals can undermine these safeguards if not properly monitored.

Rule 4513: Records of Customer Complaints

Rule 4513 obligates firms to maintain a dedicated file or record of all written customer complaints, including those submitted electronically. This log must capture details such as the date of the complaint, the complainant's name, and a concise account of the issue. Retention periods under this rule often align with other recordkeeping guidelines, typically requiring firms to keep complaint documentation for at least four years.

By systematically retaining complaint data, firms can spot patterns—for instance, recurring complaints against a particular representative or a repeated product that generates dissatisfaction. This fosters a proactive approach to addressing underlying causes—be they compliance gaps or training deficiencies. From FINRA's standpoint, the ability to audit these logs is vital to ensuring that serious complaints aren't swept under the rug or left unresolved.

Rule 4530: Reporting Certain Events

Rule 4530 mandates the prompt reporting of specific events, such as regulatory actions, criminal charges, or customer settlements above a certain monetary threshold. Firms must notify FINRA within a set number of days upon learning of these incidents, ensuring that the regulator can monitor emerging risks or patterns of misconduct. The rule often dovetails with Form U4 obligations, but 4530 is broader, requiring firm-level event reporting beyond individual-level updates.

Failure to report under Rule 4530 can be as severe a violation as the underlying event itself, because it impedes FINRA's real-time view of industry trends. Through these disclosures, FINRA can allocate resources effectively—for instance, by scheduling targeted exams or investigating a potentially fraudulent product line. Firms, therefore, must build robust pipelines between compliance, legal, and management teams, ensuring that any reportable event triggers a timely and accurate notification.

Rule 8312: FINRA BrokerCheck Disclosure

Rule 8312 authorizes FINRA to release information from the CRD (Central Registration Depository) system to the public via

BrokerCheck. This includes a representative's employment history, licensing status, and certain disciplinary records. By making such data publicly accessible, Rule 8312 promotes transparency, empowering investors to vet potential brokers or firms before opening accounts or investing funds.

In addition to mandated disclosures, the rule outlines how corrections or expungement processes occur when representatives dispute or resolve past allegations. Because BrokerCheck is a vital tool for consumer protection, FINRA closely monitors any attempts to inappropriately remove or sanitize a record. Representatives must follow established protocols, often requiring arbitration or court orders, to expunge inaccurate or unfounded complaints. Thus, Rule 8312 balances the public's right to vital information with due process for those who dispute the veracity of certain entries.

FINRA Rule	Primary Focus	Key Compliance Takeaways
1000 Series	Membership & Registration	Establishes processes for firm membership and individual qualification exams
1122	Accurate Membership/Registration Filings	Prohibits filing misleading statements; ensures integrity in regulatory disclosures
1240	Continuing Education (CE)	Mandates annual or triennial training (Regulatory Element) and firm-specific instruction (Firm Element)
2060	Fiduciary Information Usage	Bars misuse of confidential data for personal solicitation or gain
2263	Arbitration Disclosures to Employees	Informs employees about mandatory arbitration clauses

		and processes
2267	Investor Education and Protection	Requires distribution of FINRA BrokerCheck info to clients, promoting transparency
3110(e)	Background Investigations	Obligates firms to verify character, business repute, and qualifications of prospective hires
3220	Gifts to Employees of Others	Caps gifts at $100 per year to deter conflicts of interest and undue influence
3270	Outside Business Activities (OBAs)	Requires prior written notice for any external income-generating activity, enabling conflict analysis
3280	Private Securities Transactions	Governs “selling away” by requiring pre-approval for securities transactions outside the firm’s scope
4513	Customer Complaint Records	Demands systematic retention and review of written complaints, aiding oversight
4530	Reporting Certain Events	Enforces timely disclosure of regulatory actions, criminal charges, or major settlements
8312	FINRA BrokerCheck Disclosure	Authorizes public release of CRD data, bolstering investor awareness of broker/firm backgrounds

Collectively, these FINRA rules touch nearly every dimension of broker-dealer operations: from how firms and representatives enter the industry (1000 Series, 3110(e)) and stay current on regulations (1240), to how they interact with investors (2267, 4513, 4530) and external entities (2060, 3270, 3280). They underscore FINRA's broader mission of upholding ethical standards, ensuring transparency, and safeguarding consumer trust. By deeply integrating these rules into everyday compliance practices—through robust training, thorough documentation, and vigilant supervision—firms reinforce the integrity of the marketplace and maintain a stable foundation for investor protection.

5.3.3 CBOE Rule 7.10 (Fingerprinting)

CBOE Rule 7.10 sets forth fingerprinting requirements designed to ensure that every individual with access to the Chicago Board Options Exchange (CBOE) trading facilities—or who may otherwise handle or supervise cash, securities, or confidential information at a member firm—is properly vetted. These fingerprinting obligations trace back to broader federal mandates under Section 17(f)(2) of the Securities Exchange Act of 1934, but Rule 7.10 adapts those overarching principles to the specific context of CBOE membership and operations. The fundamental objective is straightforward: to prevent individuals with undisclosed criminal histories—or those who might pose a significant risk to investor funds—from occupying roles that allow them to exploit the markets or customers for illicit ends.

Scope and Applicability

Under Rule 7.10, any individual who meets the Exchange's defined criteria for "covered persons" must submit a set of fingerprints for processing by an authorized agency, typically the FBI. The definition of "covered persons" usually includes all associated persons or employees of a CBOE member firm who are directly involved in securities or options-related business, especially when such responsibilities involve handling sensitive customer data, trade orders, or physical securities. Moreover, the requirement can extend to IT staff or operations personnel who have system-level access that could allow them to initiate or conceal unauthorized transactions. The end result is a broad net: even support staff who do not actively trade may be caught under the rule if their position grants them any significant influence or oversight regarding the flow of securities or cash.

Firms are responsible for collecting fingerprints upon a new hire's onboarding or upon a role change that places an existing employee into a "covered person" category. Once the fingerprints are obtained, the firm forwards them to the relevant fingerprint processor, which then checks them against nationwide databases (such as the FBI's Criminal Justice Information Services). The outcome of the check is reported back to the employer, who must evaluate any "hits" or criminal record findings to determine whether they disqualify the individual from their intended role. Certain offenses, particularly those involving fraud or financial crime, can result in statutory disqualification under federal securities laws, thus barring the individual from working in a registered capacity without explicit regulatory clearance.

Compliance Process and Firm Obligations

Firms typically integrate Rule 7.10 requirements into their broader hiring and compliance workflows. When a candidate receives a conditional job offer for a position requiring access to CBOE trading or technology systems, the firm immediately initiates the fingerprinting procedure. Many firms contract with third-party fingerprinting vendors that use electronic scanning devices for quick and accurate submission. Once the results come back, the hiring manager and compliance department jointly review them to confirm that the applicant does not present undue risk.

Table: Typical Fingerprinting Compliance Steps

Step	Action	Purpose
1. Identify Covered Role	Determine if the prospective hire or role expansion places the individual under Rule 7.10.	Ensures that individuals handling securities, funds, or privileged info are thoroughly vetted.
2. Fingerprint Submission	Obtain and submit electronic or ink-based prints to an approved processor.	Complies with Section 17(f)(2) and CBOE requirements for background checks.
3. Results Review	Evaluate any positive matches or criminal entries that appear in the report.	Assesses whether the individual poses regulatory or reputational risks.
4. Conditional Clearance	If no disqualifying items arise, proceed with employment or role change.	Officially documents that the firm has fulfilled its due diligence duties.
5. Ongoing Updates	Track the employee's status in case future role changes trigger additional checks.	Maintains an evolving internal record ensuring that staff remain appropriately vetted.

Beyond the initial hire or role transition, CBOE members may have to periodically re-verify the records of existing employees, especially if new information surfaces about a potential criminal investigation. While Rule 7.10 does not necessarily mandate continual or annual fingerprinting updates, many firms choose to adopt a cyclical review or rely on alert systems (such as those built into the CRD system or public court databases) to stay current on changes in employees' legal statuses. Failing to conduct these checks thoroughly can expose a firm to regulatory sanctions, as well as reputational fallout if an unvetted employee later commits wrongdoing that could have been foreseen by a proper background screen.

Consequences of Non-Compliance

Failure to comply with CBOE Rule 7.10 can manifest in multiple ways. For instance, a firm might neglect to fingerprint a new hire whose position clearly meets the threshold for "covered person," or it could fail to take action when the fingerprint results reveal a disqualifying offense. Any of these oversights can trigger disciplinary actions by the CBOE or other regulators, ranging from monetary fines to the firm's potential suspension. If willful misconduct is suspected—such as deliberate misreporting or concealment of background issues—more severe penalties, such as expulsion from the Exchange or individual statutory disqualification, may apply.

Additionally, if a client or counterparty suffers financial harm because of malfeasance by an employee who should have been screened out, the firm could face civil liability in arbitration or court proceedings. The legal argument might revolve around the firm's inadequate due diligence and whether it violated industry "best practices" or explicit regulatory mandates. Thus, the cost of ignoring fingerprinting rules can extend well beyond the immediate regulatory fines and deeply impact both the firm's finances and reputation.

Interaction with Other Regulatory Requirements

Rule 7.10 does not operate in isolation; it typically intersects with SEC regulations (e.g., Rule 17f-2), FINRA requirements (especially for associated persons), and state law requirements (the so-called "Blue-Sky" laws). A robust compliance program will unify these mandates into a single, coherent process, ensuring that an individual who must register with multiple SROs or across multiple states is appropriately vetted for all jurisdictions simultaneously. For example, a representative who needs to be licensed in multiple states will likely undergo not just CBOE fingerprinting but also additional verifications mandated by FINRA or the state licensing bodies. Coordinating these processes can minimize redundant steps while reducing the possibility that critical items fall through the cracks.

Another notable synergy is with a firm's anti-money laundering (AML) compliance. While fingerprinting focuses on personal criminal history, AML programs concentrate on suspicious monetary activities, yet both share an overarching goal: preventing and detecting unethical or illegal behavior. A thorough fingerprint-based background check offers early detection of individuals with patterns of fraud or other financial crimes, which can serve as a valuable input into the firm's broader AML risk assessment. In this manner, compliance efforts addressing different rule sets reinforce each other, forging a more secure operating environment.

CBOE Rule 7.10, though straightforward in its fingerprinting mandate, has far-reaching implications for how member firms handle staffing, supervision, and risk management. By requiring all "covered persons" to undergo a background check via fingerprint submission, the rule limits the entry of potentially harmful individuals into the exchange ecosystem. Its benefits extend well beyond preventing immediate criminal activities: thorough screening fosters a culture of heightened accountability and diligence that resonates across all facets of broker-dealer operations. Firms that implement robust, repeatable processes to comply with Rule 7.10 position themselves as trustworthy participants in the marketplace, signaling to clients, regulators, and counterparties alike that they take the integrity of financial transactions seriously.

5.3.4 MSRB Rules (G-2, G-3, G-7, G-10, G-20, G-37)

The Municipal Securities Rulemaking Board (MSRB) regulates municipal securities dealers, municipal advisors, and banks engaging in underwriting or trading municipal bonds. Its rules establish professional standards to protect investors, municipal entities, and the public interest. While MSRB's regulations build upon federal securities laws, they cater to the unique structures and risks associated with municipal finance—such as varying credit profiles, tax considerations, and large-scale public infrastructure projects. This section explores several essential MSRB rules (G-2, G-3, G-7, G-10, G-20, G-37) that shape the responsibilities and conduct of municipal market participants.

An overarching theme is the MSRB's emphasis on ensuring all associated persons hold adequate qualifications (Rules G-2 and G-3) and that dealers disclose and manage conflicts ethically (Rule G-20). Additionally, G-7 focuses on record retention, while G-10 outlines investor education obligations, and G-37 guards against "pay-to-play" in the municipal underwriting process. In effect, these rules guard each phase of activity: from ensuring professional competency to deterring conflicts of interest, ensuring transparency, and maintaining robust anti-corruption safeguards.

Rule G-2: Standards of Professional Qualification

Rule G-2 mandates that any broker, dealer, or municipal securities dealer transacting in municipal securities must meet the MSRB's standards of professional qualification. This requirement extends to both individuals (e.g., municipal securities representatives) and firms. The rule integrates with the broader MSRB examination framework, demanding that associated persons successfully pass the relevant qualification exams—such as the Municipal Securities Representative Qualification Examination (Series 52) or Municipal Advisor exams—before engaging in specific municipal activities.

Failing to comply with G-2 can lead to stringent consequences. Firms may face censure or fines if they permit unqualified representatives to solicit or execute municipal bond trades. Moreover, these lapses can undermine investor confidence, as municipalities and public institutions rely heavily on the expertise of dealers to underwrite and market offerings. In practice, Rule G-2 ensures that all individuals operating in this space maintain appropriate credentials, supporting a stable, well-informed marketplace.

Rule G-3: Classification and Qualification of Municipal Securities Professionals

Rule G-3 defines various municipal securities professional categories—such as municipal securities representatives, municipal securities principals, and municipal advisors—and establishes the required qualification exams. Each category delineates permissible activities. For instance, a municipal securities principal must oversee underwriting, trading, and sales operations in municipal bonds, while municipal advisors concentrate on advising state and local governments on bond issuances. By segmenting these roles, G-3 ensures that each person's exam and registration type aligns closely with their real-world functions.

Beyond initial qualification, G-3 emphasizes continuing education. Similar to FINRA's CE requirements, municipal securities professionals must fulfill a certain amount of ongoing training. Firms must conduct annual needs analyses to keep employees informed about regulatory changes, new financial products, and evolving best practices. This framework mirrors other SRO mandates for continuing education but is specifically tailored to municipal finance nuances, such as analyzing general obligation vs. revenue bonds, or understanding complex aspects of municipal disclosure and tax law.

Rule G-7: Information Concerning Associated Persons

G-7 compels municipal securities dealers to maintain comprehensive records about associated persons, particularly regarding professional background, disciplinary history, and qualifications. This documentation includes employment histories and regulatory or legal incidents that could affect their fitness to handle municipal securities business. By instituting robust recordkeeping, G-7 aligns with parallel obligations under federal rules and FINRA guidelines, safeguarding transparency about the identities and track records of individuals entrusted with public financing deals.

Firms must ensure that these records stay current. If an associated person experiences a material change—such as a new outside business activity, regulatory action, or criminal charge—the firm is responsible for updating internal files and, if required, disclosing this to regulators. Noncompliance can trigger fines or enforcement actions, reflecting the MSRB's goal of preventing individuals with questionable histories from managing multi-million-dollar municipal transactions that affect taxpayers and local communities.

Rule G-10: Investor and Municipal Advisory Client Education

While Rule G-10 has evolved over time, its core requirement is that dealers (and, in certain contexts, advisors) provide written disclosure to clients about how they can resolve disputes and obtain educational materials. This often involves distributing information about the MSRB's role, the MSRB website, and how to submit a complaint. By ensuring clients have easy access to these resources, G-10 reinforces a culture of awareness and self-advocacy among municipal securities investors.

Rule G-10 can also shape how municipal advisors interact with their governmental clients. Advisors may be required to inform municipalities about MSRB's oversight, how to access official rule guidance, and avenues for filing grievances if they suspect unethical practices. As municipalities may not always have in-house financial experts, G-10's provisions help level the playing field, ensuring that even smaller local governments have the tools to hold advisors and dealers accountable for their recommendations.

Rule G-20: Gifts, Gratuities, and Non-Cash Compensation

Rule G-20 restricts gifts and gratuities from a municipal securities professional to employees of entities with which the professional does or seeks to do business. It sets a cap—traditionally $100 per person, per year—on most gifts, consistent with similar FINRA regulations. The aim is to prevent conflicts of interest that might arise if lavish presents sway officials or employees to steer underwriting or advisory contracts toward certain dealers or advisors.

In addition to explicit gifts, G-20 may address various forms of non-cash compensation. For instance, it delineates circumstances under which typical business entertainment—like dinners or local sporting events—may be permissible, provided the host attends and the event is reasonably related to fostering legitimate business relationships. Violations of G-20 can lead to enforcement actions and erode trust in the municipal market, as perceived pay-to-play tactics or questionable incentives undermine the fundamental principle that municipal deals should be awarded based on merit, cost-effectiveness, and public benefit.

Rule G-37: Political Contributions and Prohibitions on Municipal Securities Business

Rule G-37 is pivotal for deterring "pay-to-play" within municipal securities. Under this rule, if a municipal securities dealer or certain associated professionals—known as Municipal Finance Professionals (MFPs)—contribute above a specified de minimis threshold to a political official who can influence the award of municipal underwriting business, the firm becomes ineligible to engage in negotiated municipal securities business with that issuer for two years. This prohibition also extends to certain contributions funneled through political action committees.

Firms must publicly disclose all relevant political contributions through quarterly filings, typically using MSRB Form G-37. Noncompliance can result in bans, fines, or more severe disciplinary actions. The rule recognizes a small allowance—often $250—for contributions to officials for whom the MFP is eligible to vote, balancing the constitutional right to political participation with the necessity of preventing quid pro quo arrangements. By enforcing these disclosures and prohibitions, G-37 upholds the integrity of public bond offerings, ensuring that local governments choose underwriters or advisors free from political coercion and strictly based on merit.

Comprehensive Table of the Featured MSRB Rules

Rule	Primary Subject	Core Requirements/Implications
G-2	Standards of Professional Qualification	Ensures that anyone dealing in municipal securities is appropriately licensed and meets competency standards.
G-3	Classification and Qualification of Municipal Personnel	Defines roles (e.g., Municipal Securities Representative, Principal, Advisor) and outlines mandatory exams and continuing education.
G-7	Information Concerning Associated Persons	Mandates detailed records of each associated person's background, disciplinary history, and updates for material changes.
G-10	Investor and Municipal Advisory Client Education	Requires firms to provide disclosures on complaint processes, MSRB's role, and other educational resources for municipal customers.
G-20	Gifts, Gratuities, and Non-Cash Compensation	Restricts gifts to $100 per individual per year; prevents undue influence or conflicts in awarding municipal contracts.
G-37	Political Contributions and Prohibitions on Municipal Securities Business	Limits campaign contributions to politicians with influence over bond issuance; imposes a two-year ban if contributions exceed the de minimis threshold.

The MSRB rules (G-2, G-3, G-7, G-10, G-20, G-37) work in tandem to maintain an orderly, transparent municipal securities market by setting explicit standards for professional qualifications, recordkeeping, client disclosures, and ethical conduct. Whether preventing unqualified individuals from selling complex municipal bonds (G-2, G-3) or barring political pay-to-play (G-37), each rule shores up confidence in a market that finances critical public projects across the United States. In practice, firms weave these MSRB mandates into their operational and compliance frameworks through rigorous training, internal audits, and continuous monitoring. This ensures that municipal securities professionals are well-equipped to serve municipalities and investors ethically, while safeguarding the long-term viability of the public finance system.

5.3.5 SEC Rules and Regulations (Exchange Act of 1934, Section 3(a)(39); Rule 17f-2)

The Securities Exchange Act of 1934 (often referred to simply as the "Exchange Act") serves as a cornerstone of U.S. securities regulation, establishing the framework for the ongoing oversight of broker-dealers, exchanges, clearing agencies, and other market participants. Among its many provisions, **Section 3(a)(39)** clarifies the conditions under which an individual or entity becomes "statutorily disqualified" from participating in the securities industry, while **Rule 17f-2** spells out specific fingerprinting requirements aimed at ensuring that broker-dealers and other securities professionals are adequately vetted for prior criminal history. Together, these elements reinforce the Exchange Act's overarching goal of promoting fair, transparent markets through robust rules on who may engage in securities-related activities and how they must be supervised.

From a practical standpoint, statutory disqualification criteria (outlined in Section 3(a)(39)) capture various forms of misconduct—

ranging from certain felonies and misdemeanors to injunctions or regulatory bars—while Rule 17f-2 operationalizes the screening process by which firms identify such potential disqualifications. The net effect is a two-pronged safeguard: on one side, regulators and SROs (self-regulatory organizations) rely on the definition of statutory disqualification to keep unfit individuals out of sensitive roles; on the other, the fingerprinting mandate ensures that undisclosed criminal records come to light before those individuals can do harm.

Section 3(a)(39) of the Exchange Act: Statutory Disqualification

Section 3(a)(39) enumerates the grounds upon which a person or entity is considered "statutorily disqualified" under federal securities laws. Typical triggers include convictions for certain financial or securities-related crimes, injunctions obtained by the SEC, expulsions from self-regulatory organizations, and willful violations of securities statutes. Once disqualified, the individual cannot act as a registered or associated person of a broker-dealer or other regulated entity unless they obtain a waiver or an affirmative decision (often through an application such as FINRA's MC-400) that justifies their continued participation in the industry. Because such misconduct can significantly undermine investor trust, Section 3(a)(39) imposes a high bar for re-entry, typically requiring rigorous supervision and evidence of genuine rehabilitation.

Crucially, Section 3(a)(39) often operates in tandem with parallel rules from the SEC and SROs—for instance, FINRA's By-Laws and disciplinary rules—ensuring that every part of the U.S. securities framework applies consistent standards when assessing moral fitness. The disclosure of a statutory disqualification event on Form U4, or the discovery of a disqualifying offense during a background check, triggers immediate review. If disqualification is confirmed, the firm must decide either to sever the relationship or to seek an exemption. Noncompliance or a late disclosure can subject both the individual and the firm to disciplinary actions, reinforcing the seriousness with which regulators treat statutorily disqualifying events.

Rule 17f-2: Fingerprinting Requirements

Rule 17f-2 provides the practical mechanism for identifying individuals who may be subject to statutory disqualification. It requires that any person associated with a broker-dealer (and in some cases, other registered entities) who handles or is responsible for securities, funds, or financial records be fingerprinted. Those fingerprints are submitted to the Attorney General—through the FBI or an authorized channel—for a criminal background check. The rule extends not just to frontline registered representatives but also to certain back-office employees and technology staff who might access confidential financial or personal data. Consequently, the coverage can be quite broad, depending on each firm's internal organizational structure and the roles employees play.

Firms typically embed the Rule 17f-2 process in their overall hiring and supervisory procedures. Applicants for any covered role will usually undergo fingerprinting alongside reference checks, credit checks, and Form U4 completion. If the fingerprint results reveal a previously undisclosed crime, the firm may be obligated to file an amended U4 and evaluate whether the new information triggers statutory disqualification. Firms also need to maintain a robust internal record of these submissions and results, ensuring that they can demonstrate compliance if the SEC or an SRO examines their onboarding files. Noncompliance—such as failing to fingerprint a new hire or ignoring glaring red flags—exposes the firm to regulatory censure and potentially severe reputational harm.

Practical Interplay Between Section 3(a)(39) and Rule 17f-2

Although Section 3(a)(39) and Rule 17f-2 serve distinct functions—defining disqualifications and unearthing potential grounds for disqualification—they operate in unison to preserve market integrity. A firm's compliance department must design a workflow that quickly flags matches between an applicant's fingerprint record and the disqualifying criteria in Section 3(a)(39). This might involve a multi-step approach: first, the firm obtains the fingerprint check; second, compliance compares the results to the statutory disqualification definitions; and third, if there's a match, the firm consults internal counsel or contacts an SRO about possible next steps (e.g., filing a membership continuance application).

In addition, the synergy between these two provisions helps unify federal securities oversight with SRO rules—such as FINRA's background check mandates under Rule 3110(e) or the CBOE's fingerprinting requirements (CBOE Rule 7.10). By harmonizing multiple layers of supervision, the SEC fosters an environment in which unscrupulous individuals have fewer avenues to slip through the regulatory cracks. Investors benefit because they can place greater trust in the qualifications and ethics of securities professionals, knowing that the entire system, from government rules to exchange-level policies, is oriented toward detecting and barring high-risk actors.

Compliance Challenges and Best Practices

Implementing Section 3(a)(39) and Rule 17f-2 can be logistically complex, particularly for large firms with hundreds or thousands of employees spread across multiple jurisdictions. Human Resources (HR) and Compliance teams must coordinate to ensure that every new hire who falls under "covered" roles is fingerprinted promptly, and that reassignments or promotions are also reviewed for potential coverage. The tracking of results—especially if an individual's record emerges with ambiguous or incomplete data—can require further investigation and possible consultation with legal counsel. Meanwhile, the firm must balance thorough due diligence with fair hiring practices, respecting the privacy rights of job candidates.

To navigate these challenges, many broker-dealers adopt centralized compliance systems that automatically generate fingerprint requests and store the results in a secure, auditable format. They may also schedule periodic refresher training for supervisors, so they can detect any "red flags" that arise post-hire, prompting an updated background check if necessary. Documentation is critical: if regulators question how a statutorily disqualified individual accessed a client's account or handled securities, the firm needs to produce clear records showing either that the person was in the process of obtaining a waiver or that the firm immediately terminated or reassigned the individual upon discovery of the offense. In the face of potential enforcement actions, thorough recordkeeping often proves the deciding factor in demonstrating good-faith compliance.

Provision	Purpose	Key Takeaways
Exchange Act Section 3(a)(39)	Defines grounds for statutory disqualification (e.g., criminal convictions, regulatory bars)	Individuals who meet these criteria cannot serve in certain securities roles without an exemption or waiver
Rule 17f-2	Requires fingerprinting of certain broker-dealer personnel	Results feed into FBI checks to detect undisclosed criminal records; integral to identifying statutory disqualifications

Section 3(a)(39) and Rule 17f-2 illustrate how the SEC wields its authority under the Exchange Act of 1934 to shape the permissible composition of the securities workforce. By precisely delineating the offenses that trigger statutory disqualification and by mandating fingerprint-based background checks, the SEC ensures that participants in broker-dealer functions do not pose undue risk to clients or the broader financial system. From a compliance standpoint, successful implementation hinges on robust policies, meticulous documentation, and close collaboration between HR, legal, and compliance teams. For investors and the public, these provisions serve as a vital safety net, filtering out unethical or fraudulent actors and reinforcing confidence in the integrity of U.S. capital markets.

Chapter 6 Study Roadmap, Test-Day Tips, and Additional Resources

6.1 Recommended Study Plan

6.1.1 Timeline Suggestions (4-Week, 8-Week)

A well-structured study plan can make the difference between cramming in the final days and feeling confident on test day. Before choosing how long to spend preparing, consider your current familiarity with the material, your daily schedule, and the intensity of your other commitments. If you have extensive background in finance—or if you can devote many hours per day to studying—the **4-week plan** might be sufficient. In this accelerated route, you'll compress your reading and practice work into a tight window, which requires strong discipline to maintain momentum. Each week, you could tackle one major content area, supplementing with a daily round of practice questions to keep the concepts fresh. Toward the end of the four weeks, allow a few days for final review of any weak points, and take at least one full-length practice exam under timed conditions to replicate the pressure you'll face on the actual test day.

The **8-week plan**, by contrast, offers more breathing room for those balancing work or family obligations. You'll have the flexibility to spread content review across multiple sessions per topic, reinforcing your mastery through spaced repetition. In the early weeks, aim for manageable chunks of reading—often one or two chapters at a time—followed by targeted quiz sessions to cement your understanding. During the latter half, ramp up your practice exam schedule, gradually shifting from open-book practice to strictly timed, no-aid simulations. This gradual approach not only ensures you don't burn out but also allows you to spot knowledge gaps early, with enough time to correct course. When integrated with any supplemental online tools, such as flashcards or e-learning portals, the extended study timeline can significantly reduce test anxiety and boost comprehension.

Below is a sample comparison of how you might allocate your hours and tasks in each approach:

Plan	Recommended Duration	Reading Load	Practice Exams	Final Review Period
4-Week Plan	2–3 hours/day	Complete 1 major content area per week; keep pace	1–2 exams in final week	3–5 days of intense review at the end
8-Week Plan	~1–2 hours/day	1–2 chapters per week; spaced repetition	3–4 exams spread over last month	1–2 weeks of lighter, methodical review

Regardless of which timeline you choose, stay flexible. If you find yourself struggling with a particular concept—such as calculating yields on various fixed-income products—add extra study sessions or shift priorities until you're comfortable. Combine reading with hands-on exercises, like writing out sample problems or discussing the concepts with a study partner, to engage multiple learning styles. By following a structured schedule, whether it's a four-week sprint or an eight-week marathon, you'll position yourself for a more efficient and less stressful exam preparation experience.

6.1.2 Integrating Reading, Practice Questions, and Online Tools

A balanced study plan blends active reading of textbook chapters with consistent self-testing through practice questions, followed by periodic reinforcement using interactive tools. Start by carving out dedicated reading sessions—perhaps one chapter or subchapter at a time—using highlighting or note-taking to lock in key concepts. Soon after finishing a section, test your retention with targeted practice questions, which help you spot areas that may require a second look. This immediate cycle of "read, quiz, review" enables you to address misunderstandings before they become ingrained. It also breaks up the reading into more engaging segments, so you're less likely to zone out during heavier topics.

To deepen your mastery, take advantage of the e-learning platform's unlimited exam simulator, digital flashcards, and printable mock exams. After reading a chapter on, say, trading practices or margin accounts, launch a custom quiz with 10–15 questions in the simulator to gauge how well you've absorbed the material. If you spot repeat trouble areas—like specific margin rules—use the digital flashcards for quick daily drills on definitions and formulas. Periodically, integrate a full-length printable exam under exam-like conditions to replicate real test pressure. Because all these tools are accessible on both desktop and mobile, you can review flashcards while commuting or squeeze in a short practice quiz during downtime. By weaving together text-based study with regular practice and digital reinforcement, you create a well-rounded approach that keeps each topic fresh and increases confidence in your overall readiness.

Below is a concise sample of how you might structure a single study session:

Study Component	Possible Activity	Benefit
Textbook Reading	Read one subchapter with highlights/notes	Establishes foundational concepts and context
Practice Questions	Launch 10–15 quiz questions in the simulator	Identifies weak spots immediately and reinforces learning
Flashcard Review	Flip through digital flashcards for formulas or definitions	Quick recall drill, suitable for short gaps in your schedule
Periodic Mock Exam Segment	Attempt a timed 20–25 question segment from a printable exam	Builds stamina and simulates real testing conditions

By systematically pairing textbook study with on-the-go mobile reviews and simulated exams, you ensure that every hour you spend is targeted and cumulative. Over time, this integrated method reduces the likelihood of last-minute cramming and fosters a deeper comprehension that endures well beyond exam day.

6.2 Test-Day Logistics

6.2.1 What to Bring (Valid ID, Confirmation Letter)

One of the first steps to a smooth exam day is having the correct identification. Test centers typically require at least one government-issued photo ID that has your name exactly matching how it appears on your exam registration. This can be a passport, driver's license, or a similar document, as long as it is both valid and unexpired. Ensuring that your ID matches your exam confirmation details avoids delays or denials at check-in, so double-check well in advance that the spelling and name format align with what you used when registering. If there is any discrepancy—such as a recently changed last name—contact the testing authority ahead of time for instructions on acceptable supporting documents or name corrections.

Along with a valid ID, you will need a printed or digital copy of your exam confirmation letter. This official confirmation usually includes a reservation or seat number and confirms the test date and location. Some test centers require you to present a physical copy, while others may let you show the email on your phone. If you're unsure which format is accepted, err on the side of caution and bring a printed version. The confirmation letter not only proves your legitimate booking but also helps the test center staff direct you to the correct room or computer station. In the event of any reservation mishap, it serves as tangible proof of your scheduled exam and can expedite any administrative fixes needed to get you checked in promptly.

Common Forms of Acceptable ID	Key Features
Driver's License	Government-issued, photo, unexpired
Passport	Photo ID, exact name match, unexpired
Military ID	Official photo ID with matching name
State-Issued ID Card	Photo ID if you do not have a license

6.2.2 Prohibited Items/Activities (Notes, Calculators, Smartphones)

On exam day, security protocols require that you leave any unauthorized materials outside of the testing room. Personal notes, study sheets, and even blank paper cannot be brought in, as the test center will typically provide you with an approved scratch pad or erasable board if necessary. Likewise, electronic devices are strictly forbidden, so items such as smartphones, smartwatches, or tablets must be turned off and stored in a designated area—often a locker—before you proceed to your station. These restrictions exist to prevent unfair advantages and to preserve the validity of every test result. Even if you believe you have a legitimate need—like using your phone for a last-minute scheduling update—it's best to store it safely and not risk being flagged for a violation that could derail your entire exam experience.

Another prohibited item is your personal calculator. Many test centers supply an on-screen calculator or provide a simple one if your exam explicitly allows it, so bringing your own device is unnecessary and not permitted. Attempting to use unauthorized notes or electronics not only violates the exam's integrity standards but can also result in immediate expulsion from the testing center, alongside potential disciplinary actions that could affect your career. If you have any questions about specific items—like a medical device you need to keep with you—contact the exam sponsor or test center well in advance to obtain written approval. By following these guidelines and leaving personal study aids behind, you help maintain a level playing field for everyone pursuing their professional credentials.

Item	Reason for Prohibition
Personal Notes	Risk of unauthorized reference to content during the exam
Personal Calculators	On-screen or test-provided calculators ensure standardized use
Smartphones/Smartwatches	Potential for messaging, internet access, or cheating

6.2.3 Checking In and Using the Testing System

Arriving at the test center, you will first check in with the administrative staff, who may require you to confirm your registration details and identity before granting you access to the exam area. This process typically involves scanning your ID, verifying your appointment time, and ensuring you've stored all prohibited items. Sometimes, you might be asked to provide a digital signature or have your photo taken for security records. Allow enough time in your schedule for these pre-exam steps, as arriving late can limit your options if procedural delays arise. The staff will then assign you to a specific workstation or testing room, guiding you past any secure boundaries into the controlled environment where the exam takes place. You must follow the proctor's instructions closely, from placing personal belongings in designated storage to carefully logging in to the correct exam platform.

Once seated at your workstation, you'll encounter a brief orientation on how to navigate the testing software. This on-screen tutorial usually covers basic features such as moving forward and backward through questions, marking items for review, and operating any built-in calculators or highlight functions. While it might be tempting to rush, it's worth taking a moment to absorb the layout and test out the tools you'll rely on throughout the exam. Some systems let you flag questions for later review, display an overview of answered versus unanswered items, or allow you to highlight passages in a question stem. These capabilities can prove invaluable, especially when managing multiple-choice questions that may require you to revisit your initial reasoning. Pay close attention to any time markers as well—many exam interfaces track your remaining minutes in a corner of the screen, helping you pace your progress and avoid a frantic end.

If you have any issue with the system—for instance, if the screen freezes or the font becomes difficult to read—notify the proctor immediately rather than attempting to troubleshoot on your own. In most centers, staff are trained to resolve minor technical glitches swiftly or to re-assign you to a different workstation if necessary. Throughout the test, aim to maintain a calm, methodical approach, leveraging any review or note-flagging functions the platform offers. By staying aware of the exam's built-in tools and promptly seeking help if something goes awry, you'll keep your focus on performing your best rather than losing valuable minutes to unnecessary distraction.

Chapter 7 Full-Mock Exams

7.1 Accessing the Complete Set of 12 Exams

We recognize that including a dozen full-length mock exams within these pages would make the printed book unwieldy. Instead, we've made all twelve practice exams—each designed to mirror the real test's length, format, and difficulty—available as downloadable PDFs on the Apex Academic Resources website. This approach allows you to print the tests at your convenience and tackle them in a realistic, paper-based format, similar to what you'll experience on test day.

Below you'll find a direct link and a QR code, both of which will take you to the download page. When you visit the site, simply locate and download any or all of the PDFs. Once printed, you can complete each exam under the time guidelines recommended in Chapter 6, marking your answers on paper to replicate the feel of an official test. Whether you choose to go through a single exam at a time or multiple in quick succession, these PDFs provide the comprehensive practice essential for confident performance.

Access Code can be found on Page 434

Scan the QR code or visit:

www.apex-academic.com/sie_exam_print

Chapter 8: Answer Keys and Detailed Explanations

8.1 Accessing Complete Explanations for All 12 Exams

Just as we've made the full-length practice tests available as downloadable PDFs, we're providing the corresponding answer keys and detailed explanations on the Apex Academic Resources website. Each set of answers clarifies the correct choice for every question and walks you through the core reasoning or steps needed to arrive at it. By reviewing these explanations, you'll uncover the precise logic behind each solution—especially valuable for questions that initially seemed perplexing or involved tricky concepts.

Below, you'll see a direct link and QR code, both of which will take you to the download page. Once there, you can print the explanations and answer keys along with the practice tests themselves, ensuring you have a complete offline set of study materials. Pairing the tests with their corresponding explanations is crucial for reinforcing your understanding of the toughest items.

Access Code can be found on Page 434

Scan the QR code or visit:

www.apex-academic.com/sie_exam_print

ACCESS CODE – ONLINE TOOLS

Unlimited Exam Simulator

Practice with our interactive exam simulator featuring a built-in timer and customizable options. Choose your exam duration, select the number of questions, and challenge yourself with randomized questions to sharpen your skills and track your progress.

Exam Flashcards

Reinforce your understanding with digital flashcards designed for quick review. Cover key topics like Capital Markets and Regulatory framework to boost your memory retention and exam confidence.

Printable Exams & Answers

Access full-length practice exams that match the real SIE exam format and detailed answer keys in PDF format. Download, print, and simulate the real test-taking experience to prepare for success.

ACCESS CODE:

A A R S I E 2 5

Chapter 9 E-Learning Platform and Supplemental Tools

Your success doesn't end with this book. To further support your preparation and mastery of the material, we've included powerful digital tools designed to enhance your study process. These resources are accessible on both mobile and desktop devices, providing flexibility and convenience.

9.1 Unlimited Exam Simulator

The unlimited exam simulator is your ultimate tool for practicing and perfecting your test-taking skills. This feature generates an unlimited number of practice exams tailored to your preferences, ensuring you always have fresh material to work with.

Key Features:

- ✓ Choose the number of questions and set the time limit.
- ✓ Randomized questions ensure no two tests are ever the same.

How It Helps:

- ✓ Builds confidence by simulating actual test conditions.
- ✓ Identifies weak areas by tracking performance over multiple attempts.

Scan the QR Code or go to:

www.apex-academic.com/sie_exam_sim

Access Code can be found on Page 434

9.2 Digital Flashcards

Our flashcard set is a convenient way to review critical concepts

Key Features:

- ✓ Includes knowledge of capital markets, products and their risks, trading, regulatory framework and more.
- ✓ Flip between terms and definitions with a single click.

How It Helps:

- ✓ Reinforces understanding through repetition.
- ✓ Quick and efficient for on-the-go study sessions.

Scan the QR Code or go to:

www.apex-academic.com/sie_flashcard

Access Code can be found on Page 434

9.3 Printable Full-Length Exams

For those who prefer a physical study option, we've included printable full-length exams. These are formatted to match the real test, offering an authentic test experience offline.

Key Features:

- ✓ Downloadable PDFs of complete practice exams.
- ✓ Includes answer keys for self-assessment.
- ✓ Matches the format, question count, and difficulty of the actual test.

How It Helps:

- ✓ Allows for focused practice without screen distractions.
- ✓ Provides a realistic testing environment when paired with a timer.

Scan the QR Code or go to:

www.apex-academic.com/sie_exam_print

Access Code can be found on Page 434

A Message From Apex Academic Resources

Dear Reader,

Creating a resource as comprehensive as this one involves a dedicated team of authors, editors, illustrators and subject matter experts — all aiming to provide a thorough, supportive guide for mastering your exam. We've worked carefully to ensure that every chapter offers practical strategies, clear explanations, and meaningful advice to help you excel in your journey toward passing the SIE exam.

If you've found this book helpful or encouraging, we would be deeply grateful for your honest review on Amazon. Your insights not only guide us in refining future editions and publications but also help fellow test-takers discover resources that meet their own learning needs. Whether you share a quick note or write a more detailed critique, your feedback truly matters to us.

Thank you for choosing our material and placing your trust in our work. We hope that our efforts have made your study process smoother and more rewarding. As you move forward in your professional endeavors, we wish you every success—and we're honored to play a small part in your achievements.

With gratitude,
The Apex Academic Resources Team

Made in the USA
Monee, IL
03 November 2025

33296892R00243